The Fourth Network

The Fourth Network

HOW FOX BROKE THE RULES
AND REINVENTED TELEVISION

Daniel M. Kimmel

Ivan R. Dee

CHICAGO 2004

Library of Congress Cataloging-in-Publication Data:
Kimmel, Daniel M.
    The fourth network : how Fox broke the rules and reinvented television / Daniel M. Kimmel.
        p. cm.
    Includes bibliographical references and index.
    ISBN 1-56663-572-1 (alk. paper)
        1. Fox Broadcasting Company—History. I. Title.

PN1992.92.F68K56 2004
384.55'455'0975—dc22
                                        2003070128

To Jerry and Rita Kimmel, my parents,
for encouraging a lifelong love of reading and writing,
but allowing me to watch television too

Contents

Acknowledgments

THERE ARE MANY PEOPLE to thank for making this book possible, but for reasons explained below, it's important to mention one source that was closed to me, that of the FOX network and its current employees. The network was under no obligation to cooperate with this book, and I went into this project assuming such assistance would not be forthcoming. While it would have been useful to have the access that Alex Ben Block enjoyed for his 1990 history *Outfoxed*, I understood that since the network was looking for credibility at that time, its needs and the author's needs nicely dovetailed. Since FOX is part of a publicly traded company as well as being part of a licensed and regulated business, I did not need their permission or cooperation to access information on them and to proceed on my own. What's more, FOX has shed many executives in its short history, and I was lucky to benefit from the perspective of many of them.

The reason for noting this lack of cooperation is the official reason that FOX gave me for refusal to participate in this project. In June 1999 I began contacting the producers of some of FOX's most important shows seeking interviews. One or more of them passed the request on to the network. When I received a call from a senior publicity executive there, I explained what I was doing, that I had no ax to grind, and that my goal was to write a balanced and objective history of FOX. I was promised tentative cooperation pending approval from higher-ups. That go-ahead never came. Instead I was told that since News Corp. owned its own publishing division, they might choose to do their own history of the FOX network someday, so they saw no reason to help with a potentially competing product.

The notion that FOX would consent to interviews only with an author working on an in-house book should be troubling not only to journalists but to anyone who treasures the free flow of information. While it's possible that the current FOX administration may have simply decided on purely pragmatic terms to decline to provide assistance for this book, fear of competition was the only explanation the network offered, and it remains a disturbing one. Given that one of the big stories at the start of the twenty-first century is that control of the media is falling into fewer and fewer hands, let's hope this isn't a sign of things to come.

On a more positive note, I want to thank the many individuals who took the time to talk with me about their experiences at or with FOX. In some cases people were exceptionally generous, clearing a large piece of their schedule for an extended interview. In other cases I was catching them on the fly, often pursuing them for months for the Q&A time I got. In the end, though, it was the interview that counted, not the effort that went into getting it. For their generosity I thank Tom Allen, Garth Ancier, Ed Ansin, Bob Bennett, Jim Benson, Tom Bergeron, Stephen J. Cannell, Michael H. Diamond, Andrew Fessel, Eric Gold, Bob Greenblatt, Lance Heflin, Doug Herzog, David Honig, Ken Johnson, Jamie Kellner, Rob Kenneally, Bob Leider, Phil Lerman, Margaret Loesch, Brian Lowry, the late Bob Mariano, Greg Meidel, Brad Moran, Patrick Mullen, Kevin O'Brien, Preston Padden, James Quello, Peter Roth, Mike Ruggiero, Lucie Salhany, Andrew Jay Schwartzman, Andi Sporkin, Paul Stupin, Anne Sweeney, Gerry Walsh, Kevin Wendle, Larry Wilmore, David Woods, Joe Young, and Ken Ziffren.

For assistance in numerous ways, from providing leads to arranging interviews to simply pointing me in the right direction, I thank Michael L. Carson, S. James Coppersmith, Ro Dooley, Jack Fitzgerald, Charlie Folds, Tim Gray, Kim Harbin, Brandy Hauman, Robin Jackson at the Federal Communications Commission, Mark J. Kern, Gayle Kirschenbaum, Paul La Camera, Roger Lyons, Sabrie L. Napier and the staff at the National Association of Broadcasters library, Laurie Shroyer, Stu Tauber, John Vitanovec, and Dina Weinberg.

Several people must be singled out for special thanks. The late television consultant Paul McCarthy was a source and interview subject for his small piece of the FOX story, convincing the new affiliates of the importance of being included on area cable television systems. But without trying to influence what I was writing, McCarthy also provided me with numerous sources as well as some useful reference material. Some of the people he directed me to were smaller players in the overall chronicle but turned out to have very important stories to tell, and I remain grateful for McCarthy's always enthusiastic advice.

Someday a doctoral student will do his or her thesis on the importance of the friend's couch to the writing of American nonfiction. Nat Segaloff and Lisa and Robert Ashton opened up their homes to me for stays of a week or more, providing not only shelter but food and transportation. This is friendship above and beyond the call of duty. Even more astonishing was that members of their households with whom I had no prior acquaintance, Ami Lachmani, and Roger Bennett respectively, were equally generous in acceding to this home invasion. I hope this book makes them feel the effort was worth it.

Authors routinely thank their agents, and I shall be no exception. But I want to single out my agent, Alison Picard, for doing something that has become quite extraordinary in today's publishing industry: she took a chance on an unknown. One possible scenario for the "five-hundred channel universe" mentioned in my concluding chapter is already playing itself out in the world of publishing, where only books by celebrities or ones that are otherwise presold seem to have the best chance of reaching readers. Alison believed I had a story worth publishing, even though I had never had an affair with a politician or committed a major crime. She sets a standard the rest of the industry would be wise to emulate.

Likewise, I'm pleased to have found a home at Ivan R. Dee. Ivan's support and suggestions were welcome, and this book has benefited from both.

I also want to thank James Robert Parish, about whom it can honestly be said that but for him this book never would have been written. His contributions were invaluable. Allan Taylor's input was equally useful. My unending gratitude is also extended to my attorney, Robert Abramoff of Burgee and Abramoff, who was always there when I needed him.

On the home front, my wife Donna and my daughter Amanda were a great support. Amanda so liked the idea of her daddy doing a book that she promised me someday to write a book and mention my name if I mentioned hers. So consider this a down payment. Also special thanks to friends and godparents Bill Jarosz and Denise Karlin for looking after Amanda when Daddy needed a little more time at the computer, and especially to Bill for helping Daddy *get* his new computer. This was essential when a national retail chain refused to replace it when it crashed ten days after purchase because I had thrown away the carton it came in. Bill, a senior executive for a major investment firm who oversees all their computer operations, diplomatically handled the retail negotiations to get the computer fixed at a time when diplomacy was the last thing on my mind. Fortunately the system was under warranty and was repaired within a week, but I do not recommend this way of starting a writing project.

Finally, my sincere thanks to the people at FOX, past and present, for making television fun again, and giving me a story to tell.

D. M. K.

Brookline, Massachusetts
February 2004

The Fourth Network

PROLOGUE

"If I found out, he was going to cancel the deal"

A FOURTH American television network? It wasn't exactly a joke. It was more like an impossible dream, almost something from the realm of science fiction, like a perpetual motion machine or spaceships that could go faster than the speed of light. Everyone knew how television worked. There were the Big Three networks, and there was everything else. Everything else included public television, independent stations, cable (once derided as "pay TV"), and home video.

How could the marketplace possibly support four networks? For most of the history of television in the United States, industry experts seriously questioned whether the marketplace could support *three* networks. After the collapse of the pioneer Dumont television network in 1955, the joke was that there was really room for only two and a half networks, with the American Broadcasting Company (ABC) considered the half. By the late 1970s, when ABC was riding high on hits like *Charlie's Angels* and *Happy Days*, no one considered it half a network anymore. Now it was the Big Three, and everyone assumed that—in the United States, at any rate—that was the natural order of things.

Dumont had been started in 1946 by Allen B. Dumont, one of the pioneers of early commercial television. Its programming lineup included a variety series with a young comedian named

3

Jackie Gleason, a religious show that made an early television star out of Bishop Fulton J. Sheen, and Monday night boxing. But without the broadcasting relationships from an established radio network, like the Columbia Broadcasting System (CBS) and the National Broadcasting Company (NBC) had, Dumont found itself unable to line up sufficient affiliates to make it a viable nationwide television operation. Indeed, although Paramount Pictures owned half of Dumont's parent company, Paramount's Los Angeles station, KTLA, declined to join the Dumont network, seeing that they could realize more revenue as an independent.

By 1955 it was clear that only ABC had the resources to be the third network, managing to attract affiliates with popular shows like *The Adventures of Ozzie and Harriet*, *Make Room for Daddy*, and *The Lawrence Welk Show*. ABC was also the first network to turn to Hollywood to fill programming slots. CBS and NBC, which were still largely based in New York, drew heavily from Broadway and nightclub talents for their shows. This edge allowed ABC to attract more stations to carry their national programming, and to prevail over Dumont, which became an increasingly weaker fourth network. Finally the Dumont Laboratories surrendered to the inevitable. They shut down the network and spun off the broadcasting operations— consisting of the few stations it owned outright—into the Metropolitan Broadcasting Company. Four years later investor John Kluge bought Metropolitan and its group of now unaffiliated independent stations, and the company was renamed Metromedia. Though only a few stations, Metromedia was an important independent group because of its locations in New York, Chicago, Philadelphia, and Washington, D.C.

Meanwhile the concept of the fourth network didn't die with the Dumont operation in 1955. It was just deemed impractical to find sufficient unaffiliated stations willing to carry a new network's programming. It couldn't be made economically feasible given that many markets at the time couldn't even support a single independent station. By the 1970s, however, someone was ready to make the attempt again. This time it was Dumont's onetime partner, Paramount Pictures. In June 1977 Barry Diller, chairman and chief executive officer; Michael Eisner, president and chief operating officer; and Jeffery Katzenberg, Diller's assistant, called a press conference to announce the launch of a fourth network. It would start slowly in early 1978, with just one or two nights of weekly programming. These shows would air at the same time throughout the country on stations owned by Paramount as well as on affiliated stations that would join the new venture. The reason they were expected to sign up was considered obvious: Paramount owned *Star Trek*, having acquired the 1960s TV series when they bought the Desilu Studios. Though the show had been a weak performer during its three-year run on NBC, it had later become a phenomenon in syndication. The deal made perfect business sense: Paramount the studio would license a new *Star Trek* series to Paramount the TV network, in a sense simply transferring assets from one pocket to another. *Star Trek* creator Gene Roddenberry was signed on to produce what was being called *Star Trek Phase II*. Most of the original cast had been signed—except for Leonard Nimoy—and scripts had been commissioned.

By year's end, however, Paramount had had a change of heart. There would be no Paramount Television Service. Instead Paramount would cash in on the science-fiction movie revival led by that year's *Star Wars* and *Close Encounters of the Third Kind*, and begin production on what would eventually become the first of several *Star Trek* feature films showcasing the entire original cast.

Meanwhile John Kluge had not been idle. He had turned Metromedia into a very profitable group of independent stations. The company also had a strong production and syndication arm, with programs like *The Merv Griffin Show*, and it occurred to some of the decision-makers there that maybe *they* were the ones to create that fourth television network. By the mid-1980s Metromedia was recognized as one of the most powerful independent TV station groups. In addition to the location of its stations in major U.S.

markets, the group had expanded its programming to include the syndication of new episodes of canceled network shows, like *Fame* and *Too Close for Comfort.*

Bob Bennett, president of Metromedia Producers Corporation, the group's production entity, perceived that there was a way to create a fourth network that would benefit the independent stations. "We were in the process ourselves of developing a fourth network. I kept denying it because I didn't want the pressure that would come from the press as we did it," he recalled. "But we started off doing a lot of things, and trying to do it ourselves and with partners."

Bennett's notion was that Metromedia could partner in the producing of new shows with other major station groups in the United States, like Hearst, Taft, and Storer. They would share the production costs among them and then have the programs to air themselves. It might have worked, but then John Kluge decided to take Metromedia private, and that set the corporation down a different road.

In 1984 the company bought back its public stock for $1.4 billion, and the effort of raising the money from the banks to finance the huge buyout was very time consuming. "No sooner than we did that then—nine months later—Kluge decided to take the banks out, and we raised another $1.4 billion with [the prominent Drexel, Burnham, Lambert broker] Michael Milken, and that was junk bonds. So that took about two years between the bank borrowing and the raising of the money from Milken on the junk bonds," said Bennett.

By 1985 Metromedia was free of stockholders and the banks, and Bennett thought they could finally move ahead with his plans to launch a fourth TV network. Instead, fate—with an assist from Michael Milken—conspired to introduce John Kluge to Rupert Murdoch. There would be a fourth network, but it would not be Metromedia's. "Milken had a party which he did annually in Los Angeles, and he would invite one of his major clients to put on a show. All these guys would be invited from all over the world, all these big-money guys," said Bennett. Metromedia was invited to put on a special presentation for Milken's guests, showcasing all their enterprises, from television to cellular radio to the Harlem Globetrotters basketball team. It was to be held on the lot of Twentieth Century–Fox, where Rupert Murdoch had finally expanded his media empire from newspapers to movies and television.

The Australian media magnate Rupert Murdoch won his first toehold in the United States in 1973 when he purchased a group of newspapers in San Antonio, Texas. It really didn't matter where; Murdoch wanted to be in America and begin building up his business there. He had examined a number of properties before deciding the price and location were right. Over the next several years he would buy his way up the media food chain, acquiring the *New York Post*, the *Boston Herald*, and the *Chicago Sun-Times* along the way. His eventual goal was to own a Hollywood studio, which would give him an entrée into the world of movies and television. He already had television interests in Australia and England, part of his News Corporation, usually referred to as News Corp. Still, it wasn't quite the same thing as owning an American studio. He had made attempts at buying Twentieth Century–Fox and Warner Bros. in the early 1980s but hadn't been able to buy up enough stock to gain leverage. By 1985 Twentieth Century–Fox once again seemed to be a place of opportunity for Murdoch.

The studio, one of Hollywood's major film production companies which dated back half a century, had been acquired in 1981 by Colorado oilman Marvin Davis and commodities trader Marc Rich, who was Davis's silent partner in the deal. Rich had a financial stake but took no role in running the studio. While Davis enjoyed the "fun" of being a movie mogul, he was shrewd enough to realize that he needed someone who knew the business well enough to actually operate it. As the studio continued to flounder in the early 1980s, Barry Diller was having problems of his own at Paramount. As chairman of Paramount Pictures, Diller had had a good relationship with Charles Bluhdorn, who was chairman of Paramount's owner, Gulf + Western. In February 1983 the fifty-six-year-old Bluhdorn, who had been fighting cancer for some time, suffered a fatal heart attack. His eventual replacement was Martin Davis (no relation to Marvin Davis), who had been a senior vice president under Bluhdorn with a reputation for being his "hatchet man." Diller chafed under Martin Davis's administration. Where he had had a solid, warm working relationship with Bluhdorn, he found Davis to be an administrator who didn't share his expansive vision for Paramount. He decided to trade one Davis for another and moved to Twentieth Century–Fox in 1984 as its chief executive officer. He would control the entire studio operation, one of the major producers of films and television shows seen throughout the world.

But Diller quickly found he liked working for Marvin Davis at Twentieth no more than he had Martin Davis at Paramount. The studio's finances were a mess. The problems stemmed both from losses on films like the Sylvester Stallone/Dolly Parton country music flop *Rhinestone* (1984), and the fact that Marc Rich, Davis's silent partner, was having problems with the law. Rich had fled the country for Switzerland, allegedly to avoid turning over certain financial records to a grand jury. (In 2001 Rich would be back in the news when he received a controversial pardon from outgoing President Bill Clinton.) Diller knew the company needed an infusion of funds to rev up film and TV production and start turning it around. Unfortunately Davis was reluctant to risk putting up his own cash, and Diller was reluctant to raise the money on junk bonds because such an approach would reflect badly on him and the studio. With each side digging in their heels, the studio not only ground to a halt but it looked like the dispute between Diller and Davis could end up in court, with Diller threatening to sue Davis for failing to live up to the terms of Diller's contract with the studio.

Davis's solution to this impasse was to bring in a new partner and let him provide the funding Diller demanded. Riding to Davis's rescue was none other than Rupert Murdoch, who clearly had other things on his mind than saving Marvin Davis. First things first, though, and the deal meant that the Australian would finally get his studio. The price tag was $250 million. Part of the sum was for acquiring Rich's 50 percent stake in the studio, which had been seized by the American government and later sold to Davis. The balance would go to the studio's operating budget.

The change in ownership in early 1985 gave Diller the leverage he needed to dig out from under Davis. His work agreement permitted him to walk in the event that the studio was sold. Instead Diller insisted that his contract be renegotiated to give him the right to quit within the first year under the new Davis/Murdoch ownership, without any reason. Murdoch agreed, and Diller found that the new owner was much more congenial to his interests than Davis was.

In March 1985, on the day of the Metromedia presentation for Michael Milken's annual investors' party, Barry Diller took advantage of the presence of both Kluge and Murdoch in Los Angeles to invite them to his office on the Fox lot for drinks. Davis was present too. Diller raised the subject of a fourth network, recalling a time in the early 1980s when he and Kluge had discussed having Paramount and Metromedia join forces. It hadn't worked out then, but they had parted on good terms. Diller knew where he was leading the conversation, because Milken had tipped him off that Kluge was preparing to sell off his television assets to concentrate on his growing cellular business.

Kluge allowed that he was indeed open to offers, though WCVB, his Boston TV station, was promised to Hearst Broadcasting as part of a previous deal. Murdoch expressed interest, but they were all due at Milken's party, so Diller suggested they meet again the next day. At that meeting Kluge named his price: $2 billion. It would be for six of the Metromedia TV stations (located in New York, Los Angeles, Chicago, Washington, D.C., Houston, and Dallas)—all except WCVB in Boston. Murdoch didn't blanch.

In fact the price was outrageous. TV stations were ordinarily selling for ten to twelve times their earnings. Kluge's asking price was on the order of fifteen to seventeen times that amount. Diller would report later, "I just thought it was crazy."

But Murdoch saw this as a golden opportunity. Metromedia's stations were Very High Frequency, or VHF, which was an important factor when most Americans still didn't have cable and Ultra High Frequency (UHF) stations required bothersome separate antennas. Metromedia's Bob Bennett, still hoping for a fourth network of his own, was deliberately kept out of the loop and was not informed of the meeting. According to Bennett, "I didn't want the company to be sold. So Kluge had told Barry Diller and Murdoch and those people that if I found out, he was going to cancel the deal."

Why would Murdoch take such a gamble? Reflecting back on that time, Bennett theorizes that people like Kluge and Murdoch are modern-day riverboat gamblers, willing to take big risks that would frighten most investors, because they think they will pay huge dividends in the long run. He recalls once dickering with the owners of KRLD in Dallas, a station Metromedia was acquiring, to lower their asking price from $14 million to $10 million. Kluge stepped in and told Bennett to buy it at $14 million because "it really doesn't make any difference." Bennett was appalled at the time, but when Metromedia sold KRLD two years later, Kluge valued it at $65 million, and Murdoch paid it. This set off a flurry of station owners demanding and getting higher prices in selling their stations. It was the first, but certainly not the last time a Fox-related action would have repercussions throughout the industry.

Before the deal could be consummated, however, Murdoch had legal matters to be resolved. One was the issue of "cross-ownership." Federal Communications Commission (FCC) rules were very strict at the time prohibiting one entity from owning a newspaper *and* a TV station in the same market, and Murdoch already owned papers in Chicago and New York. He waved the objection away, figuring that although the cross-ownership regulations would create headaches down the road, he could deal with them later.

Even with that in abeyance, Murdoch still needed FCC approval of his purchase of the Metromedia stations before he could proceed. One doesn't simply buy and sell television outlets. License transfers must be approved by this federal agency since the airwaves, in theory at least, belong to the public. Murdoch soon discovered he had newfound allies on the commission. FCC chairman Mark Fowler, an appointee of President Ronald Reagan, strongly favored deregulation in the industry. He enthusiastically supported anyone trying to shake up the established TV networks. FCC commissioner James Quello, on the other hand, was nonideological. He was a broadcasting veteran who believed that if someone were going to take a serious run at creating a fourth network, the commission could have a positive role to play in the process. After all, he felt, more competition would benefit the viewer.

In what would later prove to be a crucial conversation, Kluge and Murdoch paid a call on the commissioners in Washington to brief them informally on the upcoming deal. Quello asked Murdoch who would actually operate the stations. Murdoch replied that News Corp. would, and that he controlled 75 percent of that voting stock. "He was very straightforward with me," recalled Quello. "There wasn't any bullshit with the guy." Murdoch assured them that he was in the process of becoming an American—as he would shortly thereafter—and that the citizenship issue would be resolved before the transfer of station licenses.

Foreign ownership of American television stations was not permitted, and Murdoch was still an Australian citizen. This issue became more important when Davis opted out of the Metromedia deal; now it was Murdoch's Australian company News Corp. that would be the purchaser. As the various aspects of the deal were worked out—the Metromedia junk bonds, the selling off of WCVB in Boston and of Murdoch's Chicago newspaper—Murdoch arranged to become an American. In September 1985, accompanied by his family, Murdoch entered the courtroom of Judge Shirley Wohl Kram in New York and pledged his allegiance to the United States of America. His family did not.

Now it was just a matter of tying up loose ends. Metromedia had offered to include the Metromedia Producers Corporation (MPC) in the deal. Twentieth Century–Fox, however, was a far bigger and more established production and syndication television entity and didn't need MPC, which would simply duplicate the studio's efforts. Bennett considered making a bid for MPC himself, but then reality set in: he was a broadcaster, not a producer, and he ultimately declined. Eventually Murdoch would buy it, after all, primarily for its library. Among the shows MPC syndicated were a number of off-network series from Aaron Spelling, the most lucrative of which were the foreign syndication rights to the nighttime soap opera *Dynasty*.

And then there was Marvin Davis. By the fall of 1985 Diller was eager to move ahead with plans to launch a fourth network, having been close to the starting line several times before. Murdoch's Metromedia deal had finally made that possible. Davis was now entirely out of the picture because News Corp. rather than Fox owned the Metromedia stations, and Davis's strained relationship with Diller made continuing at Twentieth impossible. The oilman suggested to Murdoch that since Diller worked for the studio—and not News Corp.—he had no business running Murdoch's TV stations. This was simply the opening move in a new round of haggling, which ended with Davis selling out his share and Murdoch's News Corp. remaining as the sole owner not only of a group of TV stations but of Twentieth Century–Fox itself.

Now, at last, it was clear what Murdoch and Diller had in mind. Twentieth Century–Fox was reorganized under a new corporate umbrella called Fox, Inc. It included both the movie and television production operations and the six TV stations. There was also a new entity labeled the "Fox Television Network." No details were available since FCC approval was still pending. Diller said the plan was "one we felt we had to set up in anticipation of our future."

With their eyes on the future, the would-be network titans still had something to learn about operating in their present circumstances. Murdoch may have charmed the FCC, but he created unnecessary aggravation by neglecting to make the obligatory courtesy calls to congressional leaders, particularly those with jurisdiction over aspects of the broadcasting industry. Political leaders and activists on media issues were noticing that the regulatory process was proceeding to rubber-stamp the Murdoch purchase without hesitation. Texas congressman John Bryant, for one, wondered why the FCC began processing the license transfers three months *before* Murdoch became an American citizen. "The FCC is treating Murdoch with favoritism for reasons which one might assume to be political," charged Bryant.

Political or not, by November 1985 the transfers had been approved. The first serious attempt at creating a fourth network in some thirty years was about to get under way.

PART I

The Coat-Hanger Network

CHAPTER ONE

"There will only be three"

[1985–1986]

ALTHOUGH IN LATER YEARS it would sometimes seem that the launching of the FOX network was entirely the doing of Barry Diller, with Rupert Murdoch off in the background writing checks, the fact is that FOX was never a one-man show. Diller may have been the face of FOX to the industry and the public, but there were a lot of people sharing the heavy lifting behind the scenes. One individual would be cited time and again by FOX affiliate executives as the real founding father of the network. He was Murdoch and Diller's first hire.

Jamie Kellner had come up through the television ranks. His resumé included stints at CBS, Viacom, and Filmways, mostly working in the selling of old television shows to local stations. It was at Filmways where he was credited with repackaging old *Saturday Night Live* episodes into thirty-minute shows for syndication. When Filmways was acquired by Orion, Kellner was asked to stay on and thrived under the new management. Now Murdoch and Diller were offering him a rare opportunity in television: launching a brand new American TV broadcast network.

"I was thirty-eight, thirty-nine, and I'd made a lot of money already," he would recall to FOX chronicler Alex Ben Block. "It was my treat to myself to do something that was sort of the ultimate challenge."

Kellner signed on as president of the start-up network, with Diller reigning as head of Fox, Inc. The network would be housed on the Twentieth Century–Fox studio lot in West Los Angeles. In the early years space was at a premium on the lot, since much of the original Fox space had been sold off years before and had become the office and condo development Century City. Some of the TV offices, like Standards and Practices (the network "censors"), worked in trailers camped outside the executive offices. Slowly they assembled their inaugural team. David Johnson, forty-six, was put in charge of advertising and affiliate relations. A veteran of the ABC network, he had been shuffled out when that network was acquired by Capital Cities around the same time that Murdoch was buying Metromedia's stations. Johnson had been marking time as a consultant. He was soon joined by Scott Sassa who, in his late twenties, had already worked at the Walt Disney Company, the Playboy Channel, and Turner Broadcasting. Sassa had a long meeting with Kellner in February 1986 where, he said, "I told him why he would fail miserably in this task [of creating a fourth network] and . . . he gave me back good answers." They quickly won each other over, and soon Sassa was on board helping to construct the fledgling network's business plan.

The heart of any network, of course, is its programming. The arrival of another twentysomething, Garth Ancier, would be a decisive step in determining not only the kinds of shows the network would develop and air, but the creation of the network's corporate culture. When Diller and Kellner came along, Ancier was vice president of current comedy programs at NBC. The NBC comedy department was white hot at the time, airing such hit sitcoms as *Cheers*, *The Cosby Show*, *Family Ties*, *Golden Girls*, and *Night Court*. While Ancier could hardly take the credit for creating those highly successful shows, he didn't mind sharing in the luster of their continued high ratings.

Sassa had suggested that Diller and Kellner contact Ancier. The young programming executive understood the risks that Fox would be facing as a start-up network. "I'd been at NBC six and a half years and felt that when you're twenty-eight years old—which is how old I was at the time—I really thought about it. I said, 'I love NBC. I love the people here. It's going to be very emotional for me. But this is a once in a lifetime kind of thing to try out.'"

Taking a chance on Fox would be a decision that each of the executives would have to make, but some had it easier than others. When Kellner left Orion Pictures, his boss, Arthur Krim, wished him well and told him to call if it didn't work out at Fox. Ancier's departure from NBC was not quite so paternal. His superiors made it clear that they thought he was making a foolish career choice and that the notion of a fourth TV network was doomed to failure. "It was certainly intensified by the fact that my current boss at the time, Brandon Tartikoff, said, 'You know, Garth, all their stations are UHF stations?'" (Tartikoff would later tag FOX with the dismissive nickname "the coat-hanger network," suggesting that people would have to attach wire hangers to their antennas just to be able to pick up the FOX signal.) Grant Tinker, the head of NBC, pointed to the big wall chart in his office with the prime-time schedules of the Big Three networks. "I will never put a fourth column on my schedule board," he told Ancier. "There will only be three." From the lofty heights of the number one TV network, Tinker seemed to imply, it was burden enough simply to have to acknowledge the existence of CBS and ABC.

Sassa was not the only one to recommend Ancier to head programming at the new network. Kevin Wendle had already been hired by Fox, but at age twenty-six he was considered too green to head the whole programming department. (His network resumé at the time consisted primarily of eighteen months in the NBC drama department.) Wendle recalls Kellner saying, "We need someone to be your boss. Have you got any ideas? Can you make any recommendations?"

Wendle replied, "My very best friend at NBC in programming is Garth Ancier. And I think he would be the ideal candidate because he's a couple of years older than I am." They complemented each other well. At NBC, Ancier had been in charge of comedy development, Wendle had worked on drama. Ancier was a vice president, Wendle at the director level below.

Having met with Kellner's approval, the Ancier/Wendle duo was presented to Diller and Murdoch, both of whom agreed to the hiring of the team. Diller liked having young executives whom he could mold rather than more experienced players who would have their own ideas about how things should be done. "Garth and I left NBC the same day, together, as a team," says Wendle. "I remember we went in, we walked into [NBC West Coast executive] Warren Littlefield's office and told him the news. He said, 'Is this a deal that's already made, or is there anything I can say?'" They told him it was a done deal, the opportunity of a lifetime.

"In that case," Littlefield replied, "I really need you out by noon, because it's competitive."

O ne of the reasons a fourth American television network was always considered a pipe dream was that the numbers didn't add up. Deregulation of the communications industry was still in its early stages, and networks were limited to owning only a handful of stations. Of the more than a hundred stations carrying a given network like ABC or NBC, only a few were actually owned by that network. All the other stations carrying the network's particular programming were "affiliates," stations owned by independent individuals or companies which agreed to carry network programming. In return they received compensation from the network and the ability to sell local advertising spots (called availabilities or "avails") during the airing of network shows. For most of the history of the industry, there simply were not enough stations to go around. Major markets could support three network-owned or affiliated stations plus one or more independents, but some smaller markets were lucky if they had all three networks, much less room for a fourth. Those affiliates were crucial because without some means to get the broadcast signal to the TV set, a network's shows would simply be unavailable to viewers. (One of the reasons for the growth of cable television was that it provided that means to viewers who, because of distance or interference from mountainous terrain, could not clearly receive the local TV signals in their market.)

In the late 1970s and early 1980s the FCC began licensing new TV stations, and by the time Fox went affiliate hunting in 1986 there was a whole new universe of independent stations. They were UHF stations, often with high numbers on the television dial and weak ratings to go along with them. If they were lucky, local cable companies would include these stations in their package of local TV stations, but many chose not to carry such little-viewed outlets which remained available only via UHF antenna. This was the basis for Tartikoff's "coat-hanger network" comment.

The new Fox network had two immediate tasks before it: convince stations to affiliate, then persuade viewers to watch. It didn't matter how good the programming was or how clever the promotion was if viewers didn't have access to the network carrying those shows, even if they wanted to tune in. So clearly the number one priority for Fox was signing up stations. And to do that, it had to come up with a reason for independent stations to give up their independence.

Affiliate relations chief David Johnson and his team went out seeking station groups and individual owners to sign on to a network that had yet to put a single show on the air. Dealing with station groups was appealing because it meant one-stop shopping, where a pact for several stations could be negotiated with a single owner. Many stations, however, were still essentially mom-and-pop operations and had to be wooed one at a time. Meanwhile Johnson's vice president of research, Andrew Fessel, was trying to find out who was likely to be in Fox's potential audience when the network finally went on the air. Fessel had previously worked for Nielsen Media Research and loved to tease information about the viewers and their preferences out of the raw numbers. In an interview for this book, he recalled the days when the Fox executives had no idea who would tune in to their programs. "We're taking these independent stations and turning them into affiliates. Let's at least see who we got." He set up a series of focus groups consisting of viewers of independent stations to see what they liked and why they were tuning out the Big Three networks. "We knew they watched movies for the most part, rerun movies in prime time, which is what independent stations were offering at the time as competitive to the networks."

All through the spring of 1986 Fessel conducted several focus groups around the country, operating under the theory that people who were dissatisfied with Big Three programming were their most likely viewers. "What we found was a tremendous vacuum essentially—every viewer had a problem with every network. They would say things like, 'They canceled my favorite show,' or 'Their shows are all the same,' or 'They only do one show that's a hit and then everybody copies that.' There was a very strong theme of very repetitive complaints about the three networks that indicated to us that if we had innovative programming, if we had programming that focused on particular age groups, if we had programming that pushed the edge, if we had programming that we really stood behind, then we thought we could really appeal to a very strong need and interest that the consumers were indicating to us that they had."

Fessel's research became part of the pitch to potential affiliates. The marketplace was changing, with the audience becoming more segmented, the Fox team argued, and the stations were being given the opportunity to get in on the ground floor of something that was going to transform the business. In any given market, the network affiliates had more prestige than the indies, they could charge more for advertising time, and the audiences attracted to their network prime-time shows would stay tuned during other parts of their broadcast schedule. It sounded good on paper, but it was time for a dramatic announcement that would convince everyone that the new network was for real. In an unexpected move, Fox prepared to take on the king of late-night television.

For more than three decades, late night—the time period following the 11 P.M. newscast (10 P.M. in the Central time zone)—had been "owned" by NBC. CBS and ABC would attempt periodically to counterprogram with occasional, limited success, but NBC's *The Tonight Show* was the undisputed late-evening champ. It achieved success in the 1950s with host Steve Allen and later with Jack Paar. When the eccentric conversationalist Paar left in 1962, he was replaced by a game-show host named Johnny Carson. The importance of Carson in understanding American television over the next three decades cannot be overstated. He was a tastemaker in introducing new acts to home audiences. He was a public barometer in that when he decided to take shots at a politician or public figure in his nightly comic monologue, it was safe to assume that Middle America felt much the same way. *The Tonight Show* was also a major profit center for NBC because it was a one-set talk show. Even big-name guests were paid minimal scale for their appearances because they were often promoting something—a movie, a book, a concert, or simply themselves—and a shot on *The Tonight Show* was the television equivalent of hitting a home run. For NBC it was more like a grand slam. At its peak *The Tonight Show* was accountable for as much as 15 to 20 percent of the network's entire profits.

By the 1980s the venerable Carson was no longer a mere employee. Besides producing the show, he had moved it from New York to Los Angeles, scaled it back from ninety minutes to an hour nightly, cut back his own appearances over the course of the year to avoid burnout, and created a hit follow-up show that ran after *Tonight*, starring comedian David Letterman. Carson was a man deferred to in the industry and by the public because he had earned it.

When Carson took the night, or the week, off, the network had two options. They could run *The Best of Carson* (which they did for many years on Saturdays until it was replaced in 1975 by *Saturday Night Live*), or they could air a *Tonight Show* hosted by a substitute. These "guest hosts" proved to be acceptable to the viewing public as long as Carson continued to do most of the shows. Even in Carson's absence, supporting players like announcer Ed McMahon and bandleader Doc Severinsen were there to provide a sense of continuity. Of the various comedians and personalities who substituted for Carson, including comics like David Brenner and Bill Cosby, the most successful was Joan Rivers. An alumna of Chicago's famed improvisational comedy troupe, Second City, Rivers had built a successful career as a stand-up, appearing numerous times on *The Ed Sullivan Show*, *The Mike Douglas Show*, *The Merv Griffin Show*, and, of course, *The Tonight Show*. Her *shtick* was that she was a chic Jewish suburban housewife, and she complained about her marriage, being a mother, and—somewhat shocking in its day—sex. What made her different was that the few women stand-ups around then, like Phyllis Diller, played somewhat grotesque characters. Rivers, with her aggressive repartee and stylish outfits, looked like someone you'd see at the supermarket or a PTA meeting.

By 1983 the fifty-year-old Rivers had achieved stardom. She had worked in theater and in the movies (even directing Billy Crystal's movie debut, the 1978 flop *Rabbit Test*). Her one-woman shows were sellouts, and her records and books were best-sellers. In a cover story, *People* magazine had dubbed her "The First Lady of Comedy." In August 1983 Rivers reached the pinnacle of success: she was named the permanent guest host of *The Tonight Show*. In other words, when Carson was away, Rivers would play. Success was sweet, but when Rivers's contract came up for renewal in the summer of 1985, she and her producer husband Edgar Rosenberg felt that she was not being treated well. Carson's contract had just been renewed for two years, but the network offered her only one. Rivers and Rosenberg felt this was NBC's way of reminding them that keeping Rivers happy was not a top priority. With her blessing, Rosenberg had their attorney, Peter Dekom, approach the yet-to-be created Fox network to see if they might have an interest in her services. They had. In fact, they wanted her to do a talk show.

By early 1986 negotiations were getting serious, and Rivers had to make a decision. Staying at NBC and *The Tonight Show* meant security. If she left, there would be no coming back. In her memoir, *Still Talking* (1991), Rivers recounts what proved to be the turning point: "Then a friend—a real friend, [NBC vice president for special services] Jay Michelis—smuggled me a list prepared by NBC naming the ten successors if Johnny [Carson] retired. My name was not on it. I almost died." NBC's president Brandon Tartikoff denied to her that there was any such list, but for Rivers it was yet another slight by the network.

All this time the top Fox people had been turning on the charm. Diller met with Rivers several times, as did Jamie Kellner. Even Rupert Murdoch got into the act. Rivers was looking for a safety net if she were to jump from *The Tonight Show*; Fox wanted a marquee name that would give their new network instant credibility. It was a match made in television. Rivers would do a nightly, one-hour show from Los Angeles, mixing comedy, music, and interviews. In essence, Fox would clone *The Tonight Show* with one of its guest hosts behind the desk.

In retrospect the show may have been doomed from the beginning. Fox had to commit to a large amount of spending on the Rivers show. If they wanted to produce a product comparable to *The Tonight Show* they'd have to pay for it. Rivers's services alone would cost $15 million, spread out over three years. Further, Rivers and Rosenberg were to be given complete creative control. When it came time to announce the deal to the world, Rivers had two concerns. First, Diller planned on a meeting with select reporters where he could detail all the latest developments at the network— new stations, new hires, new development—and the Rivers deal would simply be one item on the agenda. Rivers felt that her signing on to the new network was a major story in and of itself, and deserved a big play. In an unpleasant meeting that Rivers admitted later poisoned the relationship with Fox right from the start, she got her way. She was told that after she and Rosenberg left the room, Diller made a face and said, "Okay, make it a zoo, make it a circus."

Her other concern was how to break the news gracefully to Carson. They had never been close—Carson was a very private person, even around longtime associates—but she felt grateful to him for what her time on *The Tonight Show*, as guest and as host, had meant to her career. She wanted to tell him herself, but it was not to be. A story this good was hard to keep quiet, and rumors were soon flying all over town. The man who may have let the cat out of the bag was, by his own admission, Fox programming executive Garth Ancier.

It was known that Fox was about to announce the host of their new late-night show. After a frustrating period in which NBC executives were not returning her calls, suddenly it was Rivers's people who were incommunicado. Brandon Tartikoff was able to put the pieces together, and he called his former employee and asked him point blank if Fox was planning to launch a late-night talk show with Rivers.

Ancier was conflicted. "I said, 'I can't comment.' I didn't want to lie to him. I also didn't want to tell him. But based upon that, he said, 'I have to take that as a yes.' And he immediately called Johnny Carson. I then called Joan. Joan tried to call Johnny, but he was on the phone with Brandon."

It was unpleasant, but when the announcement was made, Rivers was right. It was big news everywhere. And suddenly stations were calling Fox to discuss affiliation. "I consider Joan Rivers to be very critical to the setting up of that network," recalled Ancier. "It was: you can get the Joan Rivers late night show if you become a Fox affiliate. So we were able to sign affiliates much more easily at Fox than we were at WB later because we had a big hook, which was this big show that everyone thought, 'Oh, that's a pre-established hit.'"

While the forthcoming Rivers entry helped make the Fox network seem more "real" to prospective affiliates, other independent stations were more interested in calculating the odds. Fox approached

Brad Moran, owner and general manager of KJTV in Lubbock, Texas, that summer. After reviewing the presentation, he decided he had nothing to lose by affiliating with Fox. "It was more of a lark for us; the downside was minimal," he recalled. In Montgomery, Alabama, WCOV owner David Woods read about the new network in the trade papers and phoned them. "Early on they didn't have the manpower to go after small markets," said Woods. Montgomery is the nation's 113th television market. "They were really working the top 50 or top 75 at the inception." WCOV signed on as well.

The Indianapolis Fox affiliate came into the fold as part of a package deal. The network was eager to get Outlet Communication's Atlanta station since WAGA was a major market VHF station. Joe Young, at the time vice president and general manager of WXIN in Indianapolis, said his boss, the late David Henderson, insisted on expanding the deal. "The guy was smart. He said, 'If I give you Atlanta, you've got to give me Indianapolis.'"

Kellner felt that by the time they were ready to go on the air in October 1986, the Fox-owned stations would be joined by 60 to 70 affiliates, and they would be able to reach viewers in over 70 percent of the country. There are more than 200 television markets in the United States, some with as few as a single station. For a network to be viable, it would need between 150 and 200 stations and affiliates. Fox had a running start, but with a goal of approaching 100 percent coverage—or "clearance," as it is called in the industry—they obviously still had a long way to go.

Part of the problem was that other than Joan Rivers, it still wasn't clear what, exactly, these stations were signing up *for* when they agreed to become Fox affiliates. Indeed, even the name of the new network wasn't clear. At the time of the Rivers announcement, it was called FBC. Says Ancier, "Basically, we all sat around a room and, I swear to God, we had one of those boards you have where you rip the paper off, those stand up boards. And we said, all networks have three initials, let's come up with three initials that make sense here. And we had everything from UBS, Universal

[Broadcasting System], to International Broadcasting Service, all of these things that sound like ABC, NBC, CBS. And we finally decided to call it FBC, like NBC."

It would remain FBC until just before the prime-time launch in April 1987.

As for what would appear on FBC once it was indeed on the air, major TV producers were being lured to the new network with promises of great creative freedom. Ancier and Wendle went to professionals they already knew—Gary David Goldberg of *Family Ties*, James L. Brooks of *Cheers*, Ed. Weinberger of *Taxi*, Stephen J. Cannell of *The A Team*—and convinced them to take a chance by each producing a show for FBC. Unlike the Big Three, who had the time and the resources to commission pilot episodes to see if the execution was as interesting as the concept for a weekly series, Diller and company had no such luxury. If someone who could sell to the Big Three was willing to risk putting a project on this untested fourth network, that person could demand a series commitment up front. With the knowledge that they would be getting paid for at least half a season of shows instead of just a single test episode, it was worth making the effort and seeing what transpired. Brooks, for example, came up with *The Tracey Ullman Show*, a half-hour filmed variety entry featuring the British comedian then largely unknown to American viewers.

Would anyone watch? Who could tell? FBC needed product and credibility, and people like Brooks offered them both. Soon it was time for another media "circus," where all these trophy producers would be trotted out to the press to convince everyone that the fourth network was really going to happen—and soon.

Rob Kenneally, who would later join the network but who at the time was working for the studio's television production arm, recalled the press conference in Los Angeles. "They had announced and walked up on stage everybody who was anybody in the writer/

producer series world. It was, 'We are all embracing this network, we who could work anywhere have decided to come to Fox to do our next new show,'" he recalled. "So [Stephen J.] Cannell went up, [Aaron] Spelling went up, Gary David Goldberg had come up, Jim Brooks had come up. . . . And then there were these two guys who were relatively unknown. They had kind of produced *The Jeffersons*, and that was Michael Moye and Ron Leavitt. They were sort of the next rung or two down from the guys that were previously on stage.

"Unlike everyone else who had done an almost spiritual presentation of how important a fourth network was, Michael and Ron get up to the podium. Ron says to the assembled crowd, 'How many out there have children?' A bunch of people raised their hands.

"And he says, 'And how many of you guys just can't wait to get home to these little shits?' And the room erupted."

Moye and Leavitt's show was already on the FBC schedule. It was called *Married . . . With Children*.

By the summer of 1986, Murdoch, Diller, Kellner, and their team had accomplished a lot. The Metromedia stations would become the flagship stations for their network, a major star had agreed to do their late-night show, stations were signing up to carry FBC programming, and producers were readying fare for the network's spring 1987 prime-time launch. It had taken tremendous effort, but in just over a year they had made it to the point where—for the first time since Dumont had gone off the air thirty-two years earlier—a fourth television network was about to debut.

The easy part was over. Now the real work would begin.

CHAPTER TWO

"A brand that most of America knows"

[1986–1987]

The Late Show with Joan Rivers premiered on Thursday, October 9, 1986. On that day FBC became the fourth network—though, as a matter of law, it would not meet the definition of a television network by FCC standards until it had at least fifteen hours a week of programming airing on its stations and affiliates.

It might sound silly to people outside the industry, but that definition of "network" was of crucial importance to Fox and to their rivals at the Big Three. Under then current rules, networks could not own television series or be involved in their production or syndication. At this point Fox's production units—which offered shows to the major networks as well as for syndication—was much more important financially to Fox, Inc., than its fledgling "weblet," as it was called in the trade papers. CBS had had to divest its ownership interest in numerous programs, including syndicated reruns of past hits, spinning off a company called Viacom to take over that end of the business. (In a neat illustration of how times have changed since the deregulation of the TV industry in 1996, three years later CBS and Viacom announced they would rejoin forces in one of the biggest mergers in American history.) If FBC was ever defined as a network as a matter of law, it would be forced to give up either the network or its production/syndication arm. Rupert Murdoch and Barry Diller, of course, had no intention of doing either.

It had been a busy summer for the FBC executives. In July 1986 they announced that they had signed their first sponsor, Bristol-Myers, for a one-year deal. The pharmaceutical and personal care company (Bufferin, Excedrin, Clairol hair products) would pay $1.5 million for two thirty-second spots each week on *The Late Show*. Each one-hour show had ten thirty-second availabilities for national advertising, which meant that FBC could sell fifty such spots per week. Two spots wouldn't pay the rent, but it was a start. For its part, Bristol-Myers had a history of being an early sponsor of new TV ventures. In 1980 it had had the foresight to sign a ten-year deal with a cable start-up operation called CNN.

The search for stations to affiliate with FBC continued. In August 1986 Jamie Kellner announced that Fox would have 80 percent clearance by the premiere of *The Late Show*. The network was in twenty-eight of the nation's top thirty markets and was negotiating in the remaining two, Milwaukee and Boston. In the latter, Fox would eventually buy the UHF station WXNE from Pat Robertson's Christian Broadcasting Network for a reported $28 million—not the last time Robertson's media empire would be bailed out by Rupert Murdoch's checkbook. Fox would rechristen it WFXT.

Perhaps most gratifying for Fox was that the Big Three felt sufficiently threatened to publicly denigrate the efforts of Diller and Kellner. NBC released a study in late summer pointing out that the average Nielsen rating for the stations under the Fox umbrella was 2.3 while for NBC it was 11.9. (A rating point represents a percentage point of all the TV sets available for use in the entire United States or whatever submarket is being measured. In contrast, a share point represents the percentage of all those TV sets actually in operation at the time.) Kellner was quick to respond to NBC's sleight of hand, noting that the Peacock network was comparing the ratings for the independent stations when they were running old movies and TV reruns, not carrying brand-new programming.

David Johnson, Fox's vice president for marketing, affiliate relations, and advertising sales, put it bluntly, "It's self-evidently correct that independent stations don't do as well as affiliates in the prime-time ratings. That's the whole point of their signing with the FBC network."

By the time Joan Rivers debuted her show in October, anticipation was high. Perhaps unfairly, she was expected to compete with her old boss, Johnny Carson, even though they'd only be going head to head for half an hour. *The Late Show* would air from 11 P.M. to midnight—an hour earlier in the Central time zone—while Carson didn't start until after the late news at 11:30. (Several years later, local stations added another five minutes to their late newscasts and the network shows were pushed back to 11:35.) It was foolishness to think Rivers could beat Carson, especially fresh out of the starting gate, even though *The Tonight Show*'s numbers had always bounced upward when she had hosted the show. For the October 9 premiere, Rivers actually outdid Carson in the New York Nielsen ratings as well as in the competing Arbitron service ratings in Los Angeles; but in most places Carson enjoyed the higher viewership.

For her first show Rivers intended to put her personal stamp on the production. While it was everyone's goal to replicate her version of *The Tonight Show* on FBC, she felt she had not had a free hand booking guests on her NBC outings. She wanted to appeal to younger viewers. Her opening night lineup indicated what she thought would do the trick: Elton John, Cher, Pee-wee Herman, and David Lee Roth. She also did away with a *Tonight Show*–style announcer/sidekick. This would be *her* show. As the ratings started to slump in later weeks, the real question became whether younger viewers were interested in this type of TV fare at all.

As for prime time—shows during the prime viewing hours of 8 to 11 P.M.—the launch of the network was still many months away. A March 1987 premiere was announced, then it was pushed back to April. Two nights (Saturday and Sunday) were announced, then the network backtracked and said it wouldn't try to do the schedule all at once. Some shows had commenced production. Gary David Goldberg's Ubu Productions would offer a smart romantic sitcom called *Duet*, while another comedy would be based on the 1986 hit movie *Down and Out in Beverly Hills*. A teen-oriented cop show, *Jump Street Chapel*, was promised from producer Stephen J. Cannell, with a two-hour TV-movie pilot set to premiere in the spring.

The decision to start prime time on FBC on the weekends was not made lightly. Network president Jamie Kellner asked numbers wizard Andy Fessel to analyze the Big Three's schedules in terms of audience share, to see where they were strongest and where they were most vulnerable. Fessel discovered the obvious—that Sunday night had the highest levels of "homes using television," or HUTs, while Saturday night had the lowest HUT levels. But he also noticed that the Big Three were required to play by certain government rules, such as that the extra hour of prime time on Sunday from 7 to 8 P.M. had to be devoted to news or family programming. FBC, not yet officially a network, was not bound by that rule. Thus it decided to put its teen cop show, renamed *21 Jump Street*, on at 7 P.M., counterprogramming the tamer offerings of the other networks. Fessel also saw opportunities later in the evening.

Said Fessel, "On Sunday night, at 9 o'clock, when the three networks all aired the same kind of [movie] programming, what better opportunity to counterprogram. Anything different from a movie would be effective." With Sunday night offering the largest audiences, advertisers were eager to buy spots. It is often forgotten that a show doesn't have to win its time slot to be successful. If it's reaching sufficient numbers of viewers whom advertisers find valuable, that program can still be a success. Fessel suggested to Kellner that Sunday nights offered chances to counterprogram the Big Three at 7 and 9 P.M., if only they could figure out a way to bridge the gap at 8 P.M.

Saturday night offered different challenges. It had some of the lowest viewing levels of the week because many viewers were out that night. For those who stayed at home, more were being attracted to the offerings on cable, especially those premium channels offering uncut and uninterrupted movies, concerts, and sporting events with which tamer network television could not easily compete. Fessel could analyze the numbers, but he didn't know any more than anyone else as to whether Saturday or Sunday night would work best for FBC. "My recommendation, because I wasn't sure what the competitive challenges would be, was shouldn't we take two diametrically opposed opportunities and see what happened?" Fessel argued that they could use their success or failure on the weekends to figure out which way to expand. If Sunday succeeded, then they could expand to Monday and Tuesday nights. If, instead, they found a secure beachhead on Saturday nights, they might want to move backward to Friday.

Of course, that was assuming Fox could get anybody to watch at all, whatever night it was on. After its premiere in October 1986 the ratings had been slumping for *The Late Show*, and everyone involved was frantically trying to fix it. The problem was that the people involved fell into two camps, neither of which trusted or even respected the other. In her 1991 memoir *Still Talking*, Joan Rivers concedes that there was plenty of blame to go around for the show's troubles and ultimate failure, even if it wasn't clear what was motivating people to be so self-destructive. "Nobody in the drama rose above the foolishness. Not me, not [her husband] Edgar, not the chairman and CEO of Twentieth Century–Fox, Barry Diller, not any of the lesser executives. To this day, so much of what happened makes no sense to me."

The troubles had started as early as the plans for the announcement of the talk show in May 1986. At the meeting with Diller, Rivers's husband was pressing his point of view when Diller, never known for his diplomatic skills, cut him off with "Shut up!" He immediately apologized, but as far as Rivers and Rosenberg were concerned, it was obvious that they would be getting no respect from Diller now that the deal was made. Rivers felt that Rosenberg was being dismissed as "the star's husband" rather than as part of the creative team, and it was the start of the rift that would eventually sink the project.

Every issue that came up became a test of wills between the Rivers camp and the FBC executives. Should the show be done live or on tape? Rivers preferred that it be taped so that mistakes or slow spots could be edited out. Diller wanted it live to give the show a sense of spontaneity that the Carson show lacked. Diller prevailed. Mark Hudson was hired as the show's music director and composed a theme song. A dispute arose over who would own publishing rights to the music. Hudson thought it politic to cede them to Rivers, but in the end Fox claimed them as the owner of the show. The network had lavished some $2 million on constructing the permanent studio for the show, locating it at KTTV, the Los Angeles TV station Fox had acquired in the Metromedia deal. Then it belatedly tried to save money by taking away a refrigerator stocked with free beverages for the staff and replacing it with a soda machine.

Rivers and Rosenberg demonstrated they too could be recalcitrant. The building at KTTV also housed space for classrooms for child performers. Rosenberg informed Fox executive Kevin Wendle that the school would have to move elsewhere. Wendle insisted it had to stay. On another issue, Rivers was concerned about her safety and the fact that the Fox guards at KTTV were generally old, retired cops. Rosenberg told Barry Diller he wanted to bring in guards from the Gavin DeBecker security firm, which they used at their home. Diller flatly refused, but Rosenberg persisted. Eventually Diller agreed, provided that they were hired from a different private agency.

Indeed, from Diller's perspective, the dispute over the guards was the moment when the well was poisoned, before the first show had even gone on the air. Rivers and Diller had a meeting on the subject, each convinced that the other was trying to pursue this issue to demonstrate who had the real power over *The Late Show*. Finally calmed, they moved on to other subjects. At the end of the meeting, Rivers made a joke, playing little girl to Papa Diller. "Now that I've been nice, can I have my guards?"

Diller was furious. He didn't take the remark as a joke but as proof that his star had been trying to manipulate him. He would later cite this moment as the point when he lost confidence in the comedian. "Oh, I knew so quickly," he told early Fox network chronicler Alex Ben Block. "That's the terrible part. I didn't tell anybody, but I knew."

In retrospect, if there was any reason why *The Late Show* failed, it was not any one dispute, it was simply that you can't have the only program on a network consider itself separate from that entity. "Ultimately it was our first and only show, so it was under the microscope from our end," recalled Wendle. "The ratings were disappointing, but at the same time it was a new network. The fact of the matter is that if we saw that the show was on a path to improvement, and perhaps it was not so much under a microscope, we would have let it alone for a while. Perhaps it could have grown into being more successful."

It didn't help that Rivers favored shorter on-air interviews and more guests when, at the time, many performers were made to feel that if they appeared on *The Late Show* first they could forget about appearing on *The Tonight Show*. Meanwhile, when even the most well-meaning Fox executives tried to make suggestions for improving the program, the Rivers team dismissed them as if they were enemy agents. Programming head Garth Ancier pointed out that with *The Tonight Show* the network respected "their right to do the show they need to do, but [the network is] partners in it." With *The Late Show*, it was made clear that the people there did not want the partnership of the network in the creative aspects of the program.

"It was a shame," Wendle lamented, "because here was a woman with all this talent, and she was so married to her production team that she didn't want to hear ideas for how to make the show better, really. She saw any ideas that we came in with as interference. The more we suggested ways to make the show better, the more she resisted, the more friction there came between her and Fox."

"Did it get petty? You know, I'm sure it did," said Ancier. "But at the end of the day, it was mostly based on the fact that the show unit was being operated like an armed camp separate from us."

During the growing hostilities, Rivers recalled a meeting she and Rosenberg had with Diller and Kellner that had everyone yelling and growing abusive. Finally her attorney Peter Dekom sought to break the tension. "Do you realize what you are fighting about? People would buy tickets to see this." The arguments continued.

There would be periodic attempts to make peace, but it was for naught. In February 1987 Fox informed Rivers and Rosenberg that their producers' contract would not be renewed and that henceforth they would not be supervising their show. In the future, they were told, any suggestions or comments they had should be presented to *The Late Show*'s new producer who would deal with the production staff. A month later the replacement producer was named. It was Ron Vandor, a Fox network loyalist. In a meeting with Jamie Kellner, Rivers said she wouldn't work for Vandor. She was advised that if she carried out her threats she would be in breach of her contract. According to her memoir, that's the moment Diller walked into the room and told Rosenberg that not only would he no longer be executive producer of his wife's program but he was banned from the set.

"You're a tinhorn dictator. I don't need this. I'm a rich man," declared Rosenberg.

"Go fuck yourself," Diller replied tersely.

As *The Late Show* saga was heading for its messy denouement in the spring of 1987, Fox prime time was getting ready to launch. It was at this point that "FBC" was dropped in favor of the FOX logo as the emblem of the network. At the time Fox had been using the prestigious Los Angeles advertising/promotion house of Chiat Day, a relationship that would not last much beyond the first season. But by everyone's account, Chiat Day made one indelible mark on the new network. It convinced the regime to make use of the history that was already at their disposal.

"You're ignoring a brand that most of America knows: Fox and its searchlights," the agency told the network executives, according to Garth Ancier. "What you should be doing is taking advantage of the Fox brand and using the searchlights [already well known from the Twentieth Century–Fox movie logo] as your signature."

Ironically it meant that the network—which would still corporately be the Fox Broadcasting Company—would now be known by the name of a man who had had nothing to do with the studio since 1930, before it had merged in 1935 with Darryl F. Zanuck's Twentieth Century Pictures. William Fox was one of the founding moguls of Hollywood whose major accomplishments all came during the silent era. He had made Theda Bara a vamp star (even renaming Theodosia Goodman with a name that was an anagram for the mysterious "Arab Death"). He had started Fox Movietone News, one of the leading newsreel operations. But he was wiped out in the stock market crash of 1929 and was out of the business by the following year. At the time of his death at age seventy-three in 1952, he was a distant memory in the industry. Now his surname would be the signature for a bold new effort on television.

FOX prime time went on the air on Sunday, April 5, 1987. In a bold move, the executives selected two shows, *Married . . . with Children* and *The Tracey Ullman Show*, and ran one episode each three times that night, running the hour package at seven, eight, and nine. Said Ancier a few months before the premiere, "We're trying to say, 'This is what Fox Broadcasting is all about' on our first night on the air. We look at the second week as the first week, and the first week as sort of open house."

It was also an open house for reporters covering the network's debut. Brian Lowry covered FOX first for the *Hollywood Reporter* and then for *Variety*. He recalled FOX's premiere night, which was held on the rooftop of the Fox Plaza Building, then under construction: "They were extraordinarily lavish in their press stuff. I remember them throwing this huge party where they bought the 'HOLLY-WOOD' sign and turned it into 'FOX.' It's the first time I remember anybody doing that." That's not all they did to impress the media. "The thing that I always remember, it seemed like their PR department was full of twenty-year-old runway models," said Lowry. "Everyone there looked really young and really gorgeous."

Who decided which shows would be the first prime-time face of FOX? "Everyone was in on that decision, from Jamie [Kellner] to Barry [Diller] to Rupert [Murdoch]," recalled Ancier. "All of us agreed to try that as a way to get these two shows sampled [by viewers]. We thought that both of those shows had interesting elements to them that would appeal to different audiences. . . . So we thought, let's try to give these shows as much sampling as possible."

It was a good night for FOX. The cumulative ratings numbers for the shows demonstrated that there had been a lot of curiosity about the new network which led to a great number of viewers trying out FOX's wares. In fact, at 7 P.M. *Married . . . with Children* had actually come in second in the ratings in New York City, trailing only CBS's *60 Minutes.* Unfortunately it wasn't such a good night for Joan Rivers. She wasn't invited to the party. Her public relations person called and insisted that she had to be there, if only to counteract the rumors that were starting to circulate that *The Late Show* was being canceled. The network agreed on one condition: that her husband Edgar Rosenberg would not accompany her.

The next week, on Sunday, April 12, 1987, *21 Jump Street* premiered as a two-hour made-for-TV movie. The notion was to appeal to teen viewers with an action-oriented show that might offer the possibility of promoting the young cast members into TV stars. It was produced by Stephen J. Cannell, who was one of the hottest people in the business during the 1980s. His credits as writer, co-creator, and/or executive producer include *The Rockford Files*, *The A Team*, *Hunter*, and *Wiseguy*. He was one of several big TV producers whom Garth Ancier and Kevin Wendle had convinced to take a chance on doing a show for the new network.

Cannell developed an idea with Patrick Hasburgh, one of his up-and-coming staff writers. They pitched the show to Ancier, but the FOX executive said it wasn't right for the network. "It's not young enough," Ancier told them. "We want really, really young."

Suddenly on the spot without a show to propose, Cannell recalled a meeting he had had with Mike Post, the composer best known for his TV themes for shows like *Hill Street Blues* and *L.A. Law*. Post's home had been robbed recently, and while filling out a report at the police station he had seen a teenager doing what he assumed was his homework. Why a kid would be doing his studies at the police station didn't enter into his thoughts until the young man got up and took out his gun and badge. It turned out that the baby-faced "kid" was actually an undercover cop. Cannell had filed away the anecdote and now pulled it out of his mental file for Ancier.

"I hadn't even talked this over with Patrick [Hasburgh]," Cannell recalled. He was winging it. "I flipped it out at [Ancier], and he went, 'I love it.'"

Cannell and Hasburgh went back to their offices to begin fleshing out the concept. The first thing they did was to contact Mike Post to see if they could track down the young cop he had encountered. They did, and got a firsthand tour of the police program that used young-looking undercover cops to target drug dealers at high schools. The law enforcers' base of operations was an old church near the main headquarters of the Los Angeles Police Department, and so the projected action drama was dubbed *Jump Street Chapel*. Barry Diller didn't like it.

"He thought it might feel like it was going to be religious or something," said Cannell. It was not the last time Diller would interfere with the show.

The pilot was in production when Diller phoned Cannell. He had seen the early footage and didn't like actor Jeff Yagher in the lead role of Tommy Hanson. He wanted him replaced.

"I always hate to do that to an actor. It's so hard on their careers," Cannell said.

"I don't care. We need to do it," Diller replied.

Cannell agreed with Diller. It wasn't Yagher's fault. He was just miscast in the key part. They hurriedly rescheduled the production then ongoing in Vancouver, British Columbia—shooting in Canada would prove economical for several FOX shows—and shot around the Hanson character for five days while conducting a hurried search to replace Yagher. Cannell and his team used the KTTV soundstage that was then under construction for *The Late Show* to do the tests, and one of the actors they saw was a newcomer named Johnny Depp. The search was over. They had found their Hanson, and FOX had found its first star.

As April turned to May, FOX continued to roll out its shows. *Duet* and *Down and Out in Beverly Hills*, two half-hour sitcoms, filled out their Sunday evening schedule. Now that they were finally operating in prime time, the FOX executives no longer had an interest in prolonging their pain in dealing with Joan Rivers. She had done what they had hired her to do—give the new network some instant legitimacy—but hadn't been able to move beyond that. In other circumstances her show might have been given a chance to grow, now that FOX had a prime time on which to promote it, but there was just too much bad blood.

On Friday, May 15, 1987, Rivers did her final broadcast. She had been informed through her attorney the week before that FOX was letting her go. It had been kept secret until the parties could work out a settlement. If booking show guests had been tough before, it would have been impossible once people knew the program was being canceled. In fact the show wasn't being dumped. It was

Rivers herself who was being dismissed. She got a $2 million settlement on her $15 million contract. There were talks of lawsuits and countersuits, but at this point everyone was completely burned out on the subject.

"But still I was staggered, devastated," Rivers wrote later. "For that money I never would have left Carson and given up the foundation of my life, lost my status, lost fans, been forced to live forever with the perception that my show was a failure."

What was incredible is that FOX dropped Rivers in the midst of the May ratings sweeps. The "sweeps" are the periodic measurements of the home TV audience that are used to establish advertising rates. Stations save up their blockbuster movies, special episodes of regular programs, exploitative news series, and other extravaganzas for the sweeps period in order to set the highest possible standard for advertisers. Firing Rivers at this juncture assured a one-night spike in the ratings for her final show, and then the need to go back to square one with the fill-in format of different "guest hosts" each weeknight. Among those who took a turn were iconoclastic rock star Frank Zappa, *Three's Company* veteran co-star Suzanne Somers, and *Golden Girl* Estelle Getty.

"You just don't make a change like that in the middle of a ratings book [the report of the "sweeps" period], and if the FOX people were thinking like broadcasters, they wouldn't have done it," said one disgruntled general manager—Dennis Thatcher of WOIO, FOX's Cleveland affiliate.

The Late Show would go on without Rivers. Indeed, it would briefly grab attention with guest host Arsenio Hall, who would go on to do a rival show in syndication. For Rivers, though, the pain from the experience was far from over. In August 1987 Edgar Rosenberg committed suicide in a Philadelphia hotel room with a combination of sedatives and alcohol. By her own account, it would be some time before Rivers would recover emotionally and professionally from what had turned into one of the worst years of her life.

From the viewpoint of the FOX affiliates, their experience with *The Late Show* had been a mixed bag, but they liked what they were now seeing on Sunday nights. One station executive told *Variety*, "FOX had given us a legitimate prime-time atmosphere on the weekend."

The station owners knew it would take a few years to pay off in a big way, but already they could charge more for their advertising spots on Sunday nights, since they were now perceived to be offering original programming. National sales were moving too. At the "upfront," the annual showcase for advertisers where each network announces its schedule and urges sponsors to get on board early, FOX had lined up $20 million in ads for the upcoming 1987–1988 season from such name sponsors as Clorox, Anheuser-Busch, Kraft, Gallo Wines, and McDonald's. It hoped eventually to reach $100 million in sales, but with program licensing fees—what FOX paid for the rights to air the shows—expected to cost $150 million, the network would still be operating at a loss. Rupert Murdoch's insurance was the fact that Fox, Inc., also owned six major FOX stations. As with the affiliates, the network-owned stations had local ad "avails" which were now much more valuable than when the stations had been independents.

In one more sign that FOX was looking at the long-term picture rather than the immediate bottom line, the network shocked the industry with the announcement that it would air television's Emmy Awards show in the fall of 1987. The annual Emmys broadcasts had rotated among the Big Three for more than thirty years and were considered a loss leader. The evening's ad revenue never made up for the cost of the show, but it was a great way to promote the network's own lineup to viewers. The Academy of Television Arts and Sciences had wanted to raise the license fee charged to the networks from $750,000 to $875,000, but was turned down. FOX stepped in and offered more than a $1 million per year for the rights to the Emmys over three years as well as for the broadcast rights to the

Television Hall of Fame presentations, which the other networks hadn't really wanted at all.

When the deal was announced, the Big Three were furious. Brian Lowry, then covering FOX for the *Hollywood Reporter*, recalls, "They were threatening to boycott the Emmys that first year. The networks were somewhat disdainful. I don't think they considered FOX initially a network, just a ragtag lineup of stations."

As its first television season drew to a close, FOX had begun to make waves. It had also begun what would become a way of life at the network: the departure of top executives. Scott Sassa, who had helped create the company's business plan and was put in charge of advertising and promotion, had been shuffled to a minor post after Diller lost confidence in him. Sassa had started to burn out under the pressure of the new job. The young executive had a major television career ahead of him working with Ted Turner at his premium TNT cable channel and then at NBC. When he left FOX, however, he might have thought to leave the door open. Within the next few years, nearly everyone he had worked with in setting up the operation—with the exception of Rupert Murdoch himself—would be following him to the exit.

CHAPTER THREE

"Why should I buy you?"

[1987–1988]

	THE FOX FALL PRIME-TIME SCHEDULE					
	7:00	7:30	8:00	8:30	9:00	9:30
Sunday	21 Jump Street		Werewolf	Married . . . with Children	Tracey Ullman	Duet
Saturday			Mr. President	Women in Prison	The New Adventures of Beans Baxter	Second Chance

ANDY FESSEL noticed something odd about the TV ratings during the run of *The Late Show* while Joan Rivers was still on it. Everyone understood that FOX was a start-up operation and that the numbers would be low in its early stages. What Fessel couldn't figure out was why the Dallas, Texas, ratings were higher than the national average for the talk show. As head of research it was his job to have the numbers make sense, and he couldn't make heads or tails of this. It was as if Joan Rivers, a native New Yorker, had a special connection with the Texas audience.

Fessel called ASI Market Research, a number-crunching consulting firm in Los Angeles, and asked, "Why are some of these stations doing better than others?"

"Collect every piece of data you can about these markets," he was advised. "We'll run an analysis of it."

After the statisticians performed their magic with the material Fessel sent, one variable popped out: Dallas had a higher cable penetration of households than comparable markets at that time. The FOX network was comprised of mostly UHF stations, which traditionally had earned lower ratings. That wasn't happening in Dallas. "What does UHF mean? Higher channel numbers, lesser quality signal. What eradicates both of those? It's cable. Cable puts everyone on an equal quality signal, and cable can also change channel numbers," explained Fessel. The notion that, say, channel 68 on the UHF dial didn't *have to* be channel 68 on the cable box would be revolutionary.

The report to Fessel began a marketing campaign that would change the relationship between broadcasters and cable operators, although at the time only FOX had figured it out. Indeed, many of the FOX stations had to be dragged kicking and screaming into the cable era, because as broadcasters they had spent their entire careers working under the assumption that cable was the enemy. If a viewer was watching a pay service like HBO, they weren't in the audience of the over-the-air broadcasters, and the latter's ratings would drop. Lower ratings equaled lower rates for advertising. As far as TV station owners were concerned, cable TV was a threat to their very existence. Now FOX was telling them that cable was their friend.

The logic was impeccable. Broadcasting was about attracting large audiences with programming and then selling specified audiences to advertisers by allowing them to purchase commercial time on particular shows. Getting people to watch was the key. It didn't matter how good the programming was if the viewer was relying on their choices on cable and the local company wasn't carrying the local FOX affiliate. Cable operators in the mid-1980s had a limited amount of channel space on their systems. If there was a distant or weak local independent station that few people were watching, it was easy enough to drop it and pick up a more appealing channel like Home Shopping Network or MTV instead. So what FOX set out to do was convince local stations to woo and win over their local cable companies, and to convince the cable companies that it made good business sense for them to carry the local FOX station. It wouldn't be as easy as it sounded.

Although some stations would do the job themselves, two outside consultants took on the task of getting the FOX affiliates onto their local cable systems. Paul McCarthy was a Massachusetts-based cable consultant. In the mid-1980s he had worked at the new Disney Channel and then at the since-defunct Entertainment Channel where his task was getting cable systems to carry the service. With the growth of independent UHF stations, McCarthy went out on his own doing the same job for local broadcasters around the United States. McCarthy signed on with FOX as a consultant to troubleshoot the process for the affiliates. Mike Ruggiero, an Indiana-based consultant, essentially did the same thing, but he worked directly for the individual TV stations, many of them brand-new FOX affiliates.

The first thing FOX did was to generate detailed reports on the cable status of every single one of their stations: what systems they were on, what systems they were missing from, what channel number they had been assigned by the cable supplier, and what channel numbers the other affiliates had. "This FOX cable report is actually very historical," recalled McCarthy. "Before this no network had ever provided their affiliates . . . a report on where they stood with cable." Such was the near total lack of knowledge in this area, even among veteran broadcasters, that most general managers didn't know they were missing from some of their area cable systems.

Under FCC rules of the time, cable operators had to carry only "significantly viewed" stations. Since the commission's goal was to boost the cable industry, cable companies were not burdened with having to carry stations that viewers weren't supporting. Unfortunately for the FOX affiliates, the decision as to what stations were "significantly viewed" in a given U.S. market had been made back in 1971, when many of them weren't yet on the air. In order to gain that much-needed status, the station would have to petition the FCC and prove that for three consecutive sweeps ratings periods they had achieved a 2 share—meaning that, on average, they had 2 percent of the local television audience at any given time. Since the major sweeps were run in February, May, and November, it could take the better part of a year to generate the necessary information, and there was no guarantee in advance that any given ratings book would provide the qualifying numbers.

"Many FOX affiliates hadn't done that, hadn't gotten around to that," said McCarthy. "They didn't think it was important. You're competing in the metro area; you're making your sales. It never really occurred to them." If they were able to sell the ad time based on their urban centers, many station managers didn't worry about the people in the suburbs or surrounding rural areas who might not be able to pick up their channel on the local cable service. FOX had to educate their affiliates to rethink their position as part of a network rather than as small-time independents. "If you were out there selling advertising and you weren't on the cable system, you were dead meat," said McCarthy. According to the consultant, when a station tried to sell advertising time to, say, a local car dealer, the reaction they got was often, "I can't watch this on my local cable system. Why should I buy you?"

In an interesting loophole to the FCC rules of the time, if a station could demonstrate that it had already hit the 2 percent benchmark during its first three years of operations, it was excused from having to prove it further. This was accomplished by looking at the Arbitron records (at that time a competing ratings service to A. C. Nielsen) and—on a county by county basis—seeing how the stations had done. The result was a series of letters from FOX pointing out to its affiliates where they were not being carried on cable, though they had the right to be on those systems. All they had to do was apply.

Getting these stations to think in terms of cable was only step one. The next step was even more mind-boggling to broadcasting veterans. It was getting them to think of their stations in terms of where they were on the cable box and not where they were on the

TV dial. A station's identity, going back to the early days of radio, always began with its dial position. It made sense because listeners—and, later, viewers—had to be able to locate you. When cable came in, it followed the existing pattern. If the CBS station was on channel 2, it was also 2 on the cable box. But many FOX stations were UHF outlets, so they were at 39 or 66 or somewhere else far removed from the affiliates of the Big Three, which were VHF stations. For some cable systems, that was a problem. Perhaps they wanted that particular channel number for a cable service or, just as likely, perhaps the cable company's numbering system didn't go up that high because it didn't offer that many channels at the time. Some cable companies simply renumbered the station, so that a channel 45 on the UHF dial might become channel 6 on the cable box.

Consultant Paul McCarthy credited a broadcaster named Arnold Chase with figuring out the real importance of cable channel position. Chase had won the license for WTIC in Hartford, Connecticut, which was channel 61. He noticed that Hartford cable viewers could receive local network affiliates on channel 3 and 8, and the New York stations on channels 4, 5, and 7. He went to the cable company and asked that WTIC be put on channel 6. Said McCarthy, "It improved their ratings, marginally, almost overnight."

Andy Fessel had discovered the same situation when examining the stations like the one in Dallas where the Joan Rivers show was outperforming the national average. "We actually ran the numbers, we did a quick look, and we found that when we got a VHS channel position [of between 2 and 13], we increased an average of a rating point. Our stations who had that were a rating point higher than those who didn't. In those days that was one rating point on top of three or four, which was a really good improvement."

Again, some of the stations were reluctant to go along, according to McCarthy. "They're clinging to the notion that if you're channel 42, you want to be on 42 because that's your number. We had to educate them that what you want to do is get a different channel, right next to the other network affiliates."

Being included on cable systems and receiving a channel number assignment near the Big Three affiliates were two parts of the FOX program. The third was to get the cable companies on board. It was decided to woo them rather than follow the MTV model of urging viewers to call their local cable service and demand that the local FOX station be included. (MTV had, early on, run an ad campaign using rock stars saying, "I want my MTV.") Instead what FOX approached the cable operators as the providers of a new programming service—which in fact they were. The only difference was that, unlike Nickelodeon or ESPN, for example, which had to be bought by the cable systems that carried them, FOX was offering new programming that wouldn't cost the cable operators a dime.

The effort to win over cable operators was done at the grass roots as well as by FOX, which is where someone like consultant Mike Ruggiero was key. As opposed to McCarthy, Ruggiero was someone with no ties to the network, and his advice to the stations to get on board the cable bandwagon—and for cable operators to carry the FOX affiliates—had a good deal of authority. Here was a professional not on the FOX payroll who was able to see where the industry was heading.

All this was supplemented by a FOX effort that included attending regional cable conventions and setting up an exhibit booth just like any other cable channel. "We would bring in FOX stars where we could. We had [localized promotional] materials made up," recalled Fessel, who said the message was a simple one: "Mr. Cable Operator, what can you do? You can bring many of your subscribers, or potential subscribers, a channel that they can not easily get over the air. In many cases, in the outlying areas, you will bring them a service they really want to see."

According to Jamie Kellner, the president of the network, not everyone in the FOX executive suite approved of the cable project. One told him, "Don't get too close to those guys [the cable companies], they're dangerous." Nonetheless, Andy Fessel's notion that cable was the key to getting viewers to notice and tune into FOX would prove correct. The early effort set the stage for later innovations in the network/cable relationship that would continue to upset the way business had been done.

Now with the network in its second season, the affiliates could assess what being a FOX station really meant for them. The ability to increase ad rates for Sunday night and get taken a bit more seriously by advertisers and others were positive items. The Joan Rivers debacle had hurt the station's ad revenues, but by the fall of 1987 that was old news. After Rivers's exit, *The Late Show* continued to bump along with different hosts. FOX was promising something new and exciting in the near future for that time slot, to be called *The Wilton-North Report*. Best of all were the Sunday ratings. Although FOX was not yet on the radar as far as the Big Three were concerned, *21 Jump Street* had quickly succeeded in attracting younger viewers, with stars like Peter DeLuise and especially Johnny Depp, attracting mainstream media coverage.

At this early stage no one expected FOX to take the world by storm. The important thing was that they had, in effect, caused the desert to bloom. "Sunday night was literally a throwaway at this station," explained Patrick Mullen, who had been director of sales and then general manager of WXMI in Grand Rapids, Michigan, and is now president of Chicago-based Tribune Broadcasting. Said Mullen, "That was the night the other networks ran their biggest movies, their most powerful programs. Our ability to compete with old movies and other programming was just minimal. It was our lowest-rated night of the week. So making a commitment to FOX was a pretty easy thing to do, very honestly."

The problem, instead, was on Saturday nights. The schedule of four half-hour sitcoms was not simply not working, and *Mr. President* in particular was proving to be an embarrassing and expensive mess. The show starred the well-regarded movie and stage actor George C. Scott in his first TV series since the early 1960s when he had appeared on the issue-oriented drama *East Side, West Side*. The sitcom about the president of the United States had premiered in May 1987 and not done much business. Now, in the fall of that year, Madeline Kahn joined the cast as Scott's bizarre sister—actress Carlin Glynn, who played the First Lady, had left—and the comedy wasn't doing any better in the ratings. New shows like *Women in Prison* and *The New Adventures of Beans Baxter*, the latter about a teenage spy in Washington, D.C., didn't improve matters. The network had a problem on Saturdays, and the executives knew it. At the start of the new season, programming chief Garth Ancier wouldn't comment on plans to add a third night to the schedule, noting that FOX was still trying to fix the second night.

As the Saturday schedule fizzled, a few stations started edging toward the exit. The 1987–1988 season had begun on a happy note with Jamie Kellner able to announce that FOX now had 115 affiliates and was within reach of 85 percent of the American viewing audience. But the difference between potential audience and the number of people actually tuning in was brought home during the November sweeps. After the numbers were tallied in December, two VHF affiliates owned by Chris-Craft—KMSP in Minneapolis and KPTV in Portland, Oregon—announced they were dropping FOX's Saturday night schedule. Explained Marty Brantley, general manager of the Portland station, "We couldn't continue with the situation of the November [ratings] books, where [the syndicated *Next Generation* of] *Star Trek* at 7 was getting a 15 rating and *Mr. President* at 8 was getting only a 3."

A week later the Orlando station WOFL followed suit. "We're in the business to make money, and the FOX network just doesn't deliver the ratings on Saturday night," complained Marty Ross, the station's general sales manager to the trade publication *Variety*. WOFL would run movies instead. They would have twenty-four minutes of advertising to sell over two hours instead of the six left them by FOX for local sponsor availabilities.

This was serious trouble. Networks and affiliates always fight over clearing the schedule for network shows, since fewer stations carrying the network feed translates into a lower number of potential available viewers and therefore lower national ad rates for the network. Of course networks understood there would be occasions when a local sports or political event necessitated a preemption, but that was supposed to be a rare occurrence. The wholesale dropping of an entire night of programming, on the other hand, was a profound challenge to network authority, especially when FOX was offering only two nights of programs in total. The network convinced Chris-Craft, owners of the Minneapolis and Portland stations, to put the decision on hold to drop FOX's Saturday lineup. The new year would bring more changes to both nights of the schedule, including a series based on the hit movie of the 1960s, *The Dirty Dozen*, and an unusual deal in which a show developed and running on cable's premium Showtime channel, *It's Garry Shandling's Show*, would be repeated on FOX as new to broadcast television. By spring 1988 such flops as *Mr. President*, *Beans Baxter*, and *Women in Prison* would be off the air for good.

At the January 1988 affiliate meeting at the Century Plaza Hotel in Los Angeles, programming chief Garth Ancier promised attendees that FOX was spending $24 million to develop new shows for Saturday night. He even brought along veteran producer Aaron Spelling, who announced that a new version of his popular 1970s series *Charlie's Angels* was being planned and would be ready that summer. But the affiliates were not reassured when FOX's cutting-edge replacement for *The Late Show*, *The Wilton-North Report*, went down in flames that same month after only four weeks on the air.

What no one would dare say at the time was that FOX knew exactly what it was doing. Ancier recalled, "We made a choice early on. . . . We felt in retrospect that we had bitten off too much at FOX by starting with two nights. And so the decision was made, very early on at FOX, to take all of our bad programs, all the ones that didn't turn out very well, and put them on Saturday, and try to put the strongest night we could on Sunday night, to try to get one night working. It made Saturday night kind of a dumping ground, and it made Sunday night a much more viable night."

The theory was that once Sunday was locked up, FOX could focus on Saturday. (Years later, when Jamie Kellner and Ancier were among the people starting up the WB network, they showed they had learned their lesson well. They launched on a single night even as rival UPN began with two nights of programming.)

While Ancier was dealing with failing programs and Kellner was dealing with recalcitrant stations, Rupert Murdoch was back in the news with more potential bad tidings. The deadlines were approaching for the FCC's cross-ownership rules, which prohibited anyone from owning a daily newspaper and a broadcast outlet in the same market. Murdoch had sold the *Chicago Sun-Times* but still had the *New York Post* and the *Boston Herald*. The *Herald* became a problem when FOX acquired WFXT in Boston. Murdoch had until March 1988 to sell the *Post* and until January 1989 to divest himself of the *Herald*. At the end of the summer of 1987 Murdoch had informed a meeting of investors in Sydney, Australia, that he would not seek a permanent waiver of the FCC's rule. But until he sold the papers— or, less likely, the stations—that obviously remained a possibility.

On December 15, 1987, Massachusetts senator Edward Kennedy took steps to make sure that Murdoch sold the papers. At Kennedy's behest Senator Ernest Hollings of South Carolina inserted language into an appropriations bill that would require the FCC to enforce the cross-ownership rule for everyone. Not only was the FCC forbidden from repealing it, but it was prohibited from granting waivers to applicants. The bill passed a week later.

The action seemed clearly directed at Murdoch, since he was the only one with cross-ownership business before the commission at that time. Since Murdoch's papers were conservative critics of

Kennedy—especially his hometown *Boston Herald*—the motivation for the act was not hard to divine for many. Kennedy's fellow Democrat, New York senator Daniel Patrick Moynihan, did not agree. He and the state's junior Republican senator, Al D'Amato, wanted to leave open the possibility of an exemption for the *New York Post*, since Murdoch was keeping it operating at a loss. If the FCC rule were enforced, the paper might be deemed unsalable, and in that case Murdoch would be forced to shut it down.

In late January 1988, having no choice, the FCC denied Murdoch a waiver on the *New York Post*. The Senate then defeated the Moynihan-D'Amato proposal to repeal the Hollings amendment. Meanwhile Murdoch pressed on with his challenge to the law, appealing the FCC decision by arguing that Congress had passed a bill directed at him to his detriment. In late March the U.S. Court of Appeals in Washington, D.C., ruled 2–1 in his favor. "The Hollings amendment strikes at Murdoch with the precision of a laser beam," the court noted, overturning the law on the grounds that it unconstitutionally sought to single out Murdoch for punishment. Hollings blasted the decision, claiming, "The Appeals Court, in a split decision, arrested the policeman on the beat, while the culprit has gone free."

The victory, while sweet, was too late to save the *Post*. Murdoch had already negotiated a sale of the paper to New York real estate developer Peter Kalikow. The renewed opportunity for waivers from the cross-ownership rule wouldn't help with the *Boston Herald* either. Waivers could be granted for financial hardship, as might have been possible with the money-losing *New York Post*. Both WFXT and the *Herald* were in the black. Murdoch would end up selling the station to the Boston Celtics basketball team, then selling the paper. Eventually he would reacquire WFXT when the Celtics chose to get out of the business of operating a TV station.

By season's end, it was clear that FOX's first full season of prime-time programming had been a year of growing pains. In June of 1988 News Corp. announced that the network had bled $80 million in red ink, $30 million more than anticipated. Richard Sarazen, News Corp. director of finance, suggested that the network could be shut down within a year if things didn't improve, but he quickly retracted and claimed his remarks were taken out of context.

Both Murdoch and Barry Diller came out with forceful statements putting the best face on the situation. "We have every intention of continuing this investment for an indefinite period and remain confident of its ultimate success," said Murdoch. Diller declared, "It is unfortunate for the wrong impression to be created at this time, because we are doing in many respects, better than anticipated."

Within one year three shows, all of them already on the air, would establish FOX beyond question. It would be a long time before they were taken seriously by the Big Three, but this was the last time stories would suggest that the network was about to close its doors.

CHAPTER FOUR

"Hey, you watched the whole show"

[1988–1989]

	7:00	7:30	8:00	8:30	9:00	9:30	10:00
			THE FOX FALL PRIME-TIME SCHEDULE				
Sunday	21 Jump Street		America's Most Wanted	Married . . . with Children	It's Garry Shandling's Show	Tracey Ullman	Duet
Saturday			The Reporters		Beyond Tomorrow		

FOX'S THIRD SEASON on the air would prove to be both the best and the worst of times. By season's end several key executives—and affiliates—had departed. In contrast, the struggling network also had several TV series that finally percolated into the national consciousness. The Big Three might still ignore FOX, but the viewing public did not.

The good news had started the previous spring with the entry of *America's Most Wanted* into the Sunday-night lineup. Hosted by John Walsh, who had become a national spokesman for victims' rights after the kidnap and murder of his young son (dramatized in the 1983 TV-movie *Adam*), it set out to capture at-large criminals with the help of the viewing audience. It premiered in February

1988 on FOX's o-and-o's (owned-and-operated stations), and two months later, on April 10, was given the prime slot on Sunday night between *21 Jump Street* and *Married . . . with Children*. Two lucky breaks helped advance the show to the network.

The premiere of the series in February featured the story of David James Roberts, a prison escapee who had been sentenced to six life terms for arson-related murder. Roberts had assumed a new identity and was running a homeless shelter in New York City, home to one of the FOX-owned stations. Within days of the broadcast he was identified and taken into custody. If Roberts had hidden anywhere but in the half-dozen cities where the FOX station was an o-and-o rather than an affiliate, he might still be at large because the people who recognized him would have been unable to watch the show.

The other break was the strike called by the Writers Guild of America that shut down movie and TV production that spring. As a reality-based program, *America's Most Wanted* was not affected; it was able to go full speed ahead when FOX found itself without fresh scripts for its supernatural horror series *Werewolf*. Within a few weeks of its national debut, the show had surpassed *21 Jump Street* to become FOX's biggest hit. Some TV critics lumped it in with the growing appetite for tabloid shows like *A Current Affair* (produced and syndicated by Twentieth Century–Fox's TV production arm). The reason was that mixed in with the reporting of fugitives and the accounts of what they had done were dramatizations of the crimes. The charge of sensationalism was one that the series would have to refute constantly.

Shortly after its national premiere, Michael Linder, the show's initial executive producer, told the *Washington Times*, "I take issue with people who say it's an entertainment show. This is a weekly crime newscast that makes substantial use of docudrama."

More than a decade later, executive producer Lance Heflin was still battling the same accusations: "We've never really—to a lot of people—arrived as a legitimate television show. We're sort of stuck in that netherworld between news and entertainment. Because we do reenactments, the news industry thinks we're way too sensational, even though the real facts behind our reenactments are all assiduously researched."

The reenactments were obviously what drew in some viewers, with actors portraying the real-life criminals. In the beginning, noted Heflin, "they were a little bit over the top. You know what they did? They actually showed the reality of the [crime] situation, which is a little too much for most people." Ultimately they were toned down, and *America's Most Wanted* settled in for a long, if somewhat rocky, run on the network.

Unfortunately the success of the show was too little and too late for some of the affiliates, which saw the Saturday schedule growing weaker and likely to remain so for some time to come. More stations were grumbling about low ratings and lower advertising revenues, and the unrest finally came to a head in July 1988 when KMSP in Minneapolis, KPTV in Portland, Oregon, and WTOG in Tampa, Florida, all left the fold. The official word was that the stations had simply elected not to renew their affiliation deals, but it was more pointed than that. Bob Mariano, the network's affiliate relations person for the Midwest, recalls that FOX made it clear they were prepared to do without the Minneapolis station, even though it was a VHF outlet.

"We had to sever it because we could not say, 'It's okay for you not to carry Saturday' and ask all the other affiliates to carry Saturday," Mariano said. "FOX is a family that carries the project and makes it happen. If a major station in the Midwest doesn't carry you because they can make money in another way, that's not part of the bigger vision of the project for the network."

A signal was sent to all the other affiliates: if the network was willing to drop a prized VHF station in a major market for failing to stay on board with the "full" schedule, it wouldn't think twice about doing the same to UHF stations in smaller markets. This was an important message to get out early, when the affiliates still controlled five of seven nights of prime time, usually running movies. As FOX added additional nights of network programming, they didn't want the affiliates treating the evening lineup as a smorgasbord, where they could pick and choose what to carry. Being a network affiliate meant carrying the full load.

"We just weren't willing to accept half a marriage," said network chief Jamie Kellner at the time.

By fall 1988 it seemed that FOX was paying attention to the weak spots on its schedule. In October it ended *The Late Show*. A full-time replacement for Joan Rivers had never been found, and many stations—including FOX o-and-o's—had begun running it at midnight. The network's one serious attempt to replace it, *The Wilton-North Report*, had been a disaster, canceled in January 1988 only four weeks after its premiere. A mix of news, comedy skits, and interviews, it was described by one critic as an "unusual, unsuccessful, and generally unfunny attempt to fill the late-night slot in FOX's schedule." It was replaced by the return of *The Late Show*, which bumped along for another ten months. Finally, without fanfare, the show that had been the first offering of the fourth network was now history, and the hour was returned to the control of the local stations.

FOX now had more important things on its agenda than late-night. It had to rescue Saturday night. It had canceled its sitcoms, like the ill-fated *Mr. President*, and replaced them with *The Reporters*, a newsmagazine, and *Beyond Tomorrow*, which featured stories on future trends and inventions. The ratings, still weak, were up 50 percent over the four sitcoms replaced. What's more, news and "reality" shows were far cheaper to produce. The early failures had been a learning experience for FOX's young creative team, who were finally able to articulate a rationale for FOX beyond merely being a fourth network.

"We didn't understand . . . that when you're trying to start a new television network, you have to aim young," said Garth Ancier. "*Mr. President*, despite the fact that we had a terrific producer in Ed.

Weinberger and, obviously, George C. Scott is a huge name to get at that time to be the lead of a show—that show was not going to appeal to younger viewers. It was going to appeal to older viewers. And those viewers were simply not going to turn to a UHF station to try out a new show. Had that show been on CBS, maybe."

If FOX seemed to be getting its act together publicly, in private the executive offices were witnessing some of the ugliest infighting in TV history. When Scott Sassa left the network in the spring of 1987, Barry Diller wanted to put Kevin Wendle, the programming department's number-two guy, in charge of advertising, publicity, and promotion.

"I don't want to leave my programming connection," Wendle recalled telling Diller.

"We'll have you still in the programming group. You'll still report to Garth. And you'll still be at the table to have a say about programming," Diller replied.

Practically speaking, though, Wendle was out of the loop on programming while he turned the ad-pub-promo department around. Six months later Wendle had done so well that Diller came back and said he wanted to give him a larger role in programming. With Ancier's blessing, Wendle returned to programming in the summer of 1988, with both of them receiving promotions. In theory, nothing was supposed to have changed. Ancier was to be in charge of programming, and Wendle was to report to him. That's not what happened, however. Like a kid poking at an animal with a stick, Barry Diller's widely known management style served to goad these two friends into turning on each other. It was a breach from which they never fully recovered.

Ancier, who later called Diller a "friend" and Wendle an "acquaintance," described it this way: "I think part of Barry's management style is to have those kinds of rivalries going on between executives in the hope that the best person will rise to the top. My problem, personally, is that I don't respond to that kind of sibling-rivalry situation very well."

When Wendle returned to programming, Diller and Jamie Kellner made it clear that they wanted him to turn the department around as he had done with ad-pub-promo. "I think for the six months I was not involved in the programming, the programming department had fallen from grace a little bit through some bad luck more than anything. It wasn't through bad management," said Wendle, referring to the Saturday night shows that were flopping.

While Wendle had been preoccupied elsewhere, Ancier had come to rely on Alan Sternfeld, another NBC alumnus. But Sternfeld constantly clashed with Diller. When Wendle returned, his position on the organizational flow chart was between Ancier and Sternfeld. Diller did nothing to make the transition easier. Sternfeld told George Mair, author of the 1997 *The Barry Diller Story*, "Barry played games with Garth. I remember specific incidents where Garth would say, 'I promised so and so I'd answer them by four o'clock tomorrow. What do you want to do?' Four o'clock would roll around and Barry would make himself unavailable, and Garth would tear his hair out because he had promised to come to some conclusion by that deadline." Then, to add insult to injury, Diller would upbraid Ancier for failing to act.

Ultimately Sternfeld departed in 1988, a move that was perceived to strengthen Wendle's position and weaken Ancier's. "It wasn't a great situation," recalled Wendle with a rueful laugh. "When you have a lot of people at that time in their lives—we were all in our late twenties, incredibly ambitious, all wanting to succeed. . . . People can get bruised."

What was needed at the network was a senior executive, like Diller, to step in and exert parentlike authority. Instead he added fuel to the fire. When Wendle had all programming staffers report to him, rather than to Ancier, and then had meetings with show suppliers without including his putative boss, Ancier went to Diller and demanded to know what was going on. Diller told him he'd be included in the process "when it's appropriate."

"What am I supposed to do? What are my responsibilities?" Ancier asked.

"Just tell people you're busy," Diller replied. When asked what that meant, Diller answered, "It means you'll go to your office and say you're busy." Diller suggested Ancier work on other parts of the schedule instead of regular prime-time programming.

"It means Kevin really is in charge," said Ancier.

"We're going to give him his chance," said Diller.

Ancier was appalled. Looking back, he agreed that Diller could have settled this easily but instead chose to let the infighting continue. "What you need is two people in a situation like that who are doing the same thing. One who will tolerate it, which is Barry, and one who will take advantage of it, which is Kevin," he said. "I put at least as much blame on Kevin for his behavior during that period, which was pretty reprehensible."

For his part, Kevin Wendle felt he was put in an untenable position. "It was weird. In a way I think everyone wanted me to be the catalyst to clean up the programming department, which meant I was perceived as the hatchet man," he said—which was a role he didn't want. "I think that's what created some ill will. I think that's what was intended, and it was a difficult situation for me because I really had no choice. . . ."

To an outsider coming into this heated situation, it must have seemed like a madhouse, but for Rob Kenneally—who arrived at the network as the new senior vice president for programming that summer of 1988—it was already obvious what he was getting into. He had been at the company's production unit for a year when he was summoned to Diller's office on a Friday afternoon. As head of Fox, Inc., Barry Diller supervised all aspects of the studio, but instead of congratulating Kenneally for having just sold a show to ABC, Diller said he needed him at the network more than in the production end. As a kicker, Diller told him he didn't expect to be turned down unless Kenneally felt he wasn't up to the job. Kenneally, who was just starting his career and had no experience in network TV, told Diller he'd like some time to think it over.

"So I left his office, and I walked across the lot, because, at the time, Fox TV [the production unit] was at the rear of the lot, and I went back to my office. I was getting ready to call my wife to tell her I might have to postpone our vacation plans because Barry Diller had called me. But before I could reach my wife, the phone was ringing and my assistant ran in and she said, 'It's Barry Diller on line two.' And I picked up the phone and he goes, 'Well?'"

By the following week Kenneally was at the network, trying hard not to take sides but finding himself working closely with Kevin Wendle even though he was also dealing with Garth Ancier. "I wasn't sure which way to go," he recalled. "For the first few weeks of the job it was very tricky because there was clearly a wall between the two of them, and you were sort of self-conscious in either office to the other one."

Kenneally attended meetings with Diller, Ancier, and Wendle, and watched as Diller did nothing to calm the situation. "It was clear to an outsider coming in [that] Garth's sort of golden boy status had rubbed off a little bit and Barry was looking for new blood. At the same time I think he didn't want to relinquish control to anybody. He wanted to see who would rise to the occasion. That was his way. He didn't do anything to correct it, really. He would just have all three in a room and hopefully our mixed agendas would produce results."

In that regard, Diller proved to be right. That's precisely what happened. During that time span, plans were made for several shows that would premiere later in the 1988–1989 season or the next fall. Several of them would be among Ancier's favorites from his FOX tenure—"Some of the best shows on FOX came out of that really horrible period, *The Simpsons* and *In Living Color*." Also placed in development was a teen-oriented one-hour drama that would become *Beverly Hills 90210* and another reality-based show, *COPS*, that started on the o-and-o's. "The irony is that we were all getting better at our jobs while all this nonsense was going on around us, which is kind of too bad in retrospect, because had we been able to hold it all together, we probably would have grown even faster."

Added Kenneally, "When I say it was awkward, 'awkward' and 'impossible to do the job' are two different things. Awkward was a constant, but we worked together as a threesome."

By mid-February 1989 Ancier had had it. He had actually asked to be let out of his contract earlier, but Diller had persuaded him to stay on until his replacement could be found. Now he had been found, and it was not Kevin Wendle. Instead Peter Chernin—who had run the movie division at Lorimar Pictures and then become head of programming for cable's Showtime channel—was brought aboard. At age thirty-seven, Chernin would have seemed a TV veteran compared to Ancier and Wendle. Said Wendle, who would depart FOX a few months later, "I think it became clear to me that Peter wanted to bring in his own people."

More than a decade later the wounds of that period haven't entirely healed. Wendle, whose TV credits include producing *The Fresh Prince of Bel-Air* with musician/producer Quincy Jones and co-founding internet and media businesses including CNET and iFILM, felt he was placed in a bad situation. Ancier, now chairman of the WB, said he encounters Wendle occasionally and they're on good terms, but only to a point, "I've said to Kevin that I would probably never work with him again."

When the dust cleared at the end of the 1988–1989 season, Garth Ancier and Kevin Wendle were gone, and Peter Chernin was in. And Rob Kenneally stayed on.

Four factors helped ensure FOX's eventual success. Three were network shows, and the fourth was a person. *21 Jump Street* had been FOX's first real success, especially with the star Johnny Depp being heavily promoted in mainstream media as a teen heartthrob. *America's Most Wanted* was a surprise hit that has proved to be FOX's most enduring show to date. The third key show was *Married . . . with Children*, which had been the very first program to air on FOX in prime time. It had achieved a cult status as a somewhat tasteless family sitcom that was so well written and acted that some actually saw it as dark satire of modern suburban life rather than simply an unending stream of sex jokes. Indeed, its working title during production was *Not the Cosbys*, a reference to the then-popular NBC sitcom starring Bill Cosby. Apart from these shows, the person who helped put FOX over the top was a woman who didn't like *Married . . . with Children*. Her name was Terry Rakolta. Her protest against the show played out in ways neither she nor FOX could have planned.

Married . . . with Children had always been a favorite among the FOX executives—with the exception of Barry Diller, who had doubts about many of the FOX series that would go on to become successes. When *Married . . .* was selected to be one of the two shows to launch the network's entry into prime time in April 1987, Kevin Wendle recalls it was because it was a "show that we all look forward to watching every week that the public hasn't seen yet." The focus of the program was on the misadventures of the Bundys, a suburban Chicago family. Al (Ed O'Neill) is a loser who hates his job as a shoe salesman and dreads going home to his sex-starved wife Peg (Katey Sagal). His children are no solace either. Kelly (Christina Applegate) is, in her mother's words, "popular" with all the boys in school while Bud (David Faustino) is a geeky kid who seems destined to follow in his dad's footsteps without ever having known Al's brief moment of glory as a high school athlete.

The show's creators, Ron Leavitt and Michael Moye, had been told by Ancier and his team to be as outrageous as they could be, doing the sort of material the Big Three would never allow on the air. They immediately went too far. In one episode set for the second-season premiere (and instead pushed back later in the 1987–1988 season), the Bundys go camping with their neighbors Steve and

Marcy (David Garrison, Amanda Bearse). During the trip Peg, Marcy, and Kelly all start their menstrual periods. As if that wasn't provocative enough for prime time, in one line Al complains about PMS—premenstrual syndrome—by claiming it really stands for "Pommel Men's Scrotums." When the network's standards and practices office (the in-house censors) cut the line, Leavitt and Moye complained to Ancier.

"You told us to be free. Now you tell us not to be free. Which is it?" demanded Leavitt.

They ended up splitting the difference. The show eventually ran as written, but it was later in the season and in a later time slot.

Married . . . with Children was successful for FOX. In November 1988 it actually beat a regularly scheduled Big Three show (ABC's revival of the 1960s spy series *Mission: Impossible*) and clearly was a modest hit. It might have remained that way but for the night of January 15, 1989. The episode airing that Sunday evening had to do with the full-figured Peg buying a new bra. It wasn't extraordinarily offensive by the standards already established for the series. But for Terry Rakolta, a Michigan housewife and mother of four who was seeing the show for the first time, it was nothing less than shocking.

Rob Kenneally recalled that when he first joined the network in the summer of 1988, the future of the show was up in the air. *"Married . . . with Children* could have stayed or gone," he said. "It had no traction. It did not have national awareness."

Rakolta had tuned in knowing nothing about the sitcom except the title, which made it seem family oriented. Within minutes she had sent her pre-teen kids from the room as the on-screen discussion turned toward vibrators and what Rakolta called "deviant sexual behavior." Said Rakolta, "When I see it in my living room, right on free television, that's when I have to get involved."

She decided to complain. She started with the network, then turned to her local station. One of the people she reached was Kevin O'Brien, general manager of three FOX affiliates, including WKBD in Detroit. "She was [exercising] on a treadmill, she told me.

And she said she watched the whole program and found it disgusting," he recalled, "My response to her was, 'Hey, you watched the
whole show, did you? You found it that disgusting?'"

Rakolta told him that if the FOX people had treated her with respect she might not have been as angry as she was. When she had
reached the network offices, they referred her to one of the show's
writers who told her she should either change the channel or turn off
her set. What she did instead was recount her experiences to the
show's advertisers, a lot not known for their courageousness in such
potentially consumer-offending situations. The Gillette Company announced that they felt the episode "violated any reasonable standard
of good taste" while the pharmaceutical company Warner-Lambert
declared it "not a desirable vehicle for [our] advertising." Coca-Cola
said they would pull their ads from unacceptable episodes, which
was curious since, at the time, Coca-Cola owned Columbia Pictures
Television—the company that produced the series.

With Rakolta now banging the drums for an advertiser boycott,
FOX had to react. It promised to monitor the show more closely in
the future to prevent further embarrassment to advertisers. The
story, however, would not die. Rakolta's crusade made the *New York
Times* and it led to her appearance on ABC's late-night news show
Nightline. *Married . . . with Children* co-creator Michael Moye wanted
to debate her on the news show, but he was told to decline an invita-
tion to appear. In fact, at first FOX didn't realize what it had just been
handed. As FOX spokespeople talked of standing by the show, Moye
later recalled to writer George Mair, "All the while we were getting
phone calls from FOX saying that we had to tone it down."

As usually happens with such controversies, all the attention
made television viewers unfamiliar with the FOX series very curious
about the show. The program's ratings started to climb. Tribune's
Patrick Mullen, who had overseen several FOX affiliates, said that
Rakolta's crusade "gave it more publicity than the FOX network or
any station could afford to give it. It took it from a mediocre—at
best mediocre—performer to a very successful show for FOX."

Joe Young, another Midwestern affiliate general manager and now a regional vice president with Tribune, says that Rakolta sold the show to the heartland. "That was the best thing that ever happened to us. She came out and talked about this FOX network," he recalled. "Wow, it just took off. I think people became conditioned that FOX was going to take chances and put on different kinds of programming."

As the viewer numbers rose, the advertisers came back and the network honchos muted their grumbling toward *Married . . . with Children.* "The spike in our ratings was so noticeable that we would get calls . . . from press and/or peers in the industry saying, 'What a genius move.' Thinking we had actually orchestrated it, which of course we hadn't," said Kenneally. "We were lucky recipients in reverse. Everything she was trying to do actually backfired. People all of a sudden went to check it out. We wanted to put a bust of her in the lobby of the FOX network at one time."

The show would prove to be such a success that when the series aired its final first-run episode in mid-1997, it was the longest-running sitcom then on the air.

Looking back at the end of the 1988–1989 season, it was clear that FOX had transcended the "coat-hanger network" insult of only three years earlier. Its Sunday lineup was getting stronger, and Saturday had been boosted by the arrival of *COPS*, a cinema verité series following the work of actual police officers. It started by following just the officers of Broward County, Florida, but as it gained the respect of audiences—and real law enforcers—the producers were soon invited to shoot their episodes elsewhere. By the summer of 1989 they were doing a one-hour special on the police officers of Moscow and Leningrad.

Meanwhile at the network offices Peter Chernin had brought stability to the programming department, and the network was gearing up to launch a third night—Monday—in the fall of 1989.

Advertising sales were up at the "up front" market in June. The year before they had had $125 million in advance sales. They had hoped to double it in for the 1989–1990 season and exceeded that, hitting $300 million. Instead of reports that FOX was losing so much money that it might shut down, the fiscal word at the end of the 1988–1989 season was that it had approached break-even or might even turn a profit.

The Big Three had yet to acknowledge it, but FOX had turned the corner.

CHAPTER FIVE

"People will watch car accidents, too"

[1989–1990]

	7:00	7:30	8:00	8:30	9:00	9:30	10:00	10:30
			THE FOX FALL PRIME-TIME SCHEDULE					
Sunday	Booker		America's Most Wanted	Totally Hidden Video	Married . . . with Children	Open House	Tracey Ullman	It's Garry Shandling's Show
Monday			21 Jump Street		Alien Nation			
Saturday			COPS	The Reporters		Beyond Tomorrow	Comic Strip Live	

ONE OF THE HALLMARKS of the new network's corporate culture was the weekly "Tuesday morning meeting" held at the FOX offices. Years later, former FOX executives still speak of it with awe, trepidation, and occasional laughter. Each week the network management—programming, sales, marketing, finance, research, affiliate relations, standards and practices—would gather around a table to report on where they'd been and where they were going. Led by Barry Diller and Jamie Kellner, this wasn't just the department heads. This was nearly everyone. Many of the stories FOX veterans tell of those years come out of the Tuesday morning meetings.

They were originally set for Monday mornings, but the "overnight" ratings took forty-eight hours to produce back then, so the meetings were shifted to mid-morning on Tuesday. Research chief Andy Fessel would bring his team in extra early that day to crunch the numbers on the computer and write up their assessment of how FOX had done over the weekend in the ratings. Over time the company-wide meeting not only became a not-to-be-missed event but one that you had to arrive early for if you expected a seat at the table.

"They'd force their way into the room," recalled Fessel. "If you didn't get there early you'd stand along the walls. The room was packed. People were sitting on the tables, people were sitting on the floor. And they kept it in a small room because they wanted people to fight to get there. And everybody could be heard."

The meetings were perfect for Barry Diller's management style of pitting people against one another. Diller was known to back executives who could stand up to challenges thrown out by himself or others, and to cut staff off at the knees if they couldn't. At these weekly gatherings each department head would report, but Diller and Kellner would allow people to question and comment outside of their ordinary domain. The late Bob Mariano, the director of Midwestern affiliate relations who briefly ran the entire affiliate shop, recalled the sessions as essential to imparting the spirit of the new network to every employee. He said that the people in programming—who had enough trouble being second-guessed by Diller, Kellner, and Rupert Murdoch—suddenly found themselves dealing with comments from all sides. "A woman in the accounting department say[s], 'I'm really upset about the way women are treated on *Married . . . with Children*.' Well, the programming department has worked this all out, and we have rationalized it, and we understand that's a retro thing, and surreal, and postmodern—and what the *hell* is the accounting department woman saying she's very upset about how they're treated on *Married . . . with Children*?"

Garth Ancier, the first programming chief to face this sort of internal grilling, found the meetings useful and continued the process when he and Kellner were reunited later at the WB network. "I think the idea of having everyone in a company around a table once a week to talk about what they watch on television, what's good, what do you not like, what do you like, about what we're doing, is a great way to get everyone's feedback, because television is one of those businesses where everyone has an opinion because everyone's a customer." Indeed, Ancier felt it was "healthy" for the programming department to hear from their co-workers. "But it's hard, because people generally don't want to speak their mind about programming for fear of upsetting others, when in fact we need honest feedback."

Of course, the get-togethers could sometimes get tense, as during the Ancier/Wendle power struggle, or when Diller began interrogating an underling not prepared to respond. There was also the problem that Diller, time and again, didn't personally like the shows that were putting FOX on the map. He was embarrassed that *Married . . . with Children* had become the program most closely associated with his network. He was skeptical of almost everything except *America's Most Wanted*. When *COPS* was launched, Diller questioned programming executive Rob Kenneally, making it clear that he felt that the reality show was too lurid and exploitative, especially as the pilot episode exposed the home life of the police officers as well as their tours of duty.

Diller, knowing that Kenneally was a reserve deputy with the Los Angeles sheriff's department, asked why he was pushing *COPS*, implying that there must be some sort of ulterior motive. Kenneally insisted that the grittiness and toughness was a major selling point for the series and would help FOX where it was weakest, on Saturday nights.

"Why do you fight for this show?" Diller demanded at one meeting. "Why are you always bringing it up?"

Kenneally replied, "Because people will watch it."

Diller's response was as deadly as it would prove ultimately to be ironic: "People will watch car accidents too. Do you suggest we program those?" By the time FOX did begin scheduling car accidents in prime time, in shows like *The World's Wildest Police Videos* in the mid-1990s, Diller was long gone from the network.

One of the reasons why Tuesday staff meetings became so crucial is that they marked a break with the way networks monitored themselves. At the Big Three the focus was on months and seasons. A show that didn't work in the fall might be pulled the next January, or it might actually run out the full season, even into summer repeats. Diller was a television executive who had also worked in the movie business, and he brought a movie executive's attitude to FOX.

"Basically, the movie business is a weekend business," explained Fessel. The ads would be building to a Friday opening, the weekend grosses would come out Monday so that the movie could be promoted as "Number One Hit in the Country" during the week, and the hope was that business would stay strong the next weekend. "We ran FOX on exactly the same timetable, which was weekly."

The major part of the agenda on Tuesdays was given over to assessing the past weekend's performance. Which shows were up, and why? Did promotion play a role in the increase, and how could that be built upon? What was down? Was it the program's fault, a failure of advertising, a problem with scheduling? What was the next episode like for each show, and how could they be promoted? By meeting's end, each department would have its marching orders for the next week's programming lineup.

"We would turn around on Wednesday, the next day, and teleconference with the affiliates. We would put all this preparation together—kind of a newscast, almost," recalled Fessel. During the teleconference the affiliates would be told what was promotable, what the competition was, what was working and what wasn't. "Then—Thursday, Friday—we'd run all the promotions. Saturday, Sunday, the shows would run; and Monday, Tuesday morning we'd start all over again."

The fall 1989 season saw FOX expand to a third night of programming. As Kellner and Fessel had discussed back before
FOX first went on the air in prime time in 1987, the expansion would
follow which night was most successful. Since Sunday was clearly
playing out better for FOX, the network's new night of programming
was Monday. (If Saturday had enjoyed higher ratings, FOX would
have moved to open up Fridays.) The new Monday schedule would
lead off with what had been its strong Sunday starter, *21 Jump
Street*. Its Sunday-night slot was taken by *Booker*, a similar teen-
action show starring Richard Grieco, who had been added to *Jump
Street* the previous season as a backup in case Johnny Depp left.
Now he was being spun off into his own series.

Stephen J. Cannell, creator of *21 Jump Street*, was not happy
with the decision. "We would have been better off if we had stayed
where we were," he would say in hindsight. The series would last
two more years, but only one more on the FOX network. At the end
of the season there was a real question whether the series would be
renewed, and whether Depp would continue.

"People wanted him to go and do features. I was always concerned that at the end of year four he was going to leave," said Cannell, noting that although Depp had one more year on his contract,
actors can make things difficult if they want to get out of a show.
Then one day Depp called Cannell.

"Look, you're probably wondering what I'm going to do," said
Depp.

"Yeah, I am."

"Put your mind at rest," the actor told him. "I hope the show is
canceled because I want to go on and do features, but I do have a
contract with you, and if it gets picked up I'll be there."

Cannell was floored by the gesture. "I thought it was really
classy," he said, adding, "and then we *were* canceled."

Almost the moment that the word got out in the spring of 1990
that the show was off the FOX schedule, Cannell's office began field-
ing calls from FOX stations, including some of the FOX o-and-o's.

"What happened to *Jump Street*? That show was working for us," they said.

"Well, talk to your network."

"Well, they don't want to put it back on, but we want the show."

By the time Cannell got commitments from FOX stations in Los Angeles, New York, and Chicago, he realized that—if he wanted it—he could distribute the show himself and be cleared in the major markets. Even without Depp, whose commitment ended with the network run, there was interest in continuing the series, and so *21 Jump Street* had a fifth season, and Cannell had his first syndicated program.

There was only one thing Cannell couldn't bring himself to do. He had quietly acquired interests in three FOX stations in markets like Cleveland and Greenville, North Carolina. His plan was to put together a group of eight or nine stations located in the top twenty-five markets, and build a platform to launch his own syndicated shows at will. It never quite came off, and he eventually sold the stations, but he enjoyed his adventures on that side of the business. "It was great. I made a lot of money as a FOX affiliate. I always wanted to go to the affiliates meeting and raise my hand and say, 'Mr. Diller, why did you cancel *Jump Street*?' but I never did that," he said.

The other Monday-night premiere in the fall of 1989 was *Alien Nation*, a series about aliens who arrive on Earth in the year 1995 as escaped slaves and are slowly integrated into Earth's society. It had been based on a moderately successful 1988 film from Twentieth Century–Fox starring James Caan and Mandy Patinkin, and was developed by the company's production arm as a pilot for ABC. Series executive producer Ken Johnson was in the middle of writing the one-hour pilot when he got a call from the network. "Look, Barry [Diller] decided he doesn't want to sell it to ABC. He wants it for his own network," Johnson was told. Further, as the Fox, Inc., chairman's remarks were relayed to Johnson, Diller had insisted, "I don't want to make something that I think is this cool and give it away to

somebody else. I want it to be a FOX project. And, by the way, I want
it to be two hours."

Alien Nation would prove to be one of those offerings that every
TV network has in its history: the program that should have been a
hit but in which the network lost faith. It didn't help that—airing
Mondays at 9 P.M.—it was up against two of the ratings power-
houses of the TV schedule, Monday Night Football on ABC and
Murphy Brown on CBS. Another potential drawback was that it was
a science fiction series, which had never performed well on television. The original *Star Trek* had struggled along for three seasons
before being canceled. In the fall of 1989, the new incarnation, *Star
Trek: The Next Generation*, was beginning only its third season in
syndication, where it would prove to be a phenomenal success. But
the success of *Next Generation* simply reinforced the feelings of the
executives that the only science fiction series that would succeed
were ones that attracted the legion of loyal *Star Trek* fans.

The format of *Alien Nation* was to tell its stories through the
eyes of its two main characters, human cop Matt Sykes (Gary Graham) and his alien partner George Francisco (Eric Pierpoint). As far
as producer Johnson was concerned, this was an opportunity to deal
with social issues—whether it was discrimination against minorities,
religious issues, even intermarriage—using the alien "Newcomers"
as a metaphor for earthbound minorities. As far as the FOX executives were concerned, said Johnson, "They kept thinking it was
Lethal Weapon [1987] with *Coneheads* [1970s comic space aliens from
Saturday Night Live and a subsequent 1993 movie], which is not
what I wanted to do."

"I remember Ken Johnson being very passionate and really having a clear vision of the show. I think there was the general feeling,
certainly around our offices, that it was well done and just really interesting," said one of those executives, Paul Stupin, then executive
vice president of series programming. "I guess it had trouble finding an audience because it was a little more cerebral than other science fiction shows up to that point."

Years later, other fantastic shows that owed nothing to *Star Trek*, like the syndicated *Babylon 5*, the WB's *Buffy the Vampire Slayer*, and FOX's own *The X-Files*, would prove the theory that it takes time for such entertainment to catch on, but when they do find a following, the audience is fiercely loyal. But FOX executives kept looking for *Alien Nation* to provide that immediate big spike in the ratings, and it never happened, not even for the memorable episode in February 1990 where Matt learns that it is the Newcomer males who give birth to their offspring, and George goes into labor. The positive critical reviews and the citation from the Viewers for Quality Television weren't enough to save the series, especially when the decision was made to have the network concentrate more on comedies.

One FOX executive who was a fan of the show, Rob Kenneally, feels that *Alien Nation* was doomed because of the corporate mindset during that season. "Because of the breakout success of the previous year [of *America's Most Wanted*, *COPS*, and *Married . . . with Children*], there was an attitude from Diller that unless something was going to break out, and unless it showed signs of breakout, you would toss it to take the next one on. . . . It was just sort of staying in moderately successful but not breakout territory, and we were in breakout mentality then."

"Barry did not think the show was going to grow and, in the end, I don't think he ever got it. He just never understood what it was about. Or maybe he did and it just wasn't his cup of tea, I don't know," said Johnson. One insider also told Johnson that Diller resented the bald aliens because they looked like him, but that may have been just a joke to ease the pain of cancellation. The show's final episode, unfortunately a cliffhanger setting up a second season that wasn't to be, aired in April 1990.

Like *Star Trek*, though, *Alien Nation* became the show that would not die. It found new viewers in reruns, though there were only twenty-two episodes to run, not the sixty-five of the original *Trek*. It also found new life on cable's Sci-Fi Channel. (In one of those twists that abound in television, in the mid-1990s Sci-Fi became part of Barry Diller's post-FOX media empire.) As a result of viewers getting repeated chances to see the series, Johnson and the show's fans would get the last laugh. In 1993 the first of five *Alien Nation* TV-movies ran on FOX, featuring the original cast from the show and picking up right from the cliffhanger ending of the series. According to the producer, "We all felt it was like a gift from the gods, to get to come back after the show had been canceled. We had been off the air and separated for two years, almost three years, yet when we had the opportunity, everybody just flocked back to do it."

If the expansion to Monday was rocky for FOX, a weekend change was about to make television history. In December the weak *Beyond Tomorrow* was put out of its misery after a little over a year on the air, and *Totally Hidden Video* was shifted to Saturday in a reshuffle of that evening's schedule. That left a hole on Sundays at 8:30 P.M., which was to be filled with a type of show that hadn't worked in prime time in more than two decades: a wholly animated half-hour. Based on two-minute segments that had run on *The Tracey Ullman Show*, *The Simpsons* was about to change all the rules.

As with so many programming decisions, Barry Diller was skeptical. When Andy Fessel provided new research showing that audiences were primed for a sharply written animated comedy, Diller didn't believe it. Indeed, even as Diller, Jamie Kellner, and everyone else at FOX devoured the ratings reports—digests were prepared even for owner Rupert Murdoch—Diller was outspoken in his belief that TV programming was a creative enterprise and couldn't be reduced to numbers. "He called us the witch doctors of the television business, all hocus pocus," Fessel said. He recalled the research staff's plans to show up at one of the Tuesday meetings dressed in the appropriate witch doctor garb, complete with bones and spells, but they never quite dared to go that far with the big boss.

The genesis of *The Simpsons* came when the offbeat "Life in Hell" comic strip was brought to the attention of James L. Brooks, producer of FOX's *The Tracey Ullman Show*. Brooks met with the strip's creator, Matt Groening, and they agreed on a series of cartoon shorts involving a family to be used as a regular segment on Ullman's show. As has been widely reported, Groening's parents really are named Homer and Marge, and he does have two sisters named Maggie and Lisa, though none of them are like their cartoon counterparts. When the cartoonist was asked to devise a half-hour special or series of specials involving the Simpson family, he decided to see if he could push this opening wedge, making *The Simpsons* into a full-fledged series. Prime-time animation had had its heyday in the early 1960s, when network programming began at 7:30 P.M. instead of 8, and when there was room for something family oriented like *The Flintstones*.

"I designed *The Simpsons* to be a TV series. That was always my secret plan. The idea of putting animated characters on at prime time was considered very controversial," Groening told George Mair for his biography of Barry Diller. "I was worried that just having one shot at getting people's attention would not do it."

The first half-hour episode ran as a Christmas special in December 1989, with Homer out of money for holiday presents and trying to win a bankroll at the local dog track. The episode appears crude compared to what the series would become over the next few years, but much of the concept was already in place. There were the multitude of recurring characters that gave you a sense that the Simpsons' hometown of Springfield wasn't merely drawn, it was actually populated. There was son Bart's mouthing off, and there was that touch of sentimentality which never overwhelmed the satiric humor but let viewers know that this dysfunctional family really did love one another. The reviewer in *Variety* was more confident than Barry Diller was about the prospect of a *Simpsons* series: "[It] should fit well into the FOX lineup if the characters and situations sustain the level of this initial effort."

When *The Simpsons* began its regular run in January 1990, it caught on quickly with TV viewers, though many adults assumed it was a kids show without bothering to see for themselves. The early public impression of *The Simpsons* was that it was about bratty Bart, a kid who was "an underachiever and proud of it" and who dismissed adult concerns by advising, "Don't have a cow, man." Parents and teachers expressed concern about this supposedly negative role model, clearly not getting the joke. It would take a year or two for *The Simpsons* to be recognized for what it clearly is, one of the smartest and best-written comedies on television.

By the end of the 1989–1990 season *The Simpsons* was a key piece in FOX's programming while its parent show was breathing its last. Tracey Ullman called it quits, proud of her Emmy—the first, and so far only, one won by a FOX series—and thanked her TV home for the past four seasons "for letting somebody no one ever heard of do a show on a network that didn't exist." Though a critical darling, her innovative sketch-comedy show had never really attracted large audiences, and it never became one of FOX's signature series. Ullman's sketch humor would later find a home on cable's HBO with the series *Tracey Takes On . . .* in 1996, and still later she would return to FOX as a recurring character on *Ally McBeal*.

Part of the problem with *The Simpsons* turning into a breakout hit was that animation took a long time to produce—not the last time FOX would have a problem of this nature—and there was no way to rush new episodes into production any faster. After the initial run of thirteen episodes, all FOX could do was repeat them, over and over, until new episodes were finally ready in the fall of 1990. At one of the Tuesday meetings, the issue came up because the affiliates were complaining that the network was killing interest in this hot hit show by repeating it to death.

Rupert Murdoch was attending that week, and his practice was usually to sit quietly and observe, contributing only when it seemed absolutely necessary for him to respond. Finally someone asked how long it would be before the first of the new *Simpsons* was ready to air, and the programming people answered it would be another month. Murdoch interjected, "It's going to be a long month," which immediately broke the tension. No one was going to be fired over this mishap. If the owner of the company was counseling patience, they could all afford to be patient.

Although a television network is often defined by its prime-time offerings, in fact programming airs throughout the day. At a Big Three affiliate, non-prime-time programming included early morning news shows, soap operas, talk shows, game shows, and late-night variety shows. For an independent station the afternoon might consist of off-network reruns of past hit series or syndicated cartoon shows geared to younger viewers. It was counterprogramming, plain and simple.

In the late 1980s the hot ticket in animated kids programming for independent stations was billed as "The Disney Afternoon." It consisted of several shows, like *DuckTales*, that were produced and distributed by the Disney Company. From the viewpoint of the stations carrying it, The Disney Afternoon attracted young viewers who would have the set tuned to their channel when the older kids and adults started watching TV 5 to 7 P.M. "That was a must-have. Several years ago, that was a no-brainer. You didn't *not* want that," explained Brad Moran, owner/general manager of KJTV in Lubbock, Texas. "You wanted it because of the value that it brought to the station in terms of audience . . . [and] the ratings that it would give you from 3 to 5 that you could go out and sell to all the cereal advertisers."

The Disney Afternoon worked because it was a well-known brand name offering quality animated fare that attracted kids. It also appealed to stations because the shows were offered on a barter basis. Stations acquire shows by purchasing the rights to air them so many times, or through barter deals where they put up a portion of their commercial availabilities. In each half-hour show, Disney would require the stations to run two minutes of national advertising—time that Disney would sell and for which it would keep the proceeds—

while the remaining four minutes of commercial time in the half-hour were left to the stations to sell. By 1989 Disney dominated the market, and it decided it was time to apply pressure on stations carrying its shows to cede more of those commercial avails—meaning Disney would take more of the advertising proceeds, and less time would be available for the local broadcaster to sell.

"The syndicators that were clearing kids shows on our stations were increasing the barter load [national advertising] every year, every six months it seemed like," recalled former Grand Rapids station executive Patrick Mullen. "We went from two minutes to two and a half to three, and even threats of three and a half minutes per show in barter load. So we were losing our commercial avails, and the kids business was a huge source of revenue for all of us at that point." With only six minutes of advertising time available each half-hour, the more Disney claimed for itself the harder it was for the station to justify continuing to carry the shows. Yet as the most popular daytime fare available for children, stations were loathe to give up The Disney Afternoon to a competitor.

In 1989 station owner Harry Pappas, a California businessman who owned a group of stations in six states, including California, Nevada, and North Carolina, approached FOX president Jamie Kellner with an idea: "Why don't you do for us in kids what you're doing for us in prime time?" Kellner liked it immediately. The concept of how FOX would sell network kids programming to the affiliates was the real genius of Pappas's suggestion. Unlike anything offered by the Big Three to their affiliates, the FOX Kids Network would be co-owned by FOX and by the individual stations, with the stations sharing in the eventual profits when they occurred. That proved to be a great incentive to get the stations to run the FOX network's cartoon shows instead of cutting their own deals with syndicators like Disney.

"I basically used Harry [Pappas] to kind of front the whole thing. Ideas that come from the affiliate groups are received better by the affiliates than network ideas," said Kellner.

It was a good deal for the stations, at least on paper. The first $20 million in proceeds from national commercial sales for a sixty-five-episode kids show airing five days a week for thirteen weeks (plus reruns) would go to the producers. After that, FOX would take 15 percent as a distribution fee and the rest would be paid out to the affiliates based on their ratings. The more a local station promoted the FOX Kids Network, the better it would make out financially. Calling it a "historic arrangement," Pappas said, "It's the first time a network was ever willing to allow its stations to share in the rewards from advertising revenues."

In 1989 Jamie Kellner had another meeting, this one with Margaret Loesch, president of Marvel Productions, the Los Angeles–based television arm of Marvel Comics, home to such characters as Spiderman, the X-Men, and the Incredible Hulk. She had heard reports that FOX was about to launch an animated children's network, or at least a programming department that would develop and acquire such shows. She arrived at Kellner's office at FOX for one reason: it was another place for her to sell her shows. Eventually the conversation turned to who she thought should head a FOX Kids Network. She made a few suggestions, and then Kellner inquired, "Well, what about you?"

Loesch was surprised. More than that, she was convinced she could not possibly take the job. She had worked at ABC in the early 1970s when Barry Diller was head of programming there. She had seen him in action and had no desire to be at the wrong end of a business discussion with him. She told Kellner, "I'm very intimidated by Barry, and I don't think I would flourish working for him or the company he runs."

Kellner assured her that she would not have to answer personally to Diller. "You don't have to worry about that. I would buffer you."

So Loesch agreed. She figured it would be easy to get out of the final year of her Marvel executive employment contract. After all, what could be better for a production company than to have one of their former employees be at a network and in a position, perhaps, to buy their programs? Instead the company's owner, the financier Ron Perelman, insisted Loesch serve out her full contract. Although she had the FOX job in 1989, she wouldn't actually come on board until March 1990.

Then there was the question of where she would fit into the organizational flowchart, because she didn't want to report to Diller. Kellner suggested she work for Peter Chernin, head of programming. "I didn't know Peter. I had met him but had no relationship," she recalled. She refused, saying that although she had nothing against Chernin, she didn't want the job if she was just going to be in charge of the kids group in the programming department, where she suspected her efforts would be relegated to second-class status. She also didn't want a senior vice presidency where she had to report to Diller. So what would make her happy?

"I wanted to be as independent as possible. But I would work directly with Jamie, and report to Jamie, and I would keep Jamie completely in the loop and meet with him on a regular basis," she told Kellner. She was "totally surprised" when she got what she asked for. "It was my first insight into FOX and how they are risk-takers and how they really, in those days, empowered their executives. I think Jamie was surprised but pleased by my request."

Kellner had a request for her when she finally arrived, and it wasn't one she would find pleasing. Indeed, she would later call it "one of the most painful years of my career." He wanted her to be ready to launch FOX Kids in the fall of 1990, only six months away. Kellner knew that once FOX Kids was announced, Disney would hit as hard as possible to blunt their newest competitor. "What Margaret didn't understand was that if I had let it go for another year, and if Disney had consolidated themselves in the kids' arena more, it would have been harder to get more stations away from Disney. So getting on there quickly with one show and starting to be aggressive was what blocked Disney from taking over all my affiliates' shelf space."

Even before Loesch's appointment was official in March 1990, Disney began taking potshots at FOX. At the January meeting of the Association of Independent TV Stations, Disney executives were pointing out that FOX's first announced original offering, *Peter Pan and the Pirates*, couldn't even provide drawings of what the proposed new animated half-hour show would look like. FOX countered with an announcement that the scripts had been written, the characters "fully developed" and awaiting final approval, with everything "ready to proceed on schedule."

The hardball continued when Disney yanked its Disney Afternoon away from San Francisco FOX affiliate KTVU. General manager Kevin O'Brien charged that Disney wanted "total control of his afternoon kids block," which Disney denied, insisting it was making market-by-market decisions as to which stations would offer the best clearance (run the shows at the times Disney demanded). O'Brien would become the first affiliate president of the Kids Network, and he proved to be just as aggressive on behalf of FOX. In February 1990 he warned Seattle FOX affiliate KCPQ that it would lose its affiliation if it didn't run the FOX kids shows. Owner Bob Kelly said he was a "full partner" in the FOX effort but was also under contract to carry The Disney Afternoon. Said O'Brien, noting that there were only slots for four half-hour shows from 3 to 5, "Bob Kelly sold eight rooms for a house that has only four rooms."

By the time Loesch joined FOX, she had walked into a lawsuit. Disney sued FOX on anti-trust grounds, claiming that FOX had threatened to pull affiliation status from stations that carried The Disney Afternoon. The suit, filed in U.S. District Court in Los Angeles in February 1990, named Fox Broadcasting Company, the FOX o-and-o's, the network's affiliate board, and the Kids Network as defendants. O'Brien lashed out against Disney, calling the suit "so absurd it's comical." "Here is an organization suing us on anti-trust grounds when they have been trying for the last year to block book with their two-hour kids block."

Loesch recalled receiving a copy of a memo entitled "Margaret Loesch: FOX's Great White Hope?" that was sent to FOX affiliates across the country. "It listed all my failures. And it [claimed] my successes were really attributable to other people. For example, the fact that I was executive producer of *Jim Henson's Muppet Babies*—[that] was really Jim Henson's. And the fact that I was the executive in charge of developing *The Smurfs*—well, that was really [some] Belgians." Loesch was tempted to respond to the accusations, but wisely decided to stay out of the escalating fight.

The real battle had only just begun.

The expansion of FOX network programming into daytime in the fall of 1990 raised another issue that had been festering in the background almost from the start-up of the network. FOX was about to hit the brick wall of the "financial interest in syndicated programming" rule, known in the trade as the fin/syn rule. Fin/syn prohibited any network from having a financial interest in any syndicated programming, including repeats of old network shows. It applied to any network that broadcast more than fifteen hours of programming per week. In theory, the rule opened the doors to more independent and diverse production by allowing production companies, rather than the networks, to reap the profits of off-network syndication. (For a long-running network series, syndication is where the money is.) As noted earlier, FOX had made sure that—legally—it was *not* a television "network," regardless of how it was perceived by the public. FOX was now up to nine hours of programming per week and was planning to add another two hours in prime time in the fall of 1990. If they also added ten hours of weekday kids shows, that would be well over the fifteen-hour limit. At that point FOX could either sell off its syndicated interests or else get out of the network business. Neither option was acceptable. (Such was the concern over the situation that contracts for the

Kids Network allowed FOX to switch the status of the programming from "network" to "syndication" if it ran afoul of fin/syn.)

In June 1988 FOX had requested that the FCC grant a waiver, allowing FOX to continue to operate in violation of the rule. It noted that when Pat Robertson's Christian Broadcasting Network (CBN) started up, the FCC had ruled in 1981 that CBN would have to reach thirty hours of national programming before it would be considered a network. The Big Three, where FOX still wasn't considered a real competitor, suddenly found reason to insist that FOX was indeed a TV network. NBC argued, "There is absolutely no basis for the Commission to artificially bias the marketplace by providing FOX and its affiliates with economic advantages over their competitors." The strictly-for-profit FOX pulled back from comparing itself with Robertson's religious-oriented CBN but replied that "the 15 hour definition does frustrate the development of effective competition to the networks."

Now, in January 1990, the people making FOX's case before the FCC presented a more nuanced argument. In a two-part filing, they first asked the commission to overhaul the fin/syn regulations, and only then did they request a temporary waiver for FOX. The assumption was that the commission wouldn't approve a permanent waiver in the face of Big Three opposition. The network was in a curious position being both a producer/supplier of shows *and* a buyer/programmer. By calling for the modification of fin/syn, it had broken ranks with the other production studios and joined the Big Three. The major networks, though, were unmoved. They continued to oppose granting FOX the desired waiver.

FOX pulled out all stops in petitioning the FCC. Barry Diller and Jamie Kellner went to Washington to lobby, as did several station general managers, where they were joined by Tom Herwitz of FOX's D.C. o-and-o WTTG. Kellner argued that FOX needed immediate relief because it was already selling ads for next season when it would be coming up against the rule. "We can't wait any longer without stopping the growth of the fourth network," said Kellner in the petition.

New to the FOX team was Preston Padden, a man who would become a key player in the months and years ahead. A lawyer with many years experience in the nation's capital, he had the perfect resumé for working at FOX: he had spent twelve years as an in-house counsel for Metromedia. He left before the Murdoch buy-out in 1987 to take over as executive director of the Association of Independent TV Stations in Washington. In that capacity he had reason to deal with Jamie Kellner, who was having a hard time finding someone to run affiliate relations for FOX. David Johnson had helped set up the affiliate office but did not stay on at FOX. He was succeeded by a man named David Ferrara, and then by Bob Mariano, who briefly moved up from servicing the network's Mid-western affiliates to running the whole affiliate operation. When Mariano returned to the Midwest, Kellner took on the responsi-bility himself.

One day Kellner was walking into an advertising convention and, as he recalled, he saw Padden and "a light went off over my head—I said, 'That's the guy.'" They had a drink and then Kellner said, "You know, I've got a need and you're just the guy to fill it." Kellner hired him to handle not only affiliate relations but the net-work's government relations as well.

Padden had no time to relax once he joined the FOX team in Jan-uary 1990. He had to get right to work on dealing with the affiliates in adding a fourth night of programming as well as the coming Kids Network, *and* he had to deal with the ongoing fin/syn crisis in Washington. His multiple tasks demanded that he report to several bosses. On affiliate matters he worked under Kellner, while his Washington lobbying was overseen by Barry Diller. Padden and Diller went to the other Hollywood studios to see if they would help FOX, but they received the same reaction they got from the networks. "And so we were literally all alone," said Padden, well aware that the fate of the fourth network was hanging in the balance. "Failure was not an option."

In May 1990 Padden and FOX notched their first victory. The FCC granted the network a one-year waiver while all interested parties would cooperate with the FCC to determine what to do about fin/syn. FOX had dodged the bullet this time, but this near miss would come back to haunt them. Behind the scenes the Big Three were making an issue of FOX getting special favors when it was really a foreign company, since it was owned by Murdoch's News Corp., an Australian business. An FCC source told *Variety*, "Foreign ownership is not a particularly relevant issue."

It was, however, an issue that simply would not go away.

Before Garth Ancier left FOX in March 1989, a new comedy/variety show had been put into development for the network. But Barry Diller was so afraid of negative public reaction that it almost became the most watched show *not* on television. Keenen Ivory Wayans was a talented actor/writer who had grown up in the projects of New York City. In 1987 he was involved in a breakthrough big-screen comedy about African Americans in Hollywood called *Hollywood Shuffle* (1987), which made the career of its director/star Robert Townsend, who co-wrote the script with him. Wayans then branched out on his own with a spoof of 1970s "blaxploitation" films entitled *I'm Gonna Git You Sucka* (1988).

The following year he was invited to pitch a show to FOX. Having collaborated with Townsend on a 1988 sketch-comedy special called *Partners in Crime* for HBO, he decided to do something along the same lines for FOX. Called *In Living Color*, it would feature a multi-ethnic cast including David Allen Grier, Jim Carrey, and several members of the Wayans family, starting with Keenen's younger brother Damon and their sister Kim. It would also include a group of sexy dancers dubbed "The Fly Girls." (In one of those bizarre near misses in history, they were almost called "The Spice Girls.")

Wayans's approach to *In Living Color* was to make it personality driven, with certain characters reappearing in subsequent sketches, and to focus the weekly half-hour show squarely on the youth audience. It was thought by some critics and viewers to be a black-oriented show because of Wayans and the largely African-American cast. For Wayans, however, the guidepost was not race but youth. He wanted this to be an urban-oriented variety series that would appeal to young adults. According to Eric Gold, Wayans's manager and one of the show's producers, "The mentality of the show was rock and roll. The thing was, our mentality was hip, not black, not white. It was hiphop, it was young urban." The closest precedent was *Saturday Night Live* on NBC, and that was a late-night show, not one scheduled for prime time.

Wayans made fun of blacks, whites, women, men, gays, the disabled . . . in fact, no one was safe from the show's barbs. The comedy was broad and sometimes tasteless, but never vicious. Wayans told writer Kristal Brent Zook, "When I came along with *In Living Color* they were actually very fearful of what I was doing. But they knew it was something different."

Diller insisted that Wayans had to go before groups like the Urban League and the National Association for the Advancement of Colored People (NAACP) with samples from his show to make sure that FOX wouldn't be criticized for airing the series. Wayans rebelled. He told the network, "I don't need to meet with them. I'm a black man. I know what's in bounds and what's out of bounds." He also pointed out that ABC hadn't asked comedian Jackie Mason to go to the B'nai B'rith to see if Jews would be offended by his new sitcom *Chicken Soup*. If anyone needed to meet with black groups, he continued, it was the producers of shows that perpetuated black stereotypes.

Since Wayans refused to cooperate, Diller wouldn't air the show until he was reassured it wouldn't burn him. Programming executive Rob Kenneally, who was wildly enthusiastic for the show, understood Diller's fears. "Nobody knew," he recalls. "He was afraid—between the NAACP, the handicapped groups, and the gay groups, and others—that we would be so completely lambasted in the press that we would just rue the day we ever saw the show through."

So tapes of the show's pilot were sent to various special-interest groups, to other TV executives, to anyone whose opinion Diller respected or who managed to obtain a copy of the sample tape. "What happened was like *South Park* [before the controversial animated show debuted on Comedy Central in 1997]. The tapes got bicycled all over town. It was a must-see tape that everybody watched," said Gold.

Meanwhile *In Living Color* was a favorite demonstration tape in the FOX offices as well. Programming executive Rob Kenneally would show it to prospective show writers, and it was thought of as a "taboo, underground pilot that was never going to get on the air. And the writers would come in the room and they would howl." They couldn't believe FOX would actually air it, but when Kenneally insisted they would, the network earned a new positive cachet in the creative community.

Ultimately Barry Diller was reassured, when even the media began running stories about this hot new program that FOX was about to put on the air. Then too, the various groups who screened it said they took no particular offense since the pilot was lampooning everyone. Diller and Kellner and programming chief Peter Chernin gave the go-ahead, and *In Living Color* premiered April 15, 1990, as part of a revamped Sunday-night schedule. It took a while for the affiliates to catch on that the show would be popular with young viewers, and Kellner in particular was caught in the middle. He dealt with not only the programming people and the affiliates but also the network's standards and practices department. Series producer Gold recalled that Kellner was being supportive though he "had a very hot dilemma on his hands because he was damned if he did and he was damned if he didn't. He knew that part of the reason it was a hit show was that it was outrageous. He knew the more outrageous it was, the more shit he was getting from his stations that were not that sure yet."

The stations came around soon enough when they saw that *In Living Color* was crossing over into a mainstream hit. Wrote one reviewer, "What might have been merely an exercise in tasteless-ness redeemed itself in the best possible way—by being funny." Joe Young, manager of the Indianapolis FOX affiliate at the time, saw that the network as a whole was more urban than rural, and he sold his advertising that way. To him, this new FOX series wasn't just a black show. "I can't tell you how many white people I knew—including myself—who loved *In Living Color*. Maybe there were people who watched who wouldn't admit that they watched it, but my kids loved it. My kids were in an upper-income neigh-borhood, and their friends all watched it. We had a lot of people watching that show."

Keenen Wayans had called it right. The show appealed to urban young adults regardless of race. *In Living Color* would remain one of the network's signature shows for several years but would come to a bitter end in 1994. Unlike the dire predictions of the show crash-ing on the rocks of controversy, it instead faced something even tougher: the way business is done in Hollywood. But that was all in the future. While Diller and Kellner remained in charge, it was safe.

CHAPTER SIX

"What is this 90210?"

[1990–1991]

THE FOX FALL PRIME-TIME SCHEDULE

	7:00	7:30	8:00	8:30	9:00	9:30	10:00	10:30
Sunday	True Colors	Parker Lewis Can't Lose	In Living Color	Get a Life	Married . . . with Children	Good Grief	Against the Law	
Monday			Movie					
Thursday			The Simpsons	Babes	Beverly Hills 90210			
Friday			America's Most Wanted		DEA			
Saturday			Totally Hidden Video	Haywire	COPS	American Chronicles	Comic Strip Live	

FOX'S FIFTH SEASON on the air saw the network take a lot of gambles. Some paid off, many didn't. For the first time, though, the other TV networks were forced to react to what FOX did.

Every September the Hollywood Radio and Television Society hosts a luncheon in which each of the networks sends a top executive to discuss the state of television and its upcoming fall season. For the first time FOX was included in the event, with Peter Chernin representing the fourth network. It was a sign of respect, but as far as the Big Three were concerned, it was premature. An ABC executive there slammed FOX, claiming that *Married . . . with Children* was "vulgar" and that *The Simpsons* had "lowered the civility level of young boys all over America."

By the fall of 1990 the FOX network was still not ready to go seven nights a week, but Barry Diller and Jamie Kellner felt it was time to expand to five nights weekly. Mondays were set as a network movie night, but FOX's projected slate of two hour made-for-TV movies proved to be taking a long time to roll, so the network was put in the embarrassing position of returning Monday nights to their affiliates until January 1991. Most FOX stations still had large film libraries on hand from their independent days when movies were the mainstay of their prime-time programming. So after first establishing a beachhead on Mondays the previous season with *21 Jump Street* and *Alien Nation*, the network was forced to pull back—at least, temporarily.

This step backward may have been a major black eye for FOX, but it proved to be a minor story. Instead, all anyone could talk about—both inside and outside the TV industry—was the audacity of FOX's Thursday night schedule. It began in May 1990 when the upcoming fall season was announced. The network was taking its single biggest hit, *The Simpsons*, and moving it from Sunday to Thursdays, where it would lead off a new night of programming. Now, a successful show for FOX wasn't quite the same as a hit for the Big Three. For example, FOX's *Married . . . with Children* and *America's Most Wanted* didn't make the week's top twenty, even though they were among the highest-rated shows aired on FOX. Yet, from a programming standpoint, moving *The Simpsons* actually made sense. Such jockeying for position is common in network TV; the theory is that the strong program will bring viewers to the newer entries that follow it. What made this move different, however, was whom Bart Simpson would be facing in on-air competition. Thursday nights at 8 P.M. had been owned for several years by the upper-middle-class Huxtable family on America's number one hit, *The Cosby Show*.

"Sure there was trepidation about the move," FOX programming chief Peter Chernin told the media, "but the more we talked about it, the more excited we got."

Paul Stupin, then executive vice president of series programming at FOX, was in the room when the key decision was made. "My recollection is that Barry got up and walked over to the scheduling board and took the *Simpsons* card and put it on Thursday night. And that initial action sparked a whole lot of discussion and subsequent excitement."

No one expected *The Simpsons* to beat the veteran hit sitcom *The Cosby Show*, not even Barry Diller or Peter Chernin. "We have no illusions about that," said Chernin. "It's the other guys, the other two networks that aren't really there on Thursday nights. There's a lot of audience left over that the other two networks aren't really hitting." Chernin felt that FOX's programming had to be built on two things: having a strong lead at 8 P.M., and counterprogramming what the other guys were doing. That's why *America's Most Wanted* was moved to Friday nights and expanded to an hour. (Series co–executive producer Phil Lerman recalls executive producer Lance Heflin coming back from a meeting with FOX and telling the show's Washington, D.C.–based staff, "You're doing great, and no good deed shall go unpunished. We're going to work twice as hard.")

Even comedian Bill Cosby was impressed with the *Simpsons* announcement. "Boy, that's an amazing move," a spokesperson for the comedian said. Cosby himself acknowledged the competition in the premiere episode of *The Cosby Show*'s seventh season, when one of the youngsters on the program surprised Cosby's character by wearing a Bart Simpson mask.

Among the affiliates, *The Simpsons* move was a cause for concern. Publicly, everyone was on board. Behind the scenes, general managers at the FOX affiliates were wondering if the people operating the network had lost their minds. "I looked in the mirror one day and said, 'Rupert Murdoch is the biggest jerk I ever met in my life. Why would he ever do that?' " recalled Gerry Walsh, who had just taken over WFXT in Boston. "Hello, it was the smartest thing they ever did because they knew *Cosby* was on the way down and *Simpsons* was a unique show. . . . He did the right thing. . . . I think it was the biggest programming decision he ever made, except to get into the programming business."

Ultimately it was a gamble that would pay off. *The Simpsons* didn't have to beat *Cosby*; it merely had to be seen as competitive. Its premiere episode in September 1990—after a long summer of the initial thirteen episodes airing repeatedly—nearly tied with *Cosby* even though FOX could still only reach, at best, only 91 percent of the country. Nearly 10 percent of the country still had no access to FOX. The hype around *The Simpsons*, and the fact that it was actually beating *Cosby* among such key demographics as teenagers and men 18–49, meant that it could be used as the calling card for the network's next big gamble.

W ith FOX shows like *The Simpsons* consistently generating publicity in the media, viewers who didn't have a local FOX station were out of luck if they wanted to see what was going on. By 1990 there were still some seventy or eighty "white areas" in the United States that FOX simply couldn't reach. ("White areas" were those spots on the map without a FOX affiliate, and no station available to become one.) The nearest FOX station was often too far away to be picked up by most regional viewers. With the growing number of cable channels vying for a spot on often limited cable boxes, there was little interest in picking up distant FOX stations and importing them into the market just so that people could watch one or two shows. Then, in July 1990 FOX announced a deal with TCI, one of the country's leading cable operators.

What had happened was that, out of the blue, Preston Padden, FOX's head of affiliate relations and chief lobbyist, had received a call from Bob Thompson, TCI's vice president for government affairs.

He said the company had a problem. It was charging people for TV service, yet its customers couldn't see this FOX not-quite-a-network that had gotten Bart Simpson on the cover of *Time*. Thompson made Padden an offer he couldn't refuse.

"If you create a satellite-delivered service to bring your network to these areas where there is no broadcast affiliate, we will pay for that service every month. *And* TCI will agree to upgrade to VHF channel positions every UHF FOX affiliate across the country."

Padden was stunned. He kept waiting for the catch. Finally he asked, "Is that it?"

"Yes."

Padden had one question. "Would a kiss be too demonstrative?"

TCI's offer was like manna from heaven. First it would increase FOX's coverage so that it would approach the 100 percent of the Big Three. (The major networks consisted of roughly two hundred stations each, most of them affiliates.) Second, TCI would *pay* FOX for this service. And third, and perhaps most important, TCI would move all FOX channels—existing ones and this new service—to a channel position comparable to the established networks. Thus FOXNET was born, a cable service that existed primarily to bring broadcast network programming to cable customers who couldn't get it from a local TV station. This was yet another FOX idea that would eventually catch on with the other networks, both the Big Three and later arrivals like UPN and WB. The big hurdle now was convincing the affiliates that this wasn't a plot to eliminate them altogether and turn FOX into another cable-only service.

Padden went to Jamie Kellner to tell him about the offer, and they put together the deal. TCI would arrange for the satellite transmission of the service from FOX to TCI, and FOX would be allowed to cancel the service in a particular market if an affiliate station emerged there. "There was a little bit of fear there," recalled Kellner, who noted that a few affiliates saw this as a wedge to eventually cut them out as conduits of FOX programming to the public. "The other part of it was, this was sort of a period of cold war between broadcasters and cable operators. All you had to do was mention cable to broadcasters and they got a rash."

There was a certain irony that Padden became the man to sell this to the affiliates as well as persuading other cable companies to get on board. "He had been a cable basher," said Andy Fessel. Fessel remembered one cable marketing meeting where a cable executive had challenged Padden.

"When you were at INTV [the independent TV stations group] you used to say that cable is really bad. How can you tell us that cable is your best friend?" he was asked.

"Well, I changed jobs," he replied, wryly.

FOXNET was launched in May 1991 and demonstrated the same sort of creativity as a business deal that the best FOX programs reflected as public entertainment. It was set up as a twenty-four-hour service, but because FOX didn't provide twenty-four hours of programming, the rest of the day would be filled with syndicated programming as well as material from the Twentieth Century–Fox film and TV library. In small cable markets FOX would collect a modest fee for the service, $100 per year for a system with fewer than one thousand subscribers, and the cable company would have the right to sell the local advertising avails within the shows' airtime. In larger markets FOX offered the service at no charge and retained the local availabilities to sell themselves.

Once FOXNET was up and running, Kellner came up with another idea. Padden says, "We had noticed that where we simply had FOXNET in an area, our ratings were lower—by about half—than where we had an active over-the-air affiliate. We knew some of the difference was in missed coverage of homes [that didn't have cable], but some of the difference was the part of the value that an affiliate brings to a broadcast network."

To combat this situation, Kellner arranged to open storefronts in shopping malls for three FOXNET "stations" in Corpus Christi, Texas; Dubuque, Iowa; and Wilmington, North Carolina. For each site FOX hired a general manager, a promotions manager, a sales

manager, a traffic manager (who schedules commercials), and a secretary, and told them to act like they were a real TV station. They
sold ads. They sponsored community events. They gave FOXNET a
presence in the given region.

"We closed the ratings gaps between pure cable delivery and
pure local affiliate delivery by about half," said Padden.

It was a novel concept, and it worked. Other networks have
copied the model to fill in the gaps in their coverage. Kellner's subsequent network, the WB, used seventy or eighty such outlets. Like
the move of *The Simpsons* from Sunday to Thursday, it was a gamble that paid off.

The launch of the FOX Kids Network in the 1990–1991 season
was a gamble that not only didn't work but generated a lot of
affiliate anger in the process.

When Margaret Loesch showed up as president of FOX's new
children's operation in March 1990, she faced the sniping of the rival Disney Afternoon. But her job was to focus on programming,
and that's what she did. It was not difficult to attract potential suppliers for the prospective FOX Kids Network. "[It] was another place
to sell product, another place to expand your business," explained
Loesch. "In the '60s and '70s kids programming was totally buying
and selling at three places [the Big Three networks]. In the '80s syndication started to emerge, and there were other opportunities."
That was good news for program *distributors*, which is what she had
been. Now, as a program *buyer*, she had to figure out which shows
would give FOX a competitive edge.

Before Loesch arrived, FOX was moving ahead with an animated
show developed by Fred Silverman, the wunderkind programmer
who had scored big at CBS and ABC in the 1960s and 1970s before
finally becoming a cropper at NBC in the early 1980s with expensive
duds like *Supertrain*. Silverman had gone into independent production and was offering FOX something called *Piggsburg Pigs!* Loesch
admired Silverman. (She had worked for him earlier in her career.)

But she was convinced that this was not the show that should launch FOX Kids. She told network president Jamie Kellner, "I think we need something more classy, classic, something that would work better for us."

Instead she chose *Peter Pan and the Pirates*, from a young company called Project X Productions. The scripts and designs were impressive, and actor Tim Curry was signed to do the voice of Captain Hook. Kellner gave her the go-ahead but insisted they be set to launch in the fall of 1990. Loesch didn't believe they could be up and running in time. "I don't know how to do sixty-five half-hours in six months," she told him, but he knew that they had to move quickly if they weren't going to lose more ground to Disney.

Unfortunately the production company wasn't up to the extraordinary demands of a rush job. Animation work is highly labor intensive, even with the aid of computers and the more limited animation done for television as opposed to the fluid animated movement done for feature films. In recent years Hollywood had found it cheaper to farm out such tasks overseas. Work on *Peter Pan and the Pirates* was delegated to animation companies throughout the world, and problems struck everywhere. "We . . . had a series of incredible fiascoes," said Loesch. "We had a hurricane in Taiwan, we had a fire or a flood in the middle of every place we did work. . . . We found out the hard way that Russians had absolutely no work ethic. They wouldn't answer their phones after five o'clock. The show that was supposed to get back to us in thirteen weeks . . . took twenty-eight weeks."

Loesch again pleaded with Kellner to delay the debut, to no avail. Other series were in development for Saturday-morning showings—the traditional network kids slot—but the series order for *Attack of the Killer Tomatoes*, a new show based on the cult 1980 feature sci-fi spoof—was only thirteen episodes. To do a weekday strip (meaning five shows per week) meant sixty-five episodes. *Peter Pan and the Pirates* launched the new FOX Kids Network with only a handful of its half-hour episodes, and they were shown over and over again for several weeks, until additional episodes arrived. The final new episodes from the original order due in March 1990 didn't arrive until the spring of 1991.

Once again the affiliates found themselves in a position where they had taken a step backward. They had griped during the run of *The Late Show with Joan Rivers* and during the first two seasons of weak Saturday prime-time programming, arguing that the stations had given up advertising time they used to be able to sell themselves. What they had gotten in exchange was network programming that, as was now happening with *Peter Pan and the Pirates* in daytime, generated lower ratings than what was there in the first place. Years later, KTVU general manager Kevin O'Brien, who had become head of the FOX affiliate board, recalls *Peter Pan and the Pirates* as "a disaster, it was a bomb."

Loesch was justifiably overwhelmed by a tight budget, staff who quit, and angry affiliates. Kellner reassured her, taking the long view. "Okay, you'll fix it. You'll do something else."

It would be another year or two before the problems were fully remedied. Meanwhile Kellner and O'Brien approached Dick Robertson at Warner Bros. Television to see if they could get some of the Warners-produced kids shows on the FOX schedule, and ended up bringing over *Beetlejuice*, *Tazmania*, and *Batman: The Animated Series*, all of which were successful on FOX that season. Kellner also proposed using the weekday kids block to promote FOX's Saturday-morning shows, and vice versa. "We told everybody that anybody who wasn't in the kids business more than just on Saturday morning couldn't be there long term, and that strategy is what made the whole thing work," he explained. His goal was to take over every time slot that his stations were filling with Disney product and have them carry FOX shows instead.

Loesch grasped immediately what Kellner was proposing. "Saturday morning on the networks is an island, and it was relegated to an island. It rarely, if ever, got promotion outside of that. ABC had a little bit in their [TGIF] Friday night lineup." Her colleagues thought she was foolish to try a start-up at FOX, but she felt it was an opportunity to combine the traditional network strategies with the newer syndication approach, strengthening both in the process. "They couldn't see the future. They could not see it," she said.

Loesch's vision was 20/20 when it came to the future of kids programming on FOX. It was the present that was painful. "I built a reputation of being able to deliver and deliver quality, on time and on budget. And here I had this fiasco that followed me around for a couple of years. It was a joke."

Equally disappointing to FOX during the 1990–1991 season, and just as stressful on affiliate relations, was the network's growing insistence that FOX stations should carry a 10 P.M. (EST) newscast. It was, again, a counterstrategy to the Big Three, which ran prime-time programming until 11 P.M. and then had local news. Except on the weekends, FOX ended its prime time at 10 P.M. FOX executives felt that going to local news at that point would capitalize on the network audiences and build up the identity of the local station, since newscasts are often the local face of a TV station. The news anchors and weather forecasters and sports reporters often become local personalities, and simply by covering local news the station becomes a presence in the community.

FOX tried to make it easy for affiliates by offering to buy the equipment (cameras, editing machines, computers, etc.) they would need in bulk and then pass the savings along to them, but most of the affiliates weren't interested in absorbing the costs of such a massive project as launching a nightly newscast, even with the help of the network. The salaries of all the news people in front of and behind the camera, after all, would be borne by the affiliate, not by FOX. In June 1990, just 16 of 129 FOX affiliates ran a newscast. By March 1991 only 3 more had signed on. An unnamed former FOX executive told *Variety* at the time, "It's a huge undertaking to convince all those general managers who've been independents for so long, who say, 'What do I need it for? I've made tons of money for years counterprogramming.'" The network had launched the FOX News Service in February 1991 to provide a national news feed to the stations, but only 32 picked it up. "We went after this thing in the typical FOX gung-ho, 'go over the wall no matter what' fashion. But then some harsh economic realities set in," said Kellner to the trade press in March.

One of the realities was that not all markets were created equal. By long-standing television tradition, the Midwest and parts of the South broadcast in sync with the East, one hour earlier. David Woods, owner of the FOX affiliate in Montgomery, Alabama, still had no newscast as of late 2003. "Very few 100+ markets have 10 o'clock newscasts," he said. The United States has more than 200 television markets, ranging in size from over 6 million television-viewing households in New York City to less than 6,000 in Glendive, Montana. Montgomery, Alabama, with about 220,000 such households, ranks 113th. Size wasn't the only issue, as Wood explained. Location mattered too. "We're in the Central time zone. There's not quite the appetite [for news] at 9 P.M. Central as there is at 10."

Tribune Broadcasting's Patrick Mullen said its FOX affiliate in Grand Rapids finally launched a newscast in 1998, feeling the market was finally ready to support it financially. "It's a very, very expensive thing to do. We're in a market size [thirty-seventh] that makes sense for us. Five, eight years ago, it might not have made sense for us. . . . There's been a great deal of pressure on all the affiliates to launch a news operation. In fact, they're even now including it, apparently, in the language of affiliation agreements, that people have to do it."

In the early 1990s, though, getting the affiliates to add a newscast was a losing battle for FOX.

Of the new shows that arrived on FOX that season—like *Babes*, a sitcom about three overweight sisters sharing an apartment, and *Get a Life*, a half-hour series featuring Chris Elliot as a thirty-year-old paperboy who moves back in with his parents—only one was a breakout hit, but it would have a lasting impact. It was a new version of that old TV staple, the high school show. The only difference was, this one was set in Beverly Hills.

"Of all the shows I've done, the one I'm proudest of is *Beverly Hills 90210* . . .," wrote producer Aaron Spelling in his 1996 memoirs. "It all started with a phone call from my old friend Barry Diller. Then running the new FOX network, Barry wanted to do a show about kids in Beverly Hills and he asked me to produce it. 'Why me?' I asked.

"'You have two teenage kids, and you live in Beverly Hills.'"

Spelling's recollection might be better suited for an earlier hit of his, *Fantasy Island*. The genesis of *Beverly Hills 90210* was far more complicated. It began, in fact, when FOX asked Spelling to do not a high school series but a retread of his 1970s hit, *Charlie's Angels*. There had been casting tryouts for the new *Angels*, but when Rob Kenneally arrived in the programming department in the summer of 1988 he and Kevin Wendle had doubts about the concept. They thought it might be better to try it out as a TV movie first and see if a series about three beautiful women playing at being detective for an unseen boss would still fly a decade later.

"I went over to Aaron Spelling's office with Barry's approval to try to convince Aaron that we do *Angels '88* as a two-hour movie. If it worked, we'd do additional episodes. If not, we'd shift into something new," Kenneally, the then senior vice president of programming, recalled. "Well, I walked into this man, this legend's office, and I pitched him this idea . . . and he just went bonkers. He went bananas."

Spelling told him, "You guys came to me, I didn't come to you."

Apparently thinking that FOX was reneging on its deal, Spelling counterattacked. The powerhouse Creative Artists Agency (CAA), which represented Spelling, made it clear that they were no longer interested in steering their clients to FOX. "CAA went to war with us, and basically said they would not give us, from that point on, any new show runners [producers], any new programming whatsoever. So for a few weeks it was a standoff where one of the major talent agencies had cut the supply line," Kenneally remembered.

Meanwhile, quite apart from all this, the new executive vice president for series programming, Paul Stupin, had the notion of doing a high school series, since FOX wanted to attract young viewers. He learned that FOX had acquired the media rights to the name Beverly Hills High School for use in a feature film, and when that didn't pan out, the idea of a TV series set at the school had been floating around the lot. Stupin arrived in the fall of 1989 at FOX, having come from Tri-Star Pictures, and he thought of a young writer who had recently done the feature film *Doin' Time on Planet Earth* as someone he might bring onto the project.

"So even before I officially moved into my office at FOX, I called this writer and pitched him the idea, and I got him very interested in doing television for the first time," said Stupin. The twenty-nine-year-old writer was Darren Star. "Darren subsequently came up with the specific characters who were loosely based upon his life, of coming out from the Midwest to Los Angeles. He came up with the idea of two twins who came out to Los Angeles and headed into the world of Beverly Hills and Beverly High from the outside, with a fresh perspective on things. And he ended up basically writing a wonderful script which we had developed almost completely internally."

Meanwhile Spelling was suffering through a rough period. In 1989 ABC had canceled Spelling's remaining shows on its schedule, including the long-running *Dynasty*. At the same time his new deal at NBC soured when his first show for them, *Nightingales*, about the lives and loves of nursing students, flopped after only thirteen episodes. As *The Class of Beverly Hills*, as it was then called, was being developed, FOX needed an experienced producer to actually handle the property. It's not quite clear whose idea it was to approach Spelling to spearhead the project. Kenneally claims *he* did— with Kevin Wendle's blessing—while Stupin recalls it was programming chief Peter Chernin who actually made the pitch. Only in Spelling's account is it Barry Diller, the chairman of Fox, Inc., who was personally making the call.

The timing of Spelling's taking over the project is important because while everyone credits Paul Stupin with the idea of hiring Darren Star, the timeline may illuminate the thinking behind that decision. Bob Greenblatt, director of drama series development at FOX, was under Stupin and Kenneally, and his recollection was that Spelling was brought in early in the development process, before Star began writing a draft script. (Greenblatt does confirm that offering the show to Spelling was payback for canceling the revival of *Charlie's Angels*.) Kenneally also remembers Spelling being brought onto the project before Star, and that not everyone at the network was happy that someone whose career dated back to the 1960s show *The Mod Squad* would be in charge of their 1990s "youth" entry. Kenneally's thinking was, "Maybe the best thing to do is have Aaron work with and supervise a younger writer who is . . . of that audience."

In any event, Spelling would now produce the show and Star would write the pilot script, creating the characters and situations. Recalled Greenblatt, "Aaron and Darren met and liked each other, and they decided they would work together on creating this series. And then the process involved all of us executives in the creation of the characters. Darren and Aaron would work on that, and then they would come to us. They would pitch us the characters, the basic story line for the pilot, the fleshed-out concept for the series. We were there to give them feedback and any of our creative ideas that were interesting." In addition to his own experiences, Star was able to draw on a book by Michael Leahy that someone at the network had given him: *Hard Lessons: Senior Year at Beverly Hills High School* (1988).

The conflicting recollections about the genesis of *Beverly Hills 90210* is understandable, given that so many people participated in the process at different times. According to Greenblatt, "Aaron and

Darren would do versions of the script—Aaron wasn't writing it, but Aaron was always very creatively involved in anything he'd done—and Darren had never written a television pilot before. He had Aaron there to guide him. A pilot script was created, and ultimately Peter Chernin read it and liked it and had his own creative thoughts."

With all these "creative" executives contributing to the overall process, it's a wonder the script was ever completed, let alone shot and aired. The hardest role to cast turned out to be that of Brandon Walsh, the male half of the twin siblings whose arrival in Beverly Hills set the weekly series in motion. Paul Stupin recalled it coming down to the wire, just as it had with the casting of Johnny Depp in FOX's earlier teen hit, *21 Jump Street*, during the 1986–1987 season. "I remember to this day the casting sessions in my office where we're shooting on Monday—it's Friday—and we still didn't have the character of Brandon. And then I remember hearing from our casting person that there was a great kid coming off of some canceled ABC show [actually, NBC's *Sister Kate*] who would be coming in that afternoon by the name of Jason Priestley. He came in, he nailed the audition, he nailed the role, and we shot the pilot."

The late Bob Mariano, in affiliate relations, recalled hearing of the show while it was still in development and looking for a title. One proposal was to call it simply *90210*. That was discussed at one of the Tuesday morning meetings.

"What is this *90210*? I live in Chicago. Is that like a 911 number?"

"It's Beverly Hills."

"Never heard of it."

The show premiered at 9 P.M. on Thursday, October 4, 1990, as *Beverly Hills 90210* and almost didn't survive its first year. "It struggled a lot that first season. It was almost canceled, like almost every show on FOX at that time," said Greenblatt.

The story line of the series defies brief summary, both because of the large cast and the multiple plots involving drugs, sex, divorce, and adolescent angst. Among the more notable people who have appeared on the show are Shannen Doherty as Jason Priestley's sister Brenda, Gabrielle Carteris as the editor of the school paper (and who, in real life, would leave the series in 1995 to launch a short-lived daytime talk show), Luke Perry as yet another male heart-throb, and Tori Spelling, real-life daughter of Aaron. That last move would lead to much Hollywood gossip about nepotism until the young actress finally proved herself.

By the end of the first season the show was barely noticed by adult viewers, but in the 12–17 teen demographic it was pulling a 40 share, meaning that an estimated 40 percent of all American teenagers watching television Thursdays at 9 were tuned to FOX. After a lot of effort, both Spelling and FOX had their much-needed success.

For the affiliates, *Beverly Hills 90210* was one of the few bits of good news at season's end in the spring of 1991. *The Simpsons* hadn't failed, but it hadn't beaten *The Cosby Show* in the ratings either. The Kids Network was dying, and FOXNET was making the stations nervous. A further FCC extension of the fin/syn waiver was cheered by FOX but didn't help the affiliates very much. Better news was a decision by the FCC that the rule defining a network by fifteen hours of programming would now be interpreted as fifteen hours of weekly *prime-time* programming. It was still a barrier to expansion, since FOX was already airing thirteen hours per week over five nights of prime time, but now they had some breathing room to expand to at least one more night.

The network Monday-night movie had finally been launched, but it was programmed so haphazardly that the listings in *TV Guide* were often incorrect. The offerings ranged from goofy comedies, like *Working Trash*, which featured George Carlin and Ben Stiller as janitors at a stock brokerage who get rich investing on the inside tips they find in the garbage, to horror films like *Blood Ties*, about California vampires. Perhaps the most ambitious attempt was an effort to steal the thunder of one of the big summer movies of 1991, the Kevin Costner vehicle *Robin Hood: Prince of Thieves*. FOX acquired the U.S. television rights to a competing *Robin Hood* film, with a cast that included Jurgen Prochnow, Uma Thurman, and, as Robin, Patrick Bergin. It was a creditable effort directed by the experienced John Irvin and had been released theatrically overseas. Ultimately the problem with the FOX TV movies is that the network's young viewers preferred going out for their entertainment. It was their parents who watched the older-skewing offerings movies on the Big Three.

FOX's real problem was more than the movies. It was the fact that by expanding so quickly the network had depleted any backup shows it had, so it couldn't replace what wasn't working. In January 1991 Barry Diller had told *Variety*'s Peter Bart, "The big lesson is that for three months we started to act like the other three networks. That will not happen again. FOX is really the only true independent company around and we must continue to act that way." In branching out into other nights, FOX had started to take the season-by-season view of the Big Three instead of continuing its initial week-by-week review of what was working and what wasn't. Diller was promising a return to first principles for the network.

In cleaning up the season's mistakes and preparing for the next year, Diller would prove to be ruthlessly efficient. At one weekly Tuesday morning meeting, senior vice president for programming Rob Kenneally spoke up for *DEA* starring Tom Mason and Byron Keith Minns, an hour drama about the Drug Enforcement Agency that had been sporadically scheduled during the season and had never found an audience. Kenneally tried to enlist the support of other decision-makers in the room who he knew liked the show, but Diller cut him off by raising his hand.

"Rob?" said Diller. "*DEA*—D."

Everyone in the room laughed. And the show was canceled.

CHAPTER SEVEN

"We were throwing parties in the halls"

[1991–1992]

	7:00	7:30	8:00	8:30	9:00	9:30	10:00	10:30
			THE FOX FALL SCHEDULE					
Sunday	True Colors	Parker Lewis Can't Lose	In Living Color	Roc	Married . . . with Children	Herman's Head	The Sunday Comics	
Monday			Movie					
Thursday			The Simpsons	Drexell's Class	Beverly Hills 90210			
Friday			America's Most Wanted		The Ultimate Challenge			
Saturday			COPS	COPS	Totally Hidden Video	Get a Life		

FOX REACHED a new plateau on August 11, 1991. On that date WGMB went on the air in Baton Rouge, Louisiana, the nation's 98th-ranked television market, affiliating with the FOX network right from its start. For the first time since its inception in 1986, FOX could be seen in all of the nation's top 100 markets. This put FOX at 92 percent coverage (not counting the FOXNET cable outlets), with 137 affiliates. There were still gaps to be closed, but Rupert Murdoch, Barry Diller, and Jamie Kellner had already accomplished far more than anyone could have imagined when their proposed fourth network had been launched five years earlier.

As the fall season got under way, there was now a new kind of complaint being leveled against FOX by its rivals. Instead of the Big Three, however, it was now other Hollywood studios saying FOX did not play fair. They claimed that FOX preferred developing their shows in-house, at Twentieth Century Television, pointing to hits like *The Simpsons* and *In Living Color*. Calling the charge "bird-brained," Fox, Inc., chairman Barry Diller shot back, "The fact is that the major studios have not really demonstrated any particular desire to do business with FOX, even though it's in their best interest to do so. The people who run these companies still don't feel it's a notch in their belts to sell a show to FOX the way it is to sell to the three networks."

After a rocky season, FOX was on the offensive again. It had run new episodes of *Beverly Hills 90210* during the summer, figuring that—as an hour drama—it would score better than the repeats airing on the other networks as well as bring in new viewers who might stick around when the fall season began. It spread out its new shows over several weeks in September instead of going head to head with the Big Three during the traditional single "premiere week." And FOX began a big push to use its affiliates to create and cement a permanent image of the network in the public mind.

One way to accomplish this was the continuing effort to convince the FOX affiliates to do newscasts, even though it remained an uphill battle. Another way was what came to be known as "FOXify-ing" the station. Midwest affiliate relations manager Bob Mariano claimed he first developed the notion. "Actually, FOXification was the word I used," he recalled. The idea was to get the local station to use the FOX name in every aspect of its promotion so that the viewer would remember it and link it with the station. Mariano said he was greeted with much skepticism. "'WXIX in Cincinnati has been WXIX for [twenty] years. Change my name from WXIX?' We said that in the era of cable you'd be better off to drop it and go FOX19."

The American television industry is a much smaller world than people outside the business imagine, and when some stations had success with FOXification, word got around fast. Brad Moran, owner and general manager of KJTV, the FOX affiliate in Lubbock, Texas, reported, "People come up to me and say, 'Since FOX bought you guys, you are much better.'" FOX *hadn't* bought the station, but the public linkage between FOX and the affiliate was now complete.

The good news overall was that ratings were up and that the public, if not the industry, was beginning to think of FOX in the same terms as the Big Three. The bad news—to the affiliates—was that so was FOX. With the start of the new season, FOX announced it was joining the other networks in cutting affiliate compensation. "Comp," as it was usually called, was what the networks paid the af-filiates each year to carry their shows, and it was based on a per-centage of the national ad revenues. FOX already paid lower comp than its competitors—since it broadcast fewer network programs each week—and now it was going to cut up to 50 percent of that amount. The FOX affiliate board approved the change, contingent as it was on improved ratings, with the network cutback not to oc-cur until ratings went up, allowing stations to make up their loss by charging more for local advertising. Jamie Kellner suggested this was simply a business adjustment: "Compensation from us is not a major part of our affiliates' revenue." Indeed, the stations had re-ceived extra local ad availabilities as a tradeoff for the reduced comp. Now it would get even less, as FOX sought a quick way to cut expenses. It was a small issue, and the affiliates went along. Later it would be seen as the first of many issues where the network had re-neged on a promise on how it would deal with its affiliates, leading to damaged relations with the stations.

On the Kids Network front there was much better news. Earlier in the 1991–1992 season, just as Margaret Loesch was climb-ing out from the rubble of *Peter Pan and the Pirates*, Jamie Kellner came to her with new marching orders for FOX's Saturday mornings. At one of their weekly meetings he said, "Let's knock off NBC."

Loesch was surprised. "What?"

"I want you to knock off NBC. They're vulnerable, you can take them. I want you to program specifically to knock them off."

"I don't think . . ." she began.

Kellner cut her off. "You can do it. Be creative. Come up with the programming that will take the kids away."

He was convinced that the kids market had changed in the 1980s from one that favored the Big Three to one that favored someone who could make a major commitment to daytime kids programming. Now, in 1991, the Big Three were no longer prepared to compete in this arena. Loesch was skeptical, but Kellner was the boss. She began planning FOX's Saturday morning schedule so as to best NBC, show after show. "I thought this guy was a lunatic," Loesch reported, "but he knew advertisers [would drop NBC] as we started to pull the ratings away from them. He was absolutely right."

Kellner was more than right. He and Loesch were victorious. It helped that FOX had popular shows like *Beetlejuice*, *Batman*, and *Tiny Toons*, but that was almost beside the point. What FOX could do that NBC could not was promote the show relentlessly to young viewers during the week. On weekday afternoons NBC was running soap operas while FOX was not only running animated shows but telling young viewers they could tune in to see more of the same on Saturday mornings. In December NBC threw in the towel. It announced that it would drop its early-Saturday-morning kids programs and instead launch *Saturday TODAY*, a weekend version of its top-rated morning news show. In response, FOX announced it was expanding *its* Saturday-morning cartoon lineup from three to four hours.

The next victory for the Kids Network came in January 1992 when Disney announced it would drop its two-year-old anti-trust suit against FOX. Disney had failed to scare FOX out of launching a competitor to its Disney Afternoon block of shows. Further, it was apparent that the two companies had other ongoing business relationships apart from competing cartoons, ranging from FOX buying Disney-produced TV series to Disney wanting to get space on Fox, Inc.–owned overseas satellite services. Disney Studios president Frank Rich announced, "It is time to put this conflict behind us, and focus on the myriad good and long-standing relationships that have existed between FOX and Disney, as well as the key officers of the two companies." The last was a reference to the fact that Diller and Disney's leader, Michael Eisner, had worked together at both ABC and Paramount. In response, a FOX spokesperson referred to this as a "statesmanlike decision."

As for prime time, reporters and other industry observers were not simply noticing that FOX's numbers were up, they were paying attention to *how* they were going up. For much of American television history, the name of the game was to get the most home viewers glued to their sets watching your programming. A show that had the most viewers in a time slot "won"; the others "lost." To a large extent that was still how the game was played, but the ratings services, and the advertisers who relied on them, had become more sophisticated in determining who made up that audience. If you were trying to sell movie tickets or soft drinks or sports cars, the fact that CBS's *60 Minutes* was not only the number one show Sunday nights at 7 P.M. but also often the top-rated show in all prime time in any given week didn't really matter. The show's viewers were generally older and were not going to be customers for youth-oriented products no matter how many times they saw your ad. Advertisers concluded that they wanted younger demographics, especially 18–34 and 25–49, where they saw more likely potential buyers. (The demographic breakdowns grew increasingly complex with groups that overlapped and yet were distinct to advertisers. Someone looking to sell to men 25–54 would not automatically buy a show that rated high among adults 18–49, not only because of the slightly younger skewing age of the group but because it might contain more women than men. Movie advertisers, for example, were extremely interested in shows that ranked high in the 18–34 and 18–49 demographics, because they were the large majority of their ticket buyers.)

This is where senior vice president for research Andy Fessel and the other number wizards at FOX had a field day. Not only were they analyzing the ratings for the network executives and the sales team; they also went out to convince reporters covering the industry that FOX was doing much better than might be thought by people operating under the traditional assumptions. By these traditional standards, FOX "lost" when, say, *The Simpsons* was not first in its time slot. But Fessel argued, who cared about the overall ratings when FOX led in the demographics most important to advertisers. He convinced both his sales team and the media reporters that demographics were far more important than overall household numbers, the traditional way success had been measured. This change was an integral part of the revolution in the TV industry that FOX was pushing: a new way to view success.

Overall the FOX Thursday to Sunday schedule was less than a ratings point behind third-place CBS. What's more—and this was the really crucial information—FOX came in number one among adults 18–49, the first time the network had *ever* beaten the Big Three in any category. On Sunday, September 8, 1991, the season premiere of *Married . . . with Children* not only had its best numbers for a premiere episode (nearly 50 percent higher than the 1990 opener) but the show was the number two nationally watched show overall for the week in all of prime time. When the Big Three began their fall seasons in mid-September, FOX refused to quietly return to fourth place. Of course NBC's hits *The Cosby Show* and *Cheers* won their Thursday-night time slots, but the number two shows in those time periods were not on CBS or ABC. They were FOX's *The Simpsons* and *Beverly Hills 90210*.

Yet the other networks still didn't get it. At least one had yet to put FOX on its prime-time scheduling board—where it could see how its shows fit against FOX's offerings. That network didn't consider

FOX as competition. Fessel and his staff pushed the idea that since FOX shows were drawing heavily among the 18–25 and 18–34 demographics, the network should capitalize on it. "At the same time that CBS was trying to sell on the age wave—that everyone was turning gray [and therefore programmers and advertisers should target older viewers]—we sold generation X. We did a whole videotape about generation X, how they're not slackers," said Fessel. He even talked it over with the writer Doug Coupland, who coined the phrase "generation X" in his book of the same name, when Fessel met him on a plane. "We were out working with his concepts and the marketing information around that, to sell [advertisers] the values of 18–34 and how they were very sophisticated and very upscale. They were a unique generation." The FOX audience skewed to younger viewers, and Fessel and his team were helping sell the point that this was a good thing: FOX was reaching a young, affluent adult audience that advertisers would be hard-pressed to find watching more traditional fare on the Big Three.

If the other networks were still at sea, the people promoting new movie releases got it right away. In 1987 FOX had sold $585 million in advertising time for movie ads. Four years later, even with a downturn in ticket sales at the box office, FOX raked in $800 million. A business analyst told *Variety*, "From the movie industry's point of view, FOX is, in effect, an entirely new medium. It attracts large numbers [of potential moviegoers] without a lot of work."

By 1991 FOX had become especially successful with young males, the toughest audience to target outside of sportscasts because they watched the least television. Fessel would gleefully point out that, for example, FOX's new office-oriented sitcom *Herman's Head* (with a cast that included William Ragsdale and Hank Azaria) might rank 72nd of all prime-time shows among all viewers, but among men 18–34 it was 13th. Other top shows among men 18–34 were *Married . . . with Children* (ranked 4th), *In Living Color* (6th), and *The Simpsons* (7th). To underscore the importance of demographics, Fessel told industry reporters, "We have demo meetings and don't

even look at the household figures. Demos are really the key to us."
(The household numbers focused on all viewers; the demos were
breakdowns by age, gender, and other factors.)

Less noticed, at least at first, was that FOX was also drawing in
African-American viewers who had become alienated from standard
network fare that largely ignored the black audience. Comedies like
True Colors, *In Living Color*, and *Roc* may have drawn in white viewers, but they were huge hits among black audiences. *Roc*, for example, featured Charles S. Dutton as a Baltimore garbage collector
who matched wits with a wife (Ella Joyce), a brother who was an un-
employed musician (Rocky Carroll), and a father (Carl Gordon)
who kept a picture of Malcolm X on display. An analysis in *Variety*
in January 1991 found that *Roc*'s black audience share was 238 percent higher than its share of the general household audience, while
for the comedy-variety show *In Living Color* that figure was 187 percent. Even for a "white" show like *Parker Lewis Can't Lose* (loosely
inspired by the 1986 big-screen comedy *Ferris Bueller's Day Off*),
African-American viewership was up because it was sandwiched between *True Colors* and *In Living Color*. (*True Colors* was a sitcom best
described as an interracial version of *The Brady Bunch*. A white
woman and a black man, each with kids, married and combined
families. Stephanie Faracy was the mother while the father was
played by Frankie Faison during the first season and by Cleavon
Little during the show's second and final season.)

Fessel felt these shows served two purposes. As hip, urban shows
they attracted FOX's primary young, city audience. But with their
special appeal to African-American viewers, not only because of the
black performers but also because of the sharper, edgier content
compared to the white-bread fare on the Big Three, this increased
FOX's overall ratings. "We found that the African-American audience was extremely wide, and it was a very efficient or productive
audience in terms of generating ratings points."

From the affiliate perspective, all this was good or bad depending on one's local market. For David Woods at WCOV in

Montgomery, Alabama, it was miraculous. "The highest ratings we've ever had on this station was when we had those shows from FOX," he recalls. For Gerry Walsh at WFXT in Boston, it was uneven: "I saw a survey that said there were more blacks in Boulder, Colorado, than in the metro Boston area. As the black population started to grow [here] those shows started to work, but *Martin* [starring Martin Lawrence, which premiered in August 1992] was never as successful here as elsewhere. . . . There was a station in Augusta, Georgia, that was doing a 52 rating with *Martin*. Unbelievable. Rating points I'm talking about." That meant that more than half of *everyone* in the potential audience was tuning in. By contrast, a top-rated network show like NBC's *E.R.* usually gets a rating in the high twenties or low thirties. Walsh continued, "Some of those small markets in the South were going through the roof. But [in Boston] the people weren't there; we didn't have the eyeballs."

FOX's romance with black viewers would continue for several more years but would end badly. For the moment, though, FOX reaped the benefits of having found another underserved TV audience. African-American viewers were pleased finally to find shows that seemed to speak to them, and FOX executives were happy with the resulting increase in their ratings. As Keenen Ivory Wayans told the writer Kristal Brent Zook, "FOX changed the course of black television *unintentionally*. They didn't go out to make black shows. They went out to make alternative programming."

In a season when FOX finally seemed to have found its groove, all bets were off on February 24, 1992. That was the day Barry Diller declared his intention to leave the network he had helped found six years earlier. Throughout the industry, two questions were debated: first, why was he leaving just as he was enjoying his greatest success, and, second, could the fledgling network survive without him?

The official story was that, at age fifty, Diller was ready to strike out on his own. His actions in the years after his time at FOX have been spent in building his own media empire, beginning with a cable shopping channel and currently as chairman and CEO of USA Interactive, clearly demonstrates his desire to be his own boss. As he explained to writer Gail Sheehy, it was more complicated than that.

Rupert Murdoch, who had been content to let Diller build FOX into a network as well as run the movie studio after 1985, was now interested in taking a more hands-on approach. Diller felt that he wasn't being given his due by Murdoch. At a board meeting in early 1992 Diller realized it was Murdoch and not he who was in charge. "It wasn't my store," he told Gail Sheehy. "I acted like it was, but it wasn't mine." It was time for a showdown. Diller went to Murdoch and insisted that he be given a real financial stake in the company, in effect becoming Murdoch's partner at FOX.

Murdoch made it clear that he was not looking for a partner. "He told me, not coldly or meanly, but just realistically, 'There is in this company only one principal.'" Diller knew it was time to get out.

It was announced simultaneously in February 1992 that Murdoch himself would take over Diller's post as chairman of Fox, Inc. "They think I'm an idiot. I'll have to work hard to prove them wrong," said Murdoch in response to the skeptics.

While everyone at FOX put on a public face about how there would be continuity at the network with president Jamie Kellner and Fox Entertainment Group chairman Peter Chernin staying on, the subtext was that the network—and the movie and TV studio—was now Rupert Murdoch's baby. Murdoch and Diller had nothing but praise for each other in their public announcements, but in interviews Murdoch quashed any notion that the success of FOX was primarily Diller's doing.

"Let's put it this way. Seven years ago I bet News Corp. on buying FOX for $2 billion. It's not as if I've been asleep for seven years," he declared in a March 1992 interview. "I was responsible for the most controversial idea of all, which was the idea of putting *The*

Simpsons on Thursday. And everyone laughed at that idea except Barry." In one verbal pirouette Murdoch simultaneously bashed those who thought he lacked Diller's refinement while insisting he was not knocking Diller himself: "Without intending any criticism, go look at the taste of every movie Barry made or anybody else in Hollywood. I read today that Barry was the last gasp of morality here. That's liberal bullshit."

Still, even though Diller's departure occurred right after the announcement, it was to everyone's best interest that this be seen as a smooth transition. In a press release announcing the resignation, Diller said, "This is completely amicable. Rupert Murdoch and I have no disagreements. . . . About Mr. Murdoch I would say that if you're going to work for somebody, work for him. He's the best . . . straight, supportive, honest, and clever. And I would add that if you want to be an entrepreneur, a better example of inspiration and aspiration could not be found—anywhere."

Within the confines of the industry there was a mixture of sadness, relief, and even celebration about Diller's resignation. One executive recalled parties breaking out at the FOX offices as people who feared him realized that their nemesis was really gone. "When Barry left we were throwing parties in the halls," he said. "It's not like you had to go down every six offices to get champagne."

Getting people to assess Diller's time at FOX is difficult because he remains a major player in Hollywood, and no one wants to go on the record criticizing him. One common complaint, beyond his very abrasive management style, was that he was credited with accomplishments that more properly belonged to others. He objected to almost every hit show FOX had except *America's Most Wanted*, and yet would appear on magazine covers with Bart Simpson as if *The Simpsons* had been his own idea. But it was his eagerness to keep employees off balance, often with angry and abusive language, that was most often cited. Margaret Loesch's refusal to take the job if she had to report to Diller directly speaks volumes. One employee, formerly at CBS, recalls Diller being shocked at the person's failure to respond

in kind to Diller's abuse. Diller was told that at CBS, one treated the
head of the company, the founder William Paley, with respect, not
by shouting obscenities.

One ex-FOX executive made it clear in an interview for this book
that Diller's place in the FOX story has been built up beyond recognition by those who were on the scene. "The reality is that there
were not many ideas that came out of Barry Diller's head. The ideas
were built by five or six or seven people who figured all this stuff
out. There wasn't one show on our air that Barry Diller dreamt up.
. . . When you go through the list of what people contributed, he's
been dramatically overpaid. But that's the way Hollywood is with
people like Barry Diller."

Another executive, one who had good relations with Diller at
FOX, was critical nonetheless: "I did not like his . . . style of management by intimidation and belittlement. . . . I saw so many just
get cut off at the knees. I don't respect that kind of management."

If Diller's departure in February 1992 was greeted with cheers
in at least some of the executive offices, there were critics among
the affiliates as well. One general manager at a FOX-affiliated station
was blunt: "I think one of the real humorous outcomes of the entire
FOX experience is the fact that everyone gives Barry Diller the credit
as the father of the network, as the man who made the network.
That's untrue. [FOX president] Jamie Kellner was the real engine
that drove and created and ensured the future of the FOX network.
Barry Diller was disruptive. He didn't have much of a creative sense
at all, a very erratic manager, and, if anything, I think delayed the
final success of the FOX network. He gets far too much credit."

To be fair, many had high praise for Diller and his work at FOX,
and they *were* willing to go on record. Patrick Mullen, president of
Tribune Broadcasting, agreed with his anonymous affiliate col-
league that Kellner deserves far more credit than he gets for starting FOX, but he believes Diller deserves major credit too. "I think
Barry Diller was a very aggressive, very bold operator, made some
good moves, took some big risks with FOX. . . . Barry was part of the

business mind behind the thing and taking those financial risks, but I think Jamie Kellner was the one who was making the program decisions. . . ." Former WFXT general manager Gerry Walsh, in Boston, noted, "Rupert had the money and maybe the idea, but Barry had the brains. . . . I don't think they ever replaced Barry Diller. It would be like the Celtics replacing Larry Bird."

For all the carping, there was plenty of admiration for Diller as someone who not only worked hard to launch and build FOX but who mastered every aspect of the TV business. "He's certainly a tireless executive," said Tom Allen, then FOX's chief financial officer, "He's one of the longest-hour working guys that I was exposed to among the senior executives of FOX while I was there." Allen recalls that all the top executives had direct lines in their office from Kellner, the head of the network, and from Diller, the head of Fox, Inc.

Midwest affiliate relations manager Bob Mariano was an out-and-out fan of Diller. "He was the most brilliant intellectual entrepreneur in show business that I ever encountered," he said. "He probes and probes and probes, and learns as much as he possibly can about every facet. . . . He could spend two hours on whether [the sitcom] *Mr. President* . . . should be [shot with] three camera[s] or one camera, and what are the values of that. He gets interested in all aspects of it." What others found as a drawback—Diller's relentlessness in grilling his employees—Mariano found "exhilarating," because he felt that Diller wasn't being needlessly cruel, "You were encouraged to respond to Barry Diller. He would attack you, but it was meant to provoke whether or not you'd done your homework, whether or not you'd really thought it through. And if you have conviction and you're a courageous person, you can respond and he will totally respect it."

Trade reporter Brian Lowry, who by 1992 was covering FOX for *Variety*, recalls the Diller resignation announcement as an "enormous shock." Said Lowry, "There was a sense that he was the mastermind behind everything. What became clear at a certain point was that despite all the turmoil and their constant, every other year, executive changes, that they had finally, by that point, become established enough that they were part of the landscape."

What was really clear, however, was that however established FOX had become, they were now moving into uncharted territory. Scott Siegler, president of Columbia Pictures Television—which was supplying FOX with *Married . . . with Children*—said, "When you pitched a project to FOX, there was always a question of what the man behind the green curtain would think. With Barry gone, I don't think people will immediately know what sensibility to orient projects towards."

If it was not quite clear how the vacuum left by Diller's departure would be filled, there was one executive who was already seen as an up-and-comer. That was Stephen Chao, vice president for development for the FOX station group. Chao had never held the high-profile posts of other top FOX execs, but he was clearly marked for success. A Harvard graduate whose resumé included stints at the *National Enquirer* and in a Wall Street brokerage firm, he was hired by Murdoch in 1983 to analyze media properties Murdoch wished to acquire. While at the FOX o-and-o group, Chao had helped oversee the development of both *America's Most Wanted* and *COPS*, more than proving his worth to the network. In March 1992 he was tapped to become president of FOX News, where he would oversee both the FOX News Service and the news operations at the FOX-owned stations in the United States. Two months later Chao took over as president of the o-and-o group in total, replacing Greg Nathanson, who resigned when Chao was handed the news responsibilities rather than himself. (Nathanson had actually submitted his resignation in April 1992, but it was delayed until May so it would not be linked to Diller's resignation.)

Two future FOX network executives also had announcements related to network programming. In April, Lucie Salhany, who had become president of Twentieth Century Television in May 1991, revealed that FOX had signed comic actor Chevy Chase to host a new late-night show, to premiere in the fall of 1993. Salhany had been behind the successful launch of Arsenio Hall's syndicated late-night show at Paramount in 1989. This led to some buzz among the affiliates about FOX's reentry into late-night programming, though many of the stations took a wait-and-see attitude. Then in May 1992 Doug Herzog, the senior vice president of programming for MTV, made public a deal wherein the music video cable channel and FOX would cooperate on a series of specials. The shows would air first on FOX and then on the cable channel, like *The FOX/MTV Guide to Summer*. Explained Herzog, "The idea is to spotlight new talent on MTV and FOX and develop those people as personalities."

The June 22–23 affiliate meeting in Century City near the Fox lot should have gone smoothly. Things were looking up for the network. FOX's viewing audience was up by 30 percent over the year before, which meant that ad revenue was up as well. What was there to complain about? Of course affiliates always have some gripes, but the issues were all low-level ones that could be expected to work themselves out down the road. For example, the affiliates were still lukewarm on doing local news, and the trend in that direction was going much more slowly than FOX might have liked— but it was happening. On another front, there was some grumbling about how slowly FOX was expanding to a seven-night service. Some stations, expecting that by now the network would be fully operational every night of the week, had let the leases on their syndicated movie libraries lapse since they figured they would no longer need old feature films to fill out the schedule. Now they were scrambling for programming to cover the gaps on Tuesday and Wednesday nights. There was also skepticism about Chevy Chase and his new late-night talk show; but the comedian was set to speak to the affiliates via satellite, and he would end by convincing many of the general managers that he could, indeed, take on the demanding role of talk show host. Certainly 1991–1992 had been an eventful season, but by stressing stability and continuity,

Murdoch and his team at FOX made it clear that business-as-usual would go on without Barry Diller.

It might almost have worked, except for the bombshell announcement just before the affiliates gathered that Fox News president Stephen Chao had been summarily fired.

Before the Century City meeting, there had been a News Corp. retreat in Aspen, Colorado, on June 19, 1992. Attending were the top executives from the various divisions of the company—newspapers and publishing as well as the various Fox entities—along with several guests, including Murdoch's wife Anna and Secretary of Defense Richard Cheney and his wife Lynne, who chaired the National Endowment for the Humanities. In this buttoned-down setting, Chao elected to take his innovative, cutting-edge attitude one step too far.

Greg Meidel was there at the Aspen retreat, having arrived on the Fox lot just a few weeks before Diller left. He was president of Twentieth Television, the part of the company that syndicated off-network repeats and produced nondramatic series like *COPS* and the syndicated *A Current Affair*. Meidel remembers that the tone had changed around the Fox offices after Diller's departure, that people were looser, less guarded. "Rupert really wanted to downplay the combative style. It was a real change in there. You could sense it," he recalled. "We were always so cautious with one another, and now all of a sudden we're being encouraged to huddle up."

What Meidel recalled most about Chao's presentation in Aspen was not his firing but what he said in the presentation that got him in trouble. "First of all, Chao's speech was magnificent. The sad part about it is that most people don't remember that he did deliver a brilliant speech about how we are sometimes hypocrites. . . . Steve never got credit for the speech."

Meidel was sitting in the back of the room with Lucie Salhany, his counterpart at Twentieth Century Television, when Chao began speaking. Meidel and Salhany had known each other at Paramount, and she noticed a stranger standing at the side of the room. Meidel figured it was someone's boyfriend, not a setup for an outrageous gag. "No way," Meidel said to Salhany, "I know Chao's going to push the envelope and I admire him for that, but he's not going to have a stripper."

In fact, that's exactly what he had done. Chao challenged the audience to ignore the stripper and focus on his own remarks, which were about the hypocrisy of much media criticism. His intention was to make the point that while his audience might prefer to think of themselves as above it all, sex is what grabbed people's attention, just as the disrobing man had become their focus. William Shawcross, in his 1992 book *Murdoch: The Making of a Media Empire*, reported that Chao also intended to have a fake gunman coming out and shoot the stripper, to make a similar point about violence in the media. He was dissuaded when it was pointed out that Defense Secretary Cheney's Secret Service guards would certainly have opened fire.

Chao's point was well taken, but his choice of visual aids couldn't have been more misconceived, given the audience. When the stripper got up on stage and went into his act, says Meidel, "You never heard such nervous laughter through an entire room."

Murdoch ordered Chao to apologize, but by then it was too late. Murdoch told the attendees, "It's a terrible thing to see a brilliant young career self-destruct. And it's a bitter loss. But the point is that there are limits." Chao was fired, and the keynote address to the affiliates on the future of FOX News that should have been Chao's was now made by Murdoch himself.

Clearly the post-Diller era had begun.

PART II

The Revolving Door

CHAPTER EIGHT

"Like most businesses, this is a team sport"

[1992−1993]

	THE FOX FALL PRIME-TIME SCHEDULE							
	7:00	7:30	8:00	8:30	9:00	9:30	10:00	10:30
Sunday	Great Scott	The Ben Stiller Show	In Living Color	Roc	Married ... with Children	Herman's Head	Flying Blind	Woops!
Wednesday			Beverly Hills 90210		Melrose Place			
Thursday			The Simpsons	Martin	The Heights			
Friday			America's Most Wanted		Sightings	Likely Suspects		
Saturday			COPS	COPS	Code 3	The Edge		

ONE WOULD THINK that at least the Academy of Television Arts and Sciences would recognize that FOX was doing something different, especially after the network had been carrying the Emmy Awards for several years in spite of the fact that it was rarely a ratings winner. In February 1992, however, the Academy's board of governors rejected a measure that would have shown how FOX had really changed the rules of the game in terms of the prime-time fare being offered on network TV. The question before them was whether the sitcom cartoon *The Simpsons*, now in its fourth season, should be considered as a comedy or as an animated series. After heated debate, the decision was made by the board to leave it in the animation category. Said one Academy member, "We can't just allow animation to compete with conventional programs. Everyone has an advantage in animation, since they can have their characters do things that real life characters can't do." In a delightful bit of irony that showcased the stodginess of the Emmy board, the decision came just as the Oscar nominations were announced. On the very same day the television Academy was ghettoizing *The Simpsons* as animation, the separately constituted Academy of Motion Picture Arts and Sciences announced that Disney's feature-length *Beauty and the Beast* had been nominated for the Best Picture Oscar. It was the first full-length animated film to be so honored.

The television Academy did make an attempt to acknowledge the significance of *The Simpsons*. In August it announced that a special voiceover performance Emmy would be awarded for the first time. Unlike the normal Emmys, which the Academy membership votes on directly, the recipients of this honor were chosen by a select jury. The cast of *The Simpsons* received six Emmys. Honored were voice cast members Nancy Cartwright (the voice of Bart), Dan Castellaneta (Homer), Julie Kavner (Marge), Yeardley Smith (Lisa), and Marcia Wallace (Mrs. Krabappel). Jackie Mason was also honored as a guest star on the show, for voicing the father of Krusty the Klown, Rabbi Krustofsky.

FOX added Wednesday night to its schedule in late July 1992 with a doubleheader that would prove to be a magnet for teen viewers. Getting the jump on the Big Three by launching its fall season two months early, FOX temporarily moved *Beverly Hills 90210* back an hour to 8 P.M. to attract audiences to the network's new hour-long offering at 9: *Melrose Place*. When FOX executives saw that the shows were not only competitive in their time slots but that more than 40 percent of the audience was in the prized 18–34 demographic, the change was made permanent.

The development of *Melrose Place* was the logical outgrowth of the success of *90210*. Programming executive Rob Kenneally would leave FOX shortly before the launch of the nighttime soap opera, which was really in the hands of vice president of drama development Bob Greenblatt. Kenneally said that by this point they knew they were shooting for the younger demographics. "There were three areas we wanted to do. One was high school, which worked well. The other was college, and the third was between college and your career. Twenty-something, that was an area we were really interested in pushing forward on, and that's sort of where *Melrose Place* was born."

In his memoir, Aaron Spelling remembers the drama having an easy birth, the only one of his shows ever to be successfully spun off from another. "FOX wanted a *90210* spin-off, and when we discussed it with Darren Star [who had created the original series two seasons before], he mentioned that he used to live in an apartment complex in West Hollywood where everyone got to know each other. We thought that was a great idea for a show. . . . *Melrose* turned out to be as big a hit as *90210*."

Greenblatt remembered it being slightly more difficult. After approaching Spelling and Star, he recalled, "Aaron was very reticent early on to do a spin-off. Ultimately he decided it would probably be a good idea." Spelling and Star developed the script and even came up with the tenuous connection with *90210*. Kelly (Jenny Garth) breaks up with a construction worker (Grant Show) she had been dating on *90210* and then is invited over for a visit by the characters on *Melrose Place* to see if they can fix things up. The July premiere set this new youth-oriented show on against summer reruns on the Big Three, and it scored well in the ratings. "We figured, why don't we try when everyone else has repeats? We'll have a bit of a competitive edge. The show was on the cover of *TV Guide* before it went on the air," said Greenblatt. "It all sort of worked pretty easily."

If it seemed like it was almost too easy, it was. In September 1992, however, *Melrose Place* started facing real competition, like new episodes of the sitcoms *Seinfeld* and *Mad About You* on NBC and the Tim Allen comedy *Home Improvement* on ABC. *Melrose's* ratings dropped like a stone. Around FOX the feeling was that they had made a nice try, but perhaps it just wasn't going to work. Then Aaron Spelling and Darren Star came to programming executives with a proposition. "You know what," Spelling told them, "it's a soap opera. Let's just make it into a big, outrageous soap."

In mid-season, Spelling brought on Heather Locklear as Amanda Woodward and soon all hell broke loose—in the story line. Modeled somewhat on the Joan Collins character of Alexis on *Dynasty*, Spelling's long-lasting 1980s hit on ABC (where Locklear had been a cast member), Amanda was smart, beautiful, and a manipulator. As official *Melrose* chronicler David Wild put it, "Amanda set off a rather powerful and strange chemical reaction in the *Melrose Place* complex. All of a sudden, in this bastion of goodwill and love for thy neighbor, assorted bad guys and girls started popping up *everywhere*." With people hopping into other's beds, backstabbing and betraying each other, *Melrose* became a hit all over again. Greenblatt said if it hadn't been for Spelling's intervention, after having reluctantly agreed to do the show in the first place, it "probably would have been off the air pretty quickly."

While *Melrose* joined the roster of FOX's signature shows—programs that told their viewers they weren't watching the Big Three anymore—other attempts by the network at the youth ensemble drama quickly disappeared. The marketplace can only absorb so much of the same kind of TV fare at once. For example, when FOX launched its Tuesday schedule in January 1993, it led with *Class of '96*, a college-oriented show starring Jason Gedrick, to fit between *90210's* high schoolers and *Melrose's* twenty-somethings. It was dropped in May. Spelling had also gone to the well again with *The Heights*, a weekly drama about a struggling rock band. It spawned a hit single, "How Do You Talk to an Angel?" which was the series' theme song, but it too was canceled after a short run. While *The Heights* is little remembered, its cancellation set off a chain of events that eventually led to the destruction of one of FOX's most important shows.

When *The Heights* was canceled in November 1992—after only three months on the air—it left a hole in FOX's Thursday-night schedule. The decision was made to fill the gap with two half-hour comedies. First was *Down the Shore*, a sitcom set in a New Jersey beach house, which had been given a tryout over the summer but had not made it to the initial fall schedule. It turned out to be a weak season for new comedies on the network. Other flop series that came and went in quick succession included *Woops!*, a broad sitcom about survivors of a nuclear holocaust; *Flying Blind* with Corey Parker as a recent college graduate and Tea Leoni as the wild woman in his life; and *The Ben Stiller Show*, a critically praised sketch comedy show which had the dubious distinction of being the lowest-rated network series that season, finishing 109th. With the comedy cupboard bare, the network chose to fill the other half-hour with reruns from the 1990–1991 premiere season of *In Living Color*.

Keenen Ivory Wayans's sketch-comedy show had become a breakout success for FOX, but it had also been a source of constant headaches. Not since Joan Rivers and *The Late Show* in 1986 had something on the FOX schedule been such a continuing irritant to network operations. At first it had less to do with personalities than simply the nature of the program. There were ongoing negotiations with the standards and practices people at the network as to what would be allowed in the show and what went beyond the pale, even for FOX.

"The book we all read at the time was the history of *Saturday Night Live*, and we would quote from it . . . with the censors all the time," recalled executive producer Eric Gold. They would use earlier examples of words or situations appearing on TV as precedents for what they wanted to do. Gold said that while the standards and practices people gave them a lot of leeway, people on the show still found themselves constantly butting heads with the censors. Finally Wayans told them they should go to network president Jamie Kellner on every issue. Said Gold, "The idea was to sort of wear Jamie out. And after a point Jamie had had enough."

Kellner supported the show and didn't allow himself to be baited on the content issue. Hollywood writers have a long history of putting material in scripts that they know will never win approval, then using that material as a bargaining chip to save the items they really want to keep. Financial officer Tom Allen remembered being in a meeting with Kellner when Fox Entertainment Group chairman Peter Chernin walked in and "described a couple of scenes, skits, on the show that were hilariously funny but also obviously over the line from a standards viewpoint." The three of them laughed out loud, and then Chernin delivered the punchline: "Our standards department approved all three."

The laughter stopped dead. Kellner got up without a word and quietly left the room. Later Allen learned that Kellner left the building, went over to the trailer where standards and practices was still located on the overcrowded Fox property, and very calmly asked if he could see Don Bay, the head of the department. The two men then strolled around the lot and discussed the material and how they could resolve any problems. "That's a very telling story about how Jamie manages people," said Allen. It may also explain why Kellner was inclined to give the writers their way instead of having constantly to negotiate over what could be included in a script.

Arguments also arose over scheduling. When *In Living Color* was moved an hour earlier to 8 P.M. there was a question whether it would have less freedom than it had at the later hour. A proposal to move it to Saturday night followed a marketing report that suggested African Americans stay home in greater numbers on the weekend. "And Keenen went crazy," recalled Gold. "He kept going 'We're not black, we're young, and you don't put a young show on Saturday night. Our audience is out partying." Wayans ultimately won that round against the network too.

As the new season began, still another problem developed. Damon Wayans had guest-starred in the pilot only as a favor to his older brother and was kept on—and paid—episode by episode. (Gold recalled that it was actually a separate payment for every *sketch* he appeared in.) Now Damon was gone, and the rest of the cast were renegotiating their contracts. Jim Carrey (then known as James) wanted more money, figuring that as one of the stars of a hit series he deserved more than the $7,500 the lead cast members were getting under their current contracts. David Alan Grier said he wanted the same deal Carrey got. Tommy Davidson said he wanted the same deal Grier got.

The negotiations proceeded with Twentieth Century Television, which was producing the show for the FOX network. Wayans demanded more money for his cast, claiming they were underpaid. Production was starting, and Carrey and Grier had not reported for work, with Wayans backing them up. According to Gold, what happened next was the beginning of an irreparable breach between Wayans and his production team on the one hand and Lucie Salhany, the head of Twentieth Century Television on the other. She suggested that they fire Carrey, on the theory that that would undercut everyone else's bargaining position. Twentieth even went so far as to hold open auditions for new cast members for the show, though no one was actually hired from the resulting cattle call.

"Lucie and I got into a big fight," remembered Gold. Recalling how much Wayans fought to get Carrey on the show, Gold—who by now was also Carrey's manager—exploded, "You know it's like, 'Lucie, are you a fucking moron? You can't just replace Jim Carrey. There aren't ten Jim Carreys in the whole world. Don't you understand?'"

Carrey finally cut a deal, followed by Grier. But now the cauldron was bubbling, and if keeping Wayans happy had been a consideration, FOX never would have scheduled repeats of the show when *The Heights* was canceled. Since *In Living Color* was owned by Wayans and Twentieth Century–Fox, he and Gold felt that the network had a duty to protect Wayans's financial interest in the sketch-comedy series. Doing a third run of already repeated first-season episodes was, in their opinion, destroying the potential value of the program in later syndication. Salhany's response was that variety series had no real value in syndication, so they were essentially arguing over nothing.

Salhany recalled that they were simply following the contract that Wayans had signed, which permitted FOX to schedule additional runs of *In Living Color*. "He was furious. He blamed it on the network, when it was really Peter Chernin's decision," she said. (As head of the Fox Entertainment Group, Chernin had climbed, in effect, to a level above both Kellner at the network and Salhany at Twentieth Century Television. He oversaw the movie studio as well.)

Wayans and Gold were more than furious. They were fed up. In December 1992 they quit the show, Wayans taking his family with him. Damon had already left, and now sister Kim Wayans walked out too. They were joined by producer Tamara Rawitt. The show went on without them. It was not the last FOX would be hearing from Wayans and Gold.

If there was any question about what chairman Barry Diller had wrought at FOX, one need only compare the executive ranks there before and after his departure. Some turnover occurred under Diller from 1985 to 1992, especially in programming, where Diller's confrontational management style led to early burnout. But there was also a great deal of stability at the network. For example, Jamie Kellner had been there from the beginning, as had ratings analyst Andy Fessel. Financial officer Tom Allen had also come early on, in September 1986. Now the FOX offices at 10201 West Pico Boulevard in Los Angeles would have to be equipped with revolving doors. While those who pleased News Corp. chairman Rupert Murdoch—like Fox Entertainment Group chairman Peter Chernin—would continue and even be promoted, others would come and go quickly. If one had to determine when the curtain was rung down on the "building" phase of the FOX network, it would have to be at the start of 1993 when Jamie Kellner announced his resignation.

Kellner had brought the network from zero to seven nights a week of programming—the Monday network movie would return to the schedule in June—and gave FOX the potential to reach nearly as many viewers as the Big Three. Now there was little room to maneuver since Rupert Murdoch had decided to become a hands-on manager. Many of Kellner's fans in the business felt he was never given his due for his role in helping create FOX, though he may have had the last laugh by essentially doing it all over again when he started the WB network in 1995, eventually outfoxing FOX. Publicly he professes to have little interest in rehashing the past. "I think, like most businesses, this is a team sport," he said. "When you go through the list of people . . . all of them did exceptional work. It was not because of any one person that the network built or became successful or whatever. It was a lot of people, twenty or thirty really talented people, that helped it survive and blossom."

Kellner's replacement at FOX was none other than Lucie Salhany. At the age of forty-seven she had come up through the ranks of local television, starting as a secretary and moving into managerial positions. At Taft Broadcasting she had convinced the station group to sign up an hour talk show featuring a then unknown African-American woman named Oprah Winfrey. Salhany was known for having the right instincts. At Paramount, as president of its domestic television group, she had supported such syndicated successes as *The Arsenio Hall Show*, *Entertainment Tonight*, and *Star Trek: The Next Generation*. Barry Diller had recruited her over to Twentieth Century Television in 1991, and now Rupert Murdoch had put her in charge of the entire network, the first woman in the United States to hold such a position. She recalled, going in, that she had a good relationship with Murdoch, but admits that he could be "very difficult." She would soon find out just how difficult.

In April 1993 the trades were reporting that Chase Carey, forty-one, had been slotted as Murdoch's number two man overseeing all the Twentieth Century–Fox operations as executive vice president and chief operating officer. His position with Murdoch was considered so secure that some called him "an honorary Australian." The industry waited to see what all this executive turnover at FOX would mean. As one talent agent told *Variety*, "What I'm hearing more and more from FOX is: Sounds good, but let me run it by Rupert and we'll get back to you in a couple of days."

Earlier, in February 1993, Salhany, Murdoch, Preston Padden, and Sandy Grushow, who had taken over for Peter Chernin as head of FOX programming, met with the network affiliates at the meeting of the National Association of Television Programming Executives (NATPE), an annual convention showcasing available and upcoming syndicated programming. Chevy Chase dropped by to promote his upcoming talk show on FOX, which would be housed at the Aquarius Theatre in Hollywood, once home to the syndicated talent showcase *Star Search*. The networks would often arrange to have midwinter sessions with their affiliates in conjunction with NATPE, because most of the people who would be attending an affiliate meeting were already there. Padden took the opportunity to warn the FOX affiliate managers about preempting the network for syndicated offerings, urging them to "put the good of the team ahead of fleeting opportunities for individual stardom" and not to "revert to their old independent ways." Padden himself had been affected by the executive shuffle, taking on the title of senior vice president of government relations in addition to already being senior vice president of affiliate relations. In this instance, though, it simply acknowledged the work he was already doing.

One person who was shaken by all the changes at FOX was Margaret Loesch at the FOX Kids Network. When Diller had departed the year before, she wondered where that left network president Jamie Kellner. "I had said to Jamie, the day Barry yells at me or puts a knot in my stomach, I quit. On the other hand, Barry was very smart and [had been] very supportive," she said, noting that kids programming was not something Diller felt passionate about. "But he thought it was a good idea."

When Kellner left, she said, "I felt very alone. . . . I was really not happy when Jamie left, and he assured me that all was well. I was worried." Still, the ratings for the cartoons were up, and she had scored a success with *X Men*, based on the Marvel Comics characters. Loesch was often cited for a brilliant programming strategy with *X Men*—previewing the show during the November 1992 sweeps, to whet the kids' appetites, then holding back the series until the February 1993 sweeps, all the while heavily promoting it. "The truth is, we couldn't get the show done [on time]," Loesch admitted with a laugh. She heard herself referred to as a "strategic genius in programming" and realized she had come a ways since *Peter Pan and the Pirates* in 1990. "We had momentum, and the FOX Kids Network was starting to be the star of the network. Rupert was really starting to talk to me a lot. He was citing the success of the Kids Network in speeches, the affiliates were being very embracing," she recalled. "And then Lucie Salhany became my biggest cheerleader."

Together Loesch and Salhany would make children's programming history, but that was still in the future.

At the annual affiliate meeting in June 1993, Preston Padden showed why he was worth his weight in gold to the network. The entire television industry was in an uproar over something called "retransmission consent." Under the new federal regulations, cable companies would need permission from broadcasters to carry their television signals on their systems. For years the cable distribution companies had just picked up the broadcast signals from whichever stations they wanted and included them in their cable packages—at no cost. The FCC had permitted this in order to help the cable industry get established and grow. But that assistance was no longer needed, and in the spirit of deregulation sweeping through

Congress, cable's special waiver was dropped. Now the whole relationship between cable and broadcast outlets was about to change.

Local TV stations had two options. First, they could elect to
take "must carry" status, in which case the cable company simply
picked up the signal and included it in its basic package of services.
Indeed, the cable operator had no choice but to carry it, as a matter
of law. Smaller stations with low ratings and no bargaining power—
as well as public television stations—would automatically end up on
cable by taking this easy way out.

But the major commercial broadcasters figured this was a way to
get cable companies to start paying for the free ride they had had
for years. Network affiliates saw that premium services like HBO and
Showtime and basic channels like Lifetime and CNN were able to
charge cable companies for the privilege of carrying their services,
even as many of them also sold advertising time. The broadcasters
felt they were entitled to comparable remuneration. The cable industry, in almost a single voice, howled defiance at the notion that
they would *ever* pay for the rights to carry "free" broadcast television channels. Around the country cable companies threatened to
drop local stations before they would agree to pay for them.

Padden responded by negotiating a deal with the FOX affiliates
in which they assigned their retransmission rights to FOX. The network would then negotiate on behalf of all the FOX stations with
various cable operators. The other networks just negotiated for
their o-and-o's (owned and operated stations), leaving their affiliates
to fend for themselves, individually or as part of their own station
groups. Besides giving FOX greater leverage, it also allowed FOX to
advance its own agenda, which was to trade retransmission consent
for an agreement to carry a new FOX cable channel. Explained Padden, "The way that worked, cable operators agreed to pay twenty-
five cents per subscriber per month for [FOX cable]. As part of the
package, they got retransmission of their local FOX affiliate. We
passed along seven and a half cents out of that twenty-five cents
to the stations, providing them with value, real value, for their

retransmission consent." In other words, FOX made a deal with cable operators to buy their new cable service at a competitive rate with other cable channels. To sweeten the deal they threw in the right to carry the local FOX broadcast station. The deal allowed the cable companies to maintain that they hadn't paid a penny for the "retransmission" rights to broadcast stations, and it allowed the individual stations to see a new revenue stream heading their way as a result of the negotiations. Most important, it marked FOX's entry into original cable programming.

KTVU general manager Kevin O'Brien was very involved in the negotiations from the affiliate side. "I think the decision we made to turn over our retransmission consent rights to FOX was a brilliant one because, indeed, we were the only affiliates that got actual cash out of the deal." No station that negotiated directly with the cable operators ever realized any payments from granting retransmission consent. Indeed, the FOX affiliates would never see any actual money on the deal either, but later they would have their accounts credited against what FOX would demand they pay as their share of FOX acquiring the rights to NFL football. Still, O'Brien was right. It was more than any of the Big Three affiliates received.

Some other companies saw the wisdom of the FOX strategy. Hearst, for example, used the retransmission rights of its broadcast stations to help launch the ESPN2 sports channel, but that didn't result in payments to the individual stations. The stations that thought they would profit from "retransmission consent" learned the hard way that in spite of this bit of deregulation, nothing had really changed. In the end, not willing to risk not being carried on local cable services, consent was inevitably granted to carry the stations.

The affiliates hadn't simply trusted in FOX's benevolence in getting them something out of their dealings with the cable companies. They used their own bargaining leverage to insist that FOX offer five-year extensions on the affiliation agreements rather than renew the contracts on shorter terms. On that point FOX had to give in.

The network still needed the affiliates to go along with FOX's separate deal with cable operator TCI to begin carrying FOX programming in U.S. markets where there was no affiliate. Asked in June 1993 if the network would have acceded to the demands of the affiliates for longer contract terms if they weren't needed to sign off on the TCI project, Padden was succinct. "Honestly? No."

The 1992–1993 season ended like it had begun, with questions about which category *The Simpsons* would be allowed to compete in at the next annual Emmy awards show in August. Executive producer James L. Brooks said that the hit animated show "doesn't defy classification; classification is defying us." Series creator Matt Groening was more to the point: "It's just not that much of a thrill beating *Garfield* every year." (CBS had been running a Saturday morning children's cartoon series featuring the comic-strip cat.)

The punch line was like something out of a *Simpsons* episode. The show was finally allowed to compete in the category of comedy series . . . and then didn't get nominated.

CHAPTER NINE

"How come you make my mommy cry all the time?"

[1993–1994]

	7:00	7:30	8:00	8:30	9:00	9:30
		THE FOX FALL PRIME-TIME SCHEDULE				
Sunday	Townsend Television		Martin	Living Single	Married . . . with Children	Daddy Dearest
Monday			Movie		Movie (continues)	
Tuesday			Roc	Bakersfield P.D.	America's Most Wanted	
Wednesday			Beverly Hills 90210		Melrose Place	
Thursday			The Simpsons	Sinbad	In Living Color	Herman's Head
Friday			Adventures of Brisco County, Jr.		The X-Files	
Saturday			COPS	COPS	Front Page	

FROM END TO END, the 1993–1994 television season for FOX was the stuff of nightmares. It began with what became known as one of the most resounding flops in television history and ended with the FOX affiliates in open revolt against the network. It witnessed resignations, lawsuits, and the start of a government proceeding that might cost Rupert Murdoch his TV network altogether. It also saw the birth of a show that would become the network's biggest franchise, another thoroughly unexpected hit that put FOX on top of the heap in kids programming, and two negotiating coups that forever changed the way the broadcast television business was conducted in the United States.

As Charles Dickens nicely observed: it was the best of times; it was the worst of times.

If someone had told sixty-two-year-old Rupert Murdoch in October 1993 that the success of his seven-year-old FOX television network would be inevitable by the end of the current season, he might well have believed it. That autumn, though, he might well have been the only one who *did* believe it, for FOX was undergoing the most public sort of humiliation possible. With great fanfare and in the midst of national attention to network late-night programming, it had launched *The Chevy Chase Show*.

On paper the show had everything going for it. Chase was a TV veteran who had been the first regular cast member to break out of NBC's late-night *Saturday Night Live*. His role in the feature film *Foul Play* in 1978 had launched him into big-screen stardom. In *Variety*, Tracy Dolgin, FOX's executive vice president of marketing, was expansive: "Chevy is the most recognized, most loved performer entering late night. . . . When you start out with that kind of recognition and likability, our job is just to let people know that he will be out there in late night." Dolgin noted that his "TV Q Score," a measure of how much viewers recognized and liked various contemporary personalities, was a 42. By contrast, Jay Leno—successor to late-night TV talk-show king Johnny Carson—was a mere 8. David Letterman, who had defected from NBC to CBS and had just launched his own run on the late-night crown, was marginally better at 19.

No one at FOX thought those Q scores would translate into direct ratings. FOX's history doing five shows a week in the late-night time slot had been spotty, from the short-lived *The Late Show with Joan Rivers* in 1986–1987 to the even shorter-lived *The Wilton-North Report* that succeeded it. Indeed, FOX had the dubious distinction of having launched stand-up comic and actor Arsenio Hall in late night when he filled in after Rivers departed, and then letting him get away to a syndicated late-night show from rival

Paramount. Lucie Salhany, the executive who had launched Hall's syndicated late-night show from that studio in 1989, was now president of FOX. If she could reestablish a FOX presence in late night, her future in the TV industry would be bright.

FOX's affiliate stations went along with the network's reentry into the late-night battlefield, many of them reluctantly. Bob Leider, executive vice president of Sunbeam Television, owner of FOX's powerful Miami affiliate WSVN, explained, "Lucie brought a programming angle that, at that particular time, we thought FOX needed. It was her Paramount experience. One of her mandates that I think she imposed on herself was that she wanted to come up with a late-night show."

The problem was that the late-night market had changed markedly since Joan Rivers departed, in large part because of FOX. The FOX affiliates had increased in viewership and value, and late night was now a valuable part of the programming day for them. Many of the stations, like WSVN, were already contractually obligated to run the syndicated *Arsenio Hall* at 11 P.M. and wouldn't be able to clear time for the network's *Chevy Chase* show until midnight. Other FOX outlets around the country were rerunning sitcoms against the local newscasts and making out quite well. FOX was asking them to give up what was working for something that was unproved. The recalcitrant stations would be accused—by the network and by some fellow affiliates—of still thinking like an independent station, with complete freedom to buy syndicated shows and program their broadcast day. As affiliates they now had an obligation to run network programming, and it wasn't always a happy choice.

For their part, FOX and Chase did everything they could to win over the stations. They went all out in promoting the show, from billboards featuring Chase with a Letterman-style space in his teeth ("Ready to fill the late-night gap" the ads promised) to airplanes trailing sky banners and an advertising tie-in with Doritos chips. Chase even did a special presentation to affiliate executives at their annual meeting to demonstrate he had what it took despite his background as a writer and an actor in sketch comedy. (Leno and Letterman, by contrast, had honed their skills in stand-up comedy, and Johnny Carson had cut his teeth as a game-show host.)

Some station executives remained unconvinced. One station honcho, recalling the *Chase* show years later, put it bluntly: "I don't think any of the affiliates thought *Chevy Chase* was a very good idea because he hadn't had experience doing that. When you saw him, his deadpan kind of thing is really more akin to motion pictures than it is to doing an interview show."

In many ways Lucie Salhany's reputation as one of the rising stars in the TV industry was riding on the show's success. Before becoming head of the network, she had run Twentieth Century–Fox Television, the studio's major TV production arm, and she had pushed hard for Chase to be the host of the proposed show that Twentieth would produce. Her predecessor at the network, Jamie Kellner, had favored trying to woo Letterman from his home base at NBC. Salhany had ultimately prevailed, and now her first new season at FOX was under way with all eyes on Chase. Although publicly everyone was upbeat, Salhany was more than aware of the danger ahead.

"I should have known there was a problem earlier when nobody wanted to be involved with it other than me. As we started, everyone was very supportive, and then as we got closer nobody really wanted to work on it," she recalled. "So I was working like sixteen hours a day. I think probably after the first week is when I knew there was no hope."

No one expected Chase's nightly hour to topple Leno or Letterman, but they thought they could have an easy victory simply by doing better than NBC's new late-night entry. He was an unknown writer—whose credits included *The Simpsons*—with the unlikely name of Conan O'Brien. He had been tapped to take over Letterman's post–*Tonight Show* slot. NBC decided to bring him along gently. The network downplayed the hype and figured that with a show starting at 12:30 A.M., there was less at stake. They'd have plenty of time to work out the bugs. In contrast, Chase would have to prove himself quickly because his show would be more clearly in the public eye, running its second half-hour opposite the higher profile Leno/Letterman battle which kicked off at 11:30 P.M.

Vince Manzee, senior vice president of on-air promotion for NBC, publicly taunted rival FOX in interviews before the launch. In September, *Variety* reported him challenging FOX: "We'll all be there watching Monday night, and he'd better be funny."

Responded FOX's Dolgin, "I don't have to change perceptions. Chevy is well liked. With O'Brien, they're starting at ground zero."

The September 7 premiere from Los Angeles was, by everyone's estimation, a disaster. Chase's monologue was weak, suggesting that he and his team hadn't put in enough time to get it right. He was awkward and fawning while interviewing his frequent movie co-star Goldie Hawn—one of the guests lined up for the premiere—leading one critic to note that viewers now knew what a bad first date between the two of them would be like. Salhany observed the proceedings from the show's green room and knew they were in deep trouble. Executive producer Bruce Bodner, speaking at the time, tried to put the best face on it: "We acknowledge that we got off to a rocky start. Chevy was very nervous, not being a stand-up and never having done a talk show. He's really improving night to night, though. . . . It will take some time for the audience to get comfortable with our rhythm."

Time was precisely what they did not have. As the ratings sank, affiliates began grumbling about bumping the show past midnight. Joan Rivers's talk show had lasted seven months. Chase's future, however, could be measured in weeks. He had no problem attracting the right sort of audience. Like Letterman, his demographics were strongest among young adults, 18–24. (Leno's audience, by contrast, flowed into the 50+ category.) Unfortunately for Chase, while he was attracting the right viewers, he wasn't getting enough of them.

Meanwhile Lucie Salhany was taking flak for *Chase* from all sides. As head of the network, it wasn't her job to personally produce the show. That was the responsibility of Twentieth Century Television, a separate division. "Twentieth Television was producing. It wasn't the network. I was at the network. I shouldn't have been over there trying to save that show. But the people who were running Twentieth Television and the programming people at the network had departed at that point. They smelled that it wasn't going to work," said Salhany. "I felt a commitment both to Chevy and to the network, so I grabbed the team and said, 'Okay, guys, I'll be here.'"

As the ratings continued to drop, Salhany and the show's producers attempted to retool. New writers were brought in, including Eddie Feldman, who had worked on *The Dennis Miller Show*, which in 1992 had had an eight-month run in syndication. They also brought in a well-known television consulting firm, Frank Magid Associates, to advise them on what could be done to salvage the program. Salhany muted the show's promotion and advertising, hoping they could make the fixes and relaunch, but it was a process that should have happened long before *Chevy Chase* ever went on the air. Now their tinkering was being assessed publicly each night, albeit by a dwindling home viewership.

In an October 1993 interview with *Variety*, Salhany all but admitted defeat: "The shows weren't very good. He was very nervous. It was uncomfortable and embarrassing to watch it. Now I'm not so stupid—and neither is Chevy Chase—to think that, long term, if this show doesn't grow, that this is going to always be on the air." By the time that appeared in print, Chase was already gone.

A few days before the cancellation, Salhany got a call from Australia. It was Rupert Murdoch. He wanted to know if Salhany was doing all right. There was a big celebration for Chase's birthday planned for Los Angeles in early October. The decision to pull the plug on the show had already been made. The situation was, to say the least, awkward.

"What are you going to do?" Murdoch asked.

"I'm going to the party."

He asked if her husband, Boston restaurateur John Polcari, would be going with her. As it turned out, he wasn't in town.

Murdoch was surprised. "You're going alone?"

"Yes."

"That's unbelievable. I don't want you to go alone."

Salhany pointed out she'd hardly be facing Chase and his friends all alone as she would be surrounded by other FOX executives who would also be in attendance. And so she went.

But that was not what she remembered most about the whole experience. The buzz was that Murdoch had demanded her head over the Chase debacle. "Everybody thought Rupert was horrified and aghast," Salhany said. Indeed, as she was preparing to go alone to a party honoring a network star who was about to be summarily fired, Murdoch was anything but angry. After asking if she was surviving the disaster, he gave her advice that she has never forgotten: "Cut your losses, and don't look back."

I n the end, *The Chevy Chase Show* would be little more than a foot-note to the real late-night battle between Jay Leno on NBC and David Letterman on CBS. Other than the embarrassment, Chase had been relatively lucky. He was able to walk away from the rubble after only six weeks. For the network, though, the problems were only beginning. In fact it can be argued that the fallout from FOX's third excursion into late-night programming would never fully heal. While *The Chevy Chase Show* would soon fade into a distant and painful memory, the tensions it laid bare between the FOX network and those it dealt with would set the tone for its numerous relationships into the next century.

It began with the question of what would replace *Chevy Chase* while the network figured out what to do about the time slot from 1 1 P.M. to midnight. In a move that was almost certain to provoke a reaction, FOX scheduled two half-hour reruns of *In Living Color*. "Every time there's a problem at FOX, they use *In Living Color*," complained Eric Gold, show creator Keenen Ivory Wayans's manager and producer, about the way the repeated network runs of the show were killing its value in syndication. "I think 'strip mining' is the perfect term,'" he charged.

With Lucie Salhany now in charge of the network, Gold knew it was pointless to appeal to her. He had already lost that battle when *In Living Color*'s first season replaced the failed *The Heights* the previous year. So he and Wayans took the only viable course open to them: they sued FOX.

It was a desperate measure, and they knew that time was not on their side. The longer they were in litigation, the harder it would be to get new work. Explained Gold, "You have to realize Hollywood's not a place where if you're suing Rupert Murdoch, Time-Warner's going to say, 'Do it! Good job!' Every company looks at you and it's like, 'Oh, shit, who needs this problem with people.' So it wasn't in our best interest to be hanging out there."

On the other hand, Wayans and Gold believed that FOX was harming their ownership interests in the future use of the series by repeated showings of old episodes of *In Living Color*. Ultimately they settled out of court, with the network buying out their interests in the show. Under the terms of the settlement, they are not allowed to disclose the details. All Gold would say is that it was "not fair, not right, wasn't good—we're over it now."

Wayans and Gold have gone back to pitching shows at FOX and have worked at both the WB and NBC with ex-FOX people like Jamie Kellner and Garth Ancier. As far as Gold is concerned, this wasn't a FOX problem. It was a Lucie Salhany problem. In retrospect he said, "The person that I guess we blame for not protecting us and doing this was Lucie. She was running the studio, then she was running the network. . . . You know, she was very bad people."

Salhany has her industry supporters as well as her detractors, but all agree on one thing: when she got angry, you didn't want to be in her way. Financial officer Tom Allen was one of the Diller-Kellner regime executives who stayed on with Salhany. "I always felt we had a good relationship and I like Lucie a lot. Completely different personality [from Kellner], very fiery . . . sometimes almost a bit scary how she could switch it on and off. She would go from a colloquial conversation one second, then something could set her off, and her eyes would widen. Those beautiful blue eyes would start thinning, like the *Jungle Book* snake. I'd sit there, and not be quite sure what it was that you did that set her off, and then a moment later, everything was fine. A very, very different style."

While Gold was facing the prospect of settling matters with FOX and Salhany in court, she had other concerns. Peter Faiman, the Australian director of the 1986 international hit movie *Crocodile Dundee*, was now working at one of the FOX production units, and he thought he had the perfect answer for who should be handling the network's late night: radio shock jock Howard Stern. FOX's target viewership was young adult males, and Stern had enough "edge" for *two* FOX networks. Rupert Murdoch was cool to the idea, but he allowed initial discussions with Stern to proceed.

"There were negotiations, but Rupert didn't tell me they were going on," recalled Salhany. He sent two of his Australian cronies to meet with Stern. "It was a disaster. When they went to New York and met with him, they would go out and drink and party, but it was never serious."

Stern ultimately killed the deal himself when he hosted what came to be considered a notorious pay-per-view TV show on New Year's Eve 1993. It included, among other grotesqueries, someone eating live maggots. Murdoch couldn't help but be aware that Stern's employer, Infinity Broadcasting, had radio license purchases before the FCC that were being held up until indecency complaints against Stern could be heard. The last thing Murdoch needed was trouble with the FCC by taking on a controversial personality like Stern with all his baggage. (Stern would later land a regular TV gig when cable's E!TV started to showcase his radio broadcasts.)

Murdoch and Salhany were also feeling pressure from the affiliates. The stations didn't care whom FOX was talking to; they wanted the network to get out of the late-night business once and for all. "They wanted the time back. That's a financial decision. They were better off running infomercials or reruns of *M*A*S*H* or *Cheers* and getting more money than Rupert was giving them. But Rupert didn't want to give the time back," said Gerry Walsh, then running FOX's Boston affiliate WFXT.

Bob Leider, executive vice president at FOX's Miami affiliate WSVN, explained, "The typical affiliate owns situation comedies, and they run them between 6 and 8. And where you end up deriving extra revenue and actually paying for high-priced *Seinfeld* or *Home Improvement* is when you run it late night. It becomes a profit center for an affiliate that's up against the 11 o'clock news. It is a very major demo producer and revenue producer. . . . If the network comes in and takes that time period, the affiliates end up with half those availabilities to sell."

The affiliates clearly didn't want any late-night shows from the network, yet the network executives kept insisting they wanted to program that time slot. For Salhany, the issue wasn't whether the affiliates would air a late-night series; it was whether it was worth putting on in the first place. "Had we come up with a good show, we were going to put it on and the stations would have taken it," she insisted.

Kevin O'Brien, a former affiliates board chairman, remained skeptical. "I would find it hard to believe that FOX would ever come back into late night. It damn near broke the network. . . . Even a donkey, if he gets kicked in the ass enough, would realize they have to back off. To come into late night, I think, would be a very scary proposition."

In January 1994 FOX surrendered in the fight over the 11 P.M. time slot. Yes, it claimed, it would be back in late night, but until then the affiliates could have the time to use as they wished. In 1998 FOX tried a stealth approach to reentering the late-night wars. It used its o-and-o's to launch *The Magic Hour* in June of that year, with basketball star Magic Johnson as the host. It was syndicated nationally. Even with a highly rated appearance by would-be FOX star Howard Stern, it was gone in a matter of months.

If late-night programming proved to be nothing but headaches and heartache, the afternoon FOX Kids Network achieved its biggest success ever. This with a show that was initially considered such a loser that both Jamie Kellner and his successor as network president, Lucie Salhany, tried to convince FOX Kids Network president Margaret Loesch to go back to the drawing board.

The saga of *Mighty Morphin Power Rangers* began in the late 1980s when Israeli entrepreneur Haim Saban was sitting in a hotel room in Japan and, while surfing the TV channels, came across a show called *Zyu Rangers*. It featured kids who changed into costumed warriors to fight ridiculous-looking monsters. Since you couldn't see the kids' faces when they were warriors, he had an idea of how to sell the show in America. He would just use the action sequences and employ American kids for the sequences when they were out of costume. He paid all of $10,000 (plus future royalties, if any) for the American TV rights. Saban syndicated children's shows all over the world, but he couldn't get anyone interested in his *Zyu Rangers*. By 1992 he was meeting with Margaret Loesch, who passed on his other new offerings. Then he pulled out the tape of the show and hit paydirt. Loesch was not only interested, she had seen the program herself in Japan and thought it held potential.

Loesch was ready to move right ahead and put it on the schedule, but she found herself being second-guessed, something that hadn't happened to her often while running FOX Kids. "When I had first shown Jamie [Kellner] *Power Rangers*, he too was skeptical. But what Jamie said to me [was], 'Why don't you do a pilot?' And you know, I think it was the only time that Jamie ever roadblocked me or put a process in that I had to follow."

Kellner, as Loesch would later admit, was right. The concept had bugs that needed to be worked out, and not just the big rubber ones inhabited by Japanese stuntmen. By the time Loesch was ready to move, Kellner had left and been replaced by Salhany. They felt a personal connection, both of them being working moms in the TV business. "In many ways she was even more embracing on a personal level than Jamie," said Loesch. "She was a tough boss. She was very emotional, but very smart." Salhany finally gave the go-ahead, but when a clip of the show was presented at a meeting of FOX sales executives, the reaction was overwhelmingly negative. They urged her not to show it to the advertisers.

"I really agonized the night before the presentation to all the advertisers. I agonized, then I just said, 'I'm going to show it,'" she recalled. Again the response was overwhelmingly bad. They told her that her other current animated series, like the comic *Bobby's World* (created by actor Howie Mandel) and the superhero action series *X Men* were great. "What's with *Power Rangers*? It's horrible. It's cheesy."

The half-hour *Mighty Morphin Power Rangers* premiered in August 1993, and all the naysayers were proven wrong. It became more than a hit, it was a phenomenon. It was exactly the right time to capture the interests of a new generation of kids who had yet to latch on to a fad or TV show they could call their own. Their older brothers and sisters might have liked *Teenage Mutant Ninja Turtles*, a popular animated series based on a comic book and movie that had run in syndication and on CBS's Saturday-morning schedule in the late 1980s and early 1990s. But these amphibious superheroes were now passé. It was the *Power Rangers* who caught the attention of youngsters now. Saban had cagily held onto the American merchandising rights for the show that looked like he would never sell, and by 1994 he closed a deal with McDonald's for a reported $20 million to allow their use of *Power Rangers* as a marketing tie-in.

As for Loesch, she was now responsible for a blockbuster kids' hit, and that meant money for the FOX network and for the affiliates. Loesch had gone from being the goat, taking the fall for *Peter*

Pan and the Pirates, to the hero who had made the FOX Kids Network something to crow about. Although the kids block had often been considered the poor relation of the network, things had clearly changed. Were things different now as far as the top executives were concerned?

"Yeah, it was," said chief financial officer Tom Allen. "Thank you, *Power Rangers*."

The FOX network was also clearly excited about its Friday-night schedule. It had a new hour show that was quirky, boasting science fiction elements as well as comedy. It had a lead who seemed destined for stardom, and the production values were movie quality. Programming executive Sandy Grushow was so certain of its chances for success that he promised to eat his desk if the show's male lead didn't become a star. The name of the series was *The Adventures of Brisco County, Jr.*

"We all thought the show was going to become a big hit," recalled Bob Greenblatt, who was in charge of drama development at the time. "It was very FOX in its day. There were no westerns on at the time. . . . We were trying to do a little of *The Wild, Wild West* kind of feeling. The production value was great, a little tongue-in-cheek humor." But the 1960s CBS series *The Wild, Wild West* had been a melding of westerns—a very popular TV staple at the time—with James Bond and the then-voguish spy genre. *Brisco County* was developed by Sam Raimi, who had a big cult following after his recent *Evil Dead* horror movies. This new show, however, was coming out of nowhere. Westerns had long been out of favor on network television, so that there was no context for the spoof of a genre that many viewers did not know. Bruce Campbell was the actor from the *Evil Dead* films who was Grushow's favorite for TV stardom, but the show never clicked with viewers.

It did have the dubious distinction of being the target of an attack on television violence. In December 1993 Senator Byron Dorgan (Democrat of North Dakota) released a study done by students at Concordia College in Minnesota that named FOX the most violent TV network then on the air. During a single week's viewing, the 109 volunteer students counted 352 acts of violence on FOX, compared to 224 on ABC, 187 on NBC, and 172 on CBS. As with most such studies, this one had its flaws, but it now had the imprimatur of a United States Senator.

It turned out that research protocols on the study had not been especially rigorous. Violence had been defined as "the deliberate and hostile use of overt force by one individual against another." It made no distinction between slapstick and gunshots. Indeed, it didn't even make a distinction as to whether a show was actually on the network or not. Episodes of the new syndicated series *Star Trek: Deep Space Nine* aired on the FOX station the students had watched, and it was counted as a FOX show even though it was programmed by individual stations and the network had nothing to do with it. Indeed, in many other markets the show was on stations that competed with the local FOX affiliate. *Brisco County* was cited for 117 violent incidents per hour. "This is patently ridiculous," charged its executive producer Carlton Case. "The episode of *Brisco* monitored featured a boxing match, and they counted each punch to come up with 117 violent incidents."

Brisco County was a well made and entertaining show that simply couldn't get noticed, and it would be gone by the end of the season. It was followed on the Friday-evening schedule by a show that almost no one had high expectations for, that Greenblatt and his colleagues referred to as "a little sci-fi cult show." It was called *The X-Files*.

The story of two FBI agents assigned to check out UFOs, vampires, shapeshifters, and other supernatural monsters, *The X-Files* was the brainchild of Chris Carter, a thirty-something writer who had the reputation of being a onetime protégé of Brandon Tartikoff, when the latter was NBC's programming chief in the 1980s. Carter developed several shows, like the 1987 NBC musical comedy/drama *Rags to Riches* about a father (Joseph Bologna) who adopts five daughters. Carter was a co-producer and writer on the series, but it had done poorly and he had yet to make a name for himself. He did have a reputation for turning out sharp scripts, and that attracted the attention of Peter Roth, the former president of Stephen J. Cannell Productions. Roth had succeeded Salhany as head of TV production at Twentieth Century Television. In 1992 he sat down to a pitch meeting over lunch with Carter. The writer surveyed the TV landscape and saw that a mainstay of his childhood—spooky, unsettling genre series like *The Twilight Zone, The Outer Limits,* and *Kolchak: The Night Stalker*—were totally absent. He thought it was time to try one again.

Carter's insight was to figure out how to solve the problem that had finally sunk *Kolchak.* The 1970s series had starred Darren Mc-Gavin (who would later guest star on *The X-Files*) as a reporter who constantly "just happened to" stumble across werewolves and monsters and all sorts of creepy crawlies. Carter's solution was to avoid the contrivance of Kolchak having strange encounters every week by making his leads two FBI agents who would be *assigned* to investigate mysterious deaths and other crimes. Rather than the on-camera monsters finding Kolchak, on *X-Files* the heroes would be out there actively looking for the unknown and the unexplainable.

Roth liked the idea and worked with Carter to develop it into a series. Seeing how the show became a major profit center for FOX, Roth enjoyed pointing out that his initial production deal with Carter was "very, very cheap." Roth gave Carter "the lion's share of credit for creative content," but it was the two of them working together that got the show to series and eventual success.

"The irony of that, of course, is that the people that were at the network at the time really weren't interested in the idea. It was not a favorite in development. It almost didn't get greenlit [the go-ahead] as a pilot. It almost didn't get greenlit as a series. It was perceived to be too myopic and singular and not commercial," said Roth.

The chief roadblock appears to have been programming chief Sandy Grushow. "Everybody will take credit for it," said Lucie Salhany, who had the final word on putting it on the air. "It was no one other than Chris Carter, Peter Roth, and I. There was nobody. And

it was more those two. Sandy Grushow did not want the show."
Roth wouldn't pin the blame on Grushow for being the roadblock—at least by name—but he did imply that Grushow was "the
one who did not believe in the value of *The X-Files*." In any event,
drama development executive Bob Greenblatt recalled that by the
time the pilot was shot and the show was on the schedule, everyone
was on board.

Over the course of its first season, *X-Files* was on shaky ground,
but it showed growth. The adventures of agents Fox Mulder (David
Duchovny) and Dana Scully (Gillian Anderson) would grow even
more over the summer of 1994 and in later seasons. The two largely
unknown actors (Duchovny had appeared on *Twin Peaks* and Showtime's erotic *Red Shoe Diaries*) were the ones who became stars instead of Campbell. Now, with *Brisco* on its way out and *X-Files*
clearly the hit of FOX's new season, Grushow had a different response, telling *Variety* in April 1994, "If we hadn't been patient we
wouldn't have grown such hits as *Beverly Hills 90210* and *Melrose
Place*. This year we believed in *The X-Files* and it's turned into a hit
all by itself. We knew it would take time."

During its first five years on the air, the ratings for *X-Files* increased each season. It gave FOX what no other show had: a franchise. The "franchise" is what the industry calls, for example,
Paramount's unending stream of programming and merchandising from *Star Trek*. At last count what had begun as creator Gene
Roddenberry's vision of the future from the perspective of the
mid-1960s had spawned six television series (including one animated), ten movies, tons of T-shirts, caps, toys, and other memo-
rabilia, and more books than even the most devoted fan could
purchase. *The X-Files* has not yet reached that stage, but already
one can fill a shelf with books—authorized or not—on the show,
from episode guides to star biographies to original novels. The
1998 feature film starring Duchovny and Anderson and expound-
ing on some of the unanswered mysteries from the series was not
a huge box-office success, but it clearly indicated that the series

had a potential future on the big screen. The first *Star Trek* movie had also had uneven results.

At the fifty-sixth World Science Fiction Convention, held in Baltimore the summer the big screen film was released, a panel entitled *"The X-Files*: SF or Paranoid Fantasy" led to a group discussion as to whether the show should be considered science fiction or not. The consensus was that sometimes it was, and sometimes it wasn't. Certainly a show dealing with space aliens attempting to take over the planet, or intelligent machines that start to think for themselves, was playing with some of the classic modes of science fiction. Yet other episodes dealt with monsters, vampires, and the supernatural. It was telling that in the 1997–1998 season two well-known authors tried their hands at scripting *X-Files* installments. Science fiction novelist William Gibson (*Neuromancer, Idoru*) contributed an episode involving people merging with computers. Horror icon Stephen King turned up an original story about a doll that compelled people to kill. Science fiction, fantasy, horror—it was all grist for Carter's mill.

From FOX's perspective, *The X-Files* would prove to be their biggest success story to date. Greg Meidel, who sold the show in syndication (where it began in 1997), explained just how important it was to Murdoch's overall operation. "It's created in-house. It becomes the number one hit on your network. It then becomes a number one hit in syndication on your cable network. The weekend runs are number one on your owned-and-operated stations. It's number one on every distribution system that is owned by News Corp. throughout the world: it's number one on B-Sky-B [in Europe], it's number one in Asia, it's number one in Latin America. It is the epitome of vertical integration. If you ever wonder what a show should achieve, that is it."

While *The X-Files* would eventually be an enormously important network hit, that was still in the future. More important things were happening in the present. If there was a single turning point in the history of the FOX network, a moment when the Big Three became the Big Four, it occurred in December 1993 with the simple announcement that NFL football was coming to FOX the following season. While to the public it was another instance of Rupert Murdoch whipping out his magic checkbook and outbidding his competitors, the behind-the-scenes story was much more complicated.

"First of all you have to give Barry Diller and Jamie Kellner the credit, because they were the ones who started talking to the NFL. Jamie went into the NFL long before anyone of the new regime," explained Lucie Salhany. Talks had continued after their departures, and Salhany was not in the loop at first because she didn't know much about sports. What she did know was television, which would prove to be just as important.

"The league's perspective was that the ratings [for network football broadcasts] were going down—not horribly, but they were going down," recalled Ken Ziffren, one of the attorneys representing the NFL at the time. Baseball and hockey license fees for the broadcast TV rights to games had suffered in recent years, and team owners were convinced that football would be next. "What FOX offered us, the league, was the potential of having a bidder who needed the games, wanted the games, and was willing—in a sense—to overpay for them. The issue was whether they were qualified."

Lucie Salhany and Chase Carey led the FOX delegation to make the case to the NFL. The football league was divided into two divisions, or conferences, and suggested that FOX might be interested in the rights to their American Football Conference (AFC), whose games were then on NBC. "I didn't know that much about football, candidly," said Salhany. "So I kept thinking about it and I went back and researched it. I looked at all the markets [that had AFC teams], and I looked at where all the strength was, and it was really the NFC that was stronger." The National Football Conference (NFC) teams were located in the major markets, which was where FOX was strongest. Salhany figured they would be better off pulling in viewers already committed to their local team than in running games with out-of-town teams where viewers might feel they had no stake.

She told the NFL that if the league were really smart they'd pull the NFC games off of CBS and give them to FOX instead. "I went through all of the ratings. It was losing audience. It was dropping. And they [the NFL] had no idea about this," she said.

Ziffren noted that Murdoch, Carey, and Salhany made an impressively strong case for FOX. "I remember we had at least two sessions where all of them appeared before the owners to make presentations. [They] did an extremely effective job and tried to show the owners that they were bona fide contenders and deserved to be considered on the merits."

Salhany recalled that the FOX executives were relentless in their pursuit of a football deal. They pointed out how strong FOX was in the 18–34 male demographic—a key demographic for attracting football ticket buyers as well. She pointed out that FOX had a lot of younger viewers too, and they were the ardent fans of the future. "That's how we built the whole campaign. And we went down to pitch it in Texas, Chase and I pitched it. I had jackets made with *The Simpsons* logo and the NFL underneath. It was unbelievable. Our whole pitch was: do you know that CBS lost 40 percent of its 18–34 audience, and NBC 20 percent of 18–49, and here we are growing?" Indeed, at the time the median age for the audience of *Beverly Hills 90210* was 24.7, and for *Melrose Place* 26.5. By comparison, the median age of the viewers for CBS's hit series *Murder, She Wrote*, with Angela Lansbury was 57.4. For ABC's *Matlock*, starring Andy Griffith, it was 56.2.

When it was clear that the team owners appreciated the FOX argument, Murdoch took out his checkbook. Said Salhany, "When Rupert took over, Rupert was his most phenomenal. 'I want it, I have a vision, I'm willing to pay for it.'" FOX made a preemptive offer of $1.6 billion to acquire the rights that CBS had held for years, and now all FOX could do was wait to see if it had won.

As head of Twentieth Television, Greg Meidel was not involved in the NFL negotiations. But he was a big sports fan. Salhany had had him role-play as a team owner when she was testing out the FOX presentation to see what sorts of questions might come from the football executives. Now it was late December 1993, just before the holidays. "Everybody was on pins and needles, because we knew the decision was coming down. It was late in the afternoon. . . . A lot of people were planning to leave for the holidays, or whatever. But everyone was glued to their phones and pacing the floor." Salhany and Carey were in New York with Murdoch, waiting for the call. They would call the FOX offices in Los Angeles to see if anyone there had heard anything on the deal.

"Rupert was, 'Let's get it, let's get it.' You see him get so excited when he really does want to accomplish something. It's addictive. We were getting calls from our friends at CBS saying, 'Instead of going down to the floor of [the corporate offices at] Black Rock, they're going to the top and they're going to jump.' Because they were feeling at the time that they had lost it," said Meidel. CBS had built their Sunday schedule around afternoon professional football games leading into their prime-time evening lineup, led off by *60 Minutes*, for decades. It was inconceivable that they could lose it to FOX.

When the announcement finally came that December, it made national headlines. The inconceivable had happened. Beginning in the fall of 1994, CBS would have no football games to broadcast. For at least the next four years, those TV viewers would be tuned to FOX. As he had with so many other properties, Murdoch had paid more than the market thought it was worth because he saw a greater opportunity there. Meidel noted that while Salhany was pitching its younger viewership to the team owners, FOX was salivating over being able to address a whole new TV audience that had previously been beyond its reach. "I think the number was staggering, but about 70 percent of the viewing audience of the NFL never watched FOX. So, in the end, it was actually a bargain to acquire the rights to the NFL to promote the rest of your schedule. It was cheaper. If you went out and spent the same amount of money to promote it, it wouldn't have been as effective."

It is difficult to overestimate the impact of FOX acquiring pro football. Though the affiliates were pleased, it would set in motion a series of events that would eventually change the relationship between the network and the stations. For the moment, though, it was all fireworks and champagne. In January, CBS's pride was dealt a further blow when their NFL announcers moved to FOX. John Madden, Terry Bradshaw, and Pat Summerall signed on, along with producer Ed Goren. Summerall had been with CBS for thirty-two years, but with no other football programming to air there, CBS hadn't much use for a play-by-play announcer.

I n the NFL deal FOX guaranteed to the football league a certain level of clearance for the broadcast of the games, yet they were still reaching only 93 percent of the country. They needed more affiliates fast. In April the affiliate relations office—which some joked was "Klingon headquarters" because of its heavy-handed enforcement of network rules—announced that its affiliates would be free to drop network shows that summer for local NFC exhibition games that would not air nationally. Ordinarily an affiliate that preempted a network show could count on a call suggesting their relationship with the FOX network was in danger. Preston Padden, who had earned the nickname of "Preston the Enforcer," reasoned that there would only be one or two such games in a given market and that they would provide perfect opportunities for the FOX station to promote itself as the new home of NFC games in the fall. Padden also signed up two dozen stations as "secondary FOX affiliates" in markets with no FOX affiliate and no fourth station, so that they could carry football as well as some other FOX programming. It still wasn't enough to satisfy FOX's obligations for audience reach under their new NFL contract. The football league was happy to get a higher payment for broadcast rights, but if fewer people were able to watch the games because FOX had a more limited reach, the agreement would prove counterproductive to the team owners.

In March 1994 FOX announced a deal with the two-year-old Savoy Pictures, an independent film company headed by former Tri-Star Pictures chairman and CEO Victor A. Kaufman, and president/ COO Lewis J. Korman. FOX and Savoy would team on something to be called SF Broadcasting, which would buy FOX affiliates or buy other stations and turn them into FOX affiliates. While FOX would put up $58 million of the $100 million equity, Kaufman and Korman would control SF's voting stock. This was a creative dodge of the FCC cap on the number of stations anyone could own, since FOX already had eight stations covering nearly 20 percent of the country. The FCC rules limited networks to owning no more than twelve stations covering 25 percent.

Meanwhile financier Ron Perelman owned a group of stations called New World, most of which were CBS affiliates. He had the same idea that Bob Bennett had had in the early 1980s at Metromedia. If he banded together with other station groups, they could profitably produce shows that they would own and broadcast on their own stations. When it looked like CBS might lose football, New World approached the network about putting up capital to make sure it kept the franchise. But CBS wasn't interested, apparently assuming that no such help was necessary. So now Perelman owned important stations in major markets without football, and Murdoch had stations in the same markets *with* football. Perhaps they could work something out? Michael Milken, who had brought Murdoch and Metromedia owner John Kluge together back in 1985, now helped Perelman and Murdoch to connect.

"[Fox, Inc., chief operating officer] Chase [Carey] was the guy who brought it up. . . . Candidly, Chase was the guy who always lusted after those stations because he thought that they would make the network stronger," recalled Salhany. FOX had been interested in them a few years earlier when they were up for sale, but they couldn't make the elements work because FOX was programming only four nights a week at that point. So Perelman got them instead. Now they were in play again.

Michael H. Diamond had just signed on as vice president and general counsel for New World. When he arrived at his new office at the company on May 1, 1994, things were already buzzing. "New World had stations, Murdoch had the NFL contract but had a lot of these UHF stations in these large cities [like] Tampa, Atlanta, Detroit, Cleveland, Phoenix, Dallas—we were in a lot of important places. Murdoch had an interesting provision in his affiliation agreement with these smaller UHF stations at the time, which said that if he got a bigger station in the market he could essentially dump them. The idea was, what could we get?"

When Diamond started at New World, he was called into a meeting with Bill Bevins, the corporation's CEO. Bevins said, "We're going over to FOX to talk to them about changing our stations to FOX affiliations."

"Gee, that's something that's never been done before."

"Well, there was a station in Miami that had done that."

WSVN had lost its NBC affiliation in 1989 and became more successful as a FOX affiliate, but there had never been a TV affiliation switch on the scale Bevins was proposing, with an entire station group switching network affiliations at one time. Diamond called some colleagues at his old law firm—Skadden, Arps, Meagher & Flom—and they advised that it could be done. Diamond reported back, "We can do it. There's a time period you may have to wait. You may not be able to switch the affiliations tomorrow, but you can certainly put them on notice that you're switching, and you can get out of the affiliations."

Negotiations moved quickly. New World drove a hard deal. They wanted compensation both for the lower local ratings they would get as FOX affiliates, and which they would now have to use to sell advertising, and also for the fact that they would have to acquire additional programming to fill time periods where CBS programmed network shows and FOX offered nothing. The two sides agreed on $500 million as an "investment" in New World by FOX, meaning FOX would have an equity interest in New World but the control of the corporation would stay with New World's CEO Ron Perelman. They also agreed that the FOX o-and-o's would carry any syndicated programming developed by New World, increasing the launch platform for that effort.

"So we went in, they felt it made sense. They were drooling over the stations we had," recalled Diamond. The negotiators broke up into teams. Diamond worked on the affiliation part with Preston Padden and Lucie Salhany representing FOX. In another room, attorney Ken Ziffren, who had represented the NFL in their negotiations with FOX just a few months before, now represented New World's programming interests. Supervising the FOX team was Chase Carey. A sticking point was that many of the New World stations had their own local programs that they were loath to abandon, and they didn't want to carry that portion of the FOX programming they felt was inferior. The New World negotiators knew they had the upper hand and played it for all it was worth.

"It happened in five days. It was the most amazing thing you've ever seen. I was involved, I was in all the meetings, but at that time it was really more a legal deal putting it together," said Salhany.

The general managers of the eight New World stations were nervous because they were used to playing in the big leagues as Big Three stations. Now they would lose all the trappings of a Big Three affiliate: a network newscast, a morning show, David Letterman's late-night talk show, daytime soap operas and game shows, and all the other things CBS had provided. From their perspective, being a FOX affiliate was like being an independent, with the concomitant loss of viewership, revenue, and industry prestige. The New World negotiators tried to build in the maximum amount of freedom for their stations vis-à-vis FOX so that the managers would feel they were controlling their own destiny. Diamond recalled that one issue was the definition of a "major" sport. "We had to carry major sports because at the time they were looking to get hockey and baseball. And they wanted to make sure we had to carry major sports. It led to an argument later whether boxing and ice-skating are major sports."

The deal covered every conceivable programming decision. For example, the New World stations didn't want to carry the FOX Kids Network, since afternoon cartoons did not fit into their self-image as a soon-to-be former Big Three affiliate. They wanted the right to preempt the network to carry the Reverend Billy Graham crusade specials. Just before Memorial Day 1994 Bevins phoned Diamond to ask why the pact hadn't been closed yet. FOX was required to make a $250 million payment upon signing, and the two sides were arguing over issues like could the stations preempt the network to carry a telethon. "Do you know what the interest on $250 million is over a three-day weekend?" Bevins said to Diamond. "Get this done."

It was done. When CBS was notified that several of their major market stations were ending their affiliation to go over to FOX, the reaction was one of utter shock. "You can't do that," Diamond was told.

"You have to read the agreement," he replied. "We really can."

Coming on top of the NFL deal, the agreement between FOX and New World sent shock waves through the television business. Business simply wasn't done like this. FOX had changed the rules yet again. Before the official announcement, someone had to break the news to the FOX affiliates in the New World markets and let them know that they were about to lose the only affiliation agreement most of them had ever known. That unpleasant duty fell to Salhany and Padden.

"I thought it was so badly handled with our affiliates," said Salhany. "It was really very difficult. I had to call the affiliates, Rupert [Murdoch] didn't." Salhany and Preston Padden were in New York for the annual "upfront" presentation to the advertising community of the next season's shows. The two of them sat in a hotel room and tried to inform the affected FOX stations as gently as they could.

Recalled Padden, "The argument we made was the following, in the face of their clear disappointment: Before we started the joint effort to build the FOX network, it was a three-network economy. If you were the fourth-best station in town, you were out of luck. But because of what we had built together, it was now a four-network economy. And if you were no worse than the fourth-best station in town, you were virtually assured that there was a network for you. . . . If you're about to lose your FOX affiliation, that means you're about to gain either an ABC, CBS, or NBC affiliation."

Since the situation was so unusual, a lot of attention was paid by the affected FOX affiliates to the most obvious recent precedent, the one in Miami that New World's Bevin had cited. Bob Leider, executive vice president of Sunbeam Television, which owns WSVN in Miami, remembered getting calls from colleagues who wondered how to survive the shock of losing an affiliation. All Leider could say, pointing to WSVN's example, was "You know, listen, life goes on." It might not have been profound, but it was the truth. WSVN had thrived as a FOX station after losing its NBC affiliation of over three decades. Sunbeam's president Ed Ansin certainly could understand what the stations were going through. "It was of particular concern to the FOX affiliates because FOX was basically shifting its policy," said Ansin. "Prior to this they really were sticking with the affiliates they'd had at their inception. But now they had a change of policy and said, 'No, we're going to have to upgrade the network.' That became the goal."

In retrospect both Padden and Leider were correct. As Padden would note in 1999, "The miracle here—and it proved the argument I was making—of the [dismissed affiliates] is that not one of them sued over the disaffiliation. And not one of them failed to garner [a subsequent] affiliation with one of the then major networks."

But June 1994 was too soon to convince the stations to look at the big picture. There was plenty of bad feeling in the room at the annual FOX affiliates meeting. The dumping of loyal FOX affiliates shook up everyone because there was no telling who might be next.

This capped a year that included several high-profile flops, headed by *The Chevy Chase Show*. Rubbing salt into the wound was the fact that the New World stations had affiliation deals that granted them much more freedom than the standard agreement. In open defiance of the network—and in particular Salhany, who promised the network had not given up on late-night programming—the affiliates voted against any more excursions into late-night shows. Said one executive, "We don't want it, no matter what it is."

The affiliate board also insisted the affiliates had the authority to hire outside counsel, so that legal advice on their dealings with FOX would not come solely from the network. The network had long opposed the move. Padden had gone so far as to threaten to dissolve the affiliate body before he would allow such a thing to happen. "I kept saying to the board, 'I've never known a situation that improved because you dropped a lawyer into the middle of it.' Obviously the board was free to get a lawyer whenever they wanted. But I kept arguing that the longer we stayed on the same team, the longer we pulled together, and the longer we avoided sticking a lawyer in between us, the more progress we'd make. And I'm absolutely certain that that was the case, and I'm absolutely certain we'd have never successfully built a network had there been a lawyer stuck in the middle of our relationship." From the network perspective, an independent counsel for the affiliates meant another viewpoint that wouldn't be under their control when the inevitable disputes between the stations and the network arose.

Joe Young, then the general manager of FOX's Indianapolis affiliate, was president of the affiliate board in June 1994 when the issue came to a head. "At the time, every [network] affiliate board had legal counsel. . . . It wasn't just to go in there and give us a lawsuit," he said, noting that one of the key reasons such boards have counsel is to make sure they don't violate anti-trust laws by illegally colluding among themselves. "[FOX] had all the counsel in the world, and they wanted it all their way. It was their way, or the highway. . . . When the network started it was very give and take, but as it evolved from that, and the stronger they got, it became more of the traditional network-versus-affiliate relationship. 'I'm the network, you're lucky to have me, and if you don't like it, I'll take my affiliation elsewhere.' I cannot tell you how many conversations I and other board members had over the years where our affiliation was threatened."

The affiliates voted to retain their own counsel, independent of the network. There was so much ill-will at that moment that Padden made a tactical retreat on his threat to dissolve the board, and let the matter stand. He addressed the affiliates and told them that FOX was no longer an expansion club. It was now competing in the big leagues. "The only disappointing note is that in the big leagues, players sometimes get traded among teams," he said. "The only way to win in the major leagues of network television is to support the team that you're on."

Young recalled having a different metaphor that summed up how the affiliates felt. "There were a lot of stations that were bitter because they were getting dropped. You know, they were the ones that brought them to the dance. They were the person that Rupert took to the dance, and he left them with new partners. That was pretty lousy. But, in his grand scheme, that's what he wanted to do."

The 1993–1994 TV season wasn't over yet. One more bombshell was yet to drop. Lucie Salhany's relationship with Rupert Murdoch had never been an especially close one. She recalled one time when one of her sons, then a little boy, came up to Murdoch at a social function and asked, "How come you make my mommy cry all the time?"

She also chafed under Murdoch's management style where she was supposedly head of the network but would learn about meetings he was having with other executives to second-guess her. One day she and Sandy Grushow were trying to figure out where to schedule a new show—*Party of Five*—the next season, and went to

Murdoch to get his input. "He was caught short," she recalled, sitting there with a couple of executives in a meeting that might have included Salhany in the first place. "Rupert was always sneaking around, having people come in, and having outsiders criticize what his employees were doing. That's his favorite game."

On Memorial Day weekend 1994, Murdoch called Salhany, upset about the pilot for a new show called *Party of Five* set for the 1994–1995 season. He had screened it for the crew on his boat, and they weren't interested in a soap opera about five orphaned kids. She pointed out that she had screened it for his wife and daughter, and they liked it. "It was a fight," she recalled, "and that's when I gave up and Sandy took over."

Fox Entertainment Group chairman Peter Chernin had recommended that a consultant come in to help FOX reorganize its chain of command. According to Salhany, Chernin now wanted to merge all the film and TV production units at Twentieth Century–Fox, so that all the entertainment divisions would report directly to him while the rest of TV operations would report to Fox, Inc., chief operating officer Chase Carey. Salhany argued that all of TV should be kept together. "But everybody was jockeying for position, and it was whoever went to Rupert's on Saturday to talk to him behind the scenes. It was horrible, very political, horribly political, and I had never encountered anything like that."

At the close of the affiliate meeting in Los Angeles in June 1994, she walked over to Chase Carey and said, "Goodbye."

"What do you mean, goodbye?"

She told him she thought she was through, though no decision had yet been made. Salhany flew east to Massachusetts for an extended vacation with her family on Cape Cod. Meanwhile the reorganization plans continued, and she called Murdoch to ask, "Who's going to run the network?"

Murdoch replied, "Let me think about it. I'll call you back."

On the Friday before the Fourth of July, Murdoch called back. Again Salhany asked who would run the network. Murdoch told her that under the reorganization Chase Carey would be in charge as president of Fox Television, and she'd report to him with reduced status as simply the head of network programming.

"Well, it's not what I want, Rupert. Let's just call it a day."

"Okay."

"No hard feelings."

There were none. And then, Salhany said, she and Murdoch "had the best discussion we ever had" about the future of the network. Now that she was an outsider giving him advice, he was very interested in what she had to say.

She had been in charge all of eighteen months.

CHAPTER TEN

"I was never in doubt about what FOX intended"

[1994-1995]

THE FOX FALL PRIME-TIME SCHEDULE

	7:00	7:30	8:00	8:30	9:00	9:30
Sunday	Fortune Hunter		The Simpsons	Hardball	Married . . . with Children	Wild Oats
Monday			Melrose Place		Party of Five	
Tuesday			Movie			
Wednesday			Beverly Hills 90210		Models, Inc.	
Thursday			Martin	Living Single	New York Undercover	
Friday			M.A.N.T.I.S.		The X-Files	
Saturday			COPS	COPS	America's Most Wanted	

THERE'S NO QUESTION that without the help of the Federal Communications Commission, Rupert Murdoch's task of launching a fourth American television network in 1986 would have been infinitely more difficult, if not downright impossible. After a rocky start, FOX executives learned that they disregarded the FCC at their peril. Indeed, special efforts were made to court the Washington-based commissioners. When *Melrose Place* was launched in July 1992, a street party was held on four blocks of Melrose Avenue in Hollywood. The commissioners were invited and attended. They received all sorts of FOX promotional items, from T-shirts to tapes of the shows. None of these trivial things was enough to constitute bribery, but it was part of a courting process, and the FCC looked with favor on the new network.

Former FCC chairman Al Sikes, who by then had joined Hearst Broadcasting, told *Variety* in May 1994, "We probably sided with them more times than we didn't. They generally were favoring deregulation in areas where it was done."

Take the end result of the financial interest/syndication rule, or fin/syn, which forbade networks from having a financial interest in entertainment programming. FOX had been granted two waivers so they could continue their expansion as a network without having to give up their production studios. Then the commission obligingly changed the definition of what constituted a "network" from programming more than fifteen hours per week to more than fifteen hours *in prime time* per week. As FOX expanded to additional nights, they returned control of the post-10 P.M. time slot on Sundays to the local stations. This gave the stations a prime-time slot for local news all week long, which is what the network encouraged. It also assured that FOX would never go over fifteen hours in prime time, since they ran only two hours per night (as opposed to the Big Three's programming of 8 to 11 P.M.), with the additional 7–8 P.M. time slot on Sunday. Even as the FCC fin/syn restrictions were falling by the wayside, FOX stayed clear of crossing the line that might put the remaining rules—or future rules—into play. Fin/syn was finally allowed to expire in November 1995, with the FCC bowing to the spirit of deregulation that had been sweeping through government. It had never been applied to FOX.

Rupert Murdoch had also won his fight on the cross-ownership rule. Though he ended up selling off the *Boston Herald*, he was eventually permitted to own both the *New York Post* and FOX's flagship TV station in New York City, WNYW.

Then too, there was the ongoing matter of a complaint filed by the New York chapter of the NAACP (National Association for the Advancement of Colored People) back in November 1993. The organization challenged the license renewals of FOX-owned stations on the grounds that FOX was in violation of the FCC's foreign ownership cap, which limited foreign control of a TV station to no more than a 25 percent interest. The NAACP charged that FOX was owned by News Corp., an entirely Australian corporation. Preston Padden, putting on his Washington lobbyist hat, said it was much ado about nothing. "Those ownership issues were before the FCC eight years ago when it approved the transfer of the Metromedia stations," he said. "There is nothing new in the NAACP filing."

By the end of the 1993–1994 season, it had appeared that the FCC—dubbed the FOX Communications Commission by some industry critics—agreed with Padden, as there had been no further action on the complaint. But FOX's stunning coup with NFL football, topped by the New World deal which led to eight CBS affiliates becoming FOX stations, had put the Big Three networks on notice. FOX was not only here to stay, it had become a serious rival. The others could no longer afford to ignore the upstart network. An early shot was fired by CBS lobbyist Marty Franks: "Everywhere in the world except at the FCC, FOX and its parent News Corp. are properly regarded as the colossus they are. Somehow, though, the FCC sees them as a struggling, emerging operation."

Though neither FOX nor the FCC seemed especially concerned about the NAACP license challenge, FOX was legally required to respond. It pointed out that the ownership of FOX might appear confusing, but it really wasn't. The network was owned by Twentieth Century Holding Corporation, and 76 percent of the stock in that entity was in the hands of Rupert Murdoch, American citizen. Andrew Schwartzman, of the Media Access Project, a Washington, D.C., public interest law firm, contended that FOX was "pushing the FCC ownership rules to the limit."

FOX certainly had provoked a change in the competitive climate for the other TV networks, and the stakes were much higher now. The NFL deal worried the Big Three about their other sports franchises, such as coverage of major league baseball. The New World deal made them worry about the loyalty of their affiliates. And now when an unaffiliated station was up for grabs, FOX was very much a player. Such an instance occurred after the CBS/Westinghouse merger was announced in early 1994. One of the results of that complex deal was that WBZ-TV in Boston, a Westinghouse station that had been an NBC affiliate for more than forty years, switched to CBS. That meant NBC needed a new Boston affiliate, and the logical candidate—indeed, the *only* candidate—was WHDH, the town's former CBS station. The only problem was that FOX was also interested in the station, and WHDH was owned by Sunbeam Television, which also owned one of the country's most successful FOX affiliates, WSVN in Miami. Sunbeam eventually went with NBC in Boston, but until the agreement was signed it could have gone the other way, and NBC would have found itself in a top-ten market available only on a UHF station. (Instead FOX stayed with its UHF Boston affiliate, WFXT, eventually buying the station back from the Boston Celtics in October 1994 when the FCC raised the cap on the number of stations a network could own.)

This would be the year when the Big Three would have one last chance to cripple FOX, and they were not about to miss the opportunity.

In the wake of Lucie Salhany's departure as president of the network in July 1994, Sandy Grushow was temporarily put in charge, but by October he was gone. He was replaced by John Matoian, who took the title of president of the Fox Entertainment Group rather than of the FOX network. That change was part of the corporate reorganization that had led to Salhany's resignation. Now parts of the network that had been supervised directly by network presidents Jamie Kellner and Salhany would be out of Matoian's hands. Dealing with cable companies or government regulators were not part of his domain. Meanwhile the departing Grushow would become president of Tele-TV, a service providing an alternative to cable and satellite TV in Los Angeles and Orange counties in California before returning to head Twentieth Century Television, the company's production unit, in 1997.

Matoian was a former CBS executive—he had been senior vice president of movies and miniseries—and was an odd choice for FOX. He was seen as being more in tune with traditional broadcasting rather than with the cutting-edge, youth-oriented programming of FOX. Indeed, he was barely settled in when he canceled two new FOX shows, *Wild Oats*, about a horny photographer, and *Fortune Hunter*, a spy series. He would become annoyed at charges that, as reported in the trade press, "his tastes ran along the lines of producing movies for little old ladies." To show he could be hip and youth oriented, he announced that he had ordered a full season of two new series, *New York Undercover*, a gritty cop show, and *M.A.N.T.I.S.*, featuring a black superhero.

Leslie Moonves, soon to be running CBS but then president of Warner Bros. Television, and thus a program supplier who had every reason to praise a potential customer, said in November 1994, "Matoian is a class act. There's a sense you get from him that you can shoot a little higher brow." That's what seemed to be the problem. FOX's success had been built on the 18–34 demographic, and its strongest performers were *Beverly Hills 90210*, *Melrose Place*, and *The X-Files*, the last showing strong growth in its current second season. Matoian's taste would become apparent late in the new season with the premieres—and short runs—of *Medicine Ball*, a series about young doctors with a cast of young unknowns, and *The Great Defender*, a lawyer show starring Michael Rispoli and featuring veteran actor Richard Kiley. Both were quickly canceled. They were quirky, but they were both only slightly different versions of the fare on the Big Three.

FOX programming executive Bob Greenblatt said they were also victims of bad timing. "We always were guided by the principle that it has to be different, unique, and FOXlike. . . . *Medicine Ball* . . . suffered, unfortunately, because *E.R.* and *Chicago Hope* were big hits that season. And those were really well crafted adult ensemble shows, and we wanted to go in underneath that in terms of younger interns. I was proud of that show. I think we suffered from too many medical shows after a period where there were no medical shows."

The Great Defender would prove to be FOX's second failed attempt to do an offbeat series about a Boston-based attorney. *Against the Law*, a one-hour drama starring Michael O'Keefe, had lasted one season in 1990–1991. Their third attempt would finally succeed in 1997, but *Ally McBeal* was still a few years away.

Matoian's problem was that he had been given a job to do, but it was the wrong job. He had been told to broaden the network's audience to the 18–49 demographic, and he did that by moving FOX away from the sorts of shows that had given it its identity. Peter Roth, who would eventually succeed Matoian in running the network in 1996, was then in charge of television production at the studio, with shows being sold to all the networks. He called Matoian a "very, very smart and capable executive," but questioned why he was brought over to FOX. "I think one would have to question . . . why Rupert [Murdoch] and/or his team would hire the then-head of movies for CBS for the FOX sensibility, which was as diametrically different as one could ask for."

People pitching shows to FOX tried to get a fix on what the network under Matoian was looking for, and it soon became apparent that his orders were to make FOX more like the Big Three in terms of programming. Said Roth, "I think that the brand that has always been FOX was—for me, at least—a little less well-defined. . . . With his past, having been a CBS executive, familiar with and very successful with broad-based audiences, his charge with the responsibility of expanding the audience at FOX, naturally you're going to lose some of that very distinctive clear edge that had been uniquely FOX."

In many ways Matoian became the scapegoat for FOX's programming difficulties in the mid-1990s, even though he was trying to accomplish the job he had been hired to do. One success he got little credit for, since the show had already premiered the month before he arrived at FOX, and it wouldn't be considered a hit until after he was gone. Nonetheless, if not for John Matoian, *Party of Five* might never have made it through its first season.

"We had the idea in our development meetings to do a FOX version of a family show," recalled Bob Greenblatt, who was promoted to executive vice president of content programming in October 1994. "And we thought the way to do that was to remove the parents. We were a very young-skewing network. Wouldn't it be novel if there was a family show where the parents were gone?"

Like *Beverly Hills 90210*, *Party of Five* was a show that originated within the confines of the network and was then turned over to outside creative people to make into a series. In this case it was Christopher Keyser and Amy Lippman who got the job, having been staff writers on the early 1990s NBC show *Sisters*. They were in there pitching their own ideas to FOX, and the programming executives turned around and said, in effect, what do you think of *our* idea? Keyser and Lippman had mixed feelings about a dramatic series about five orphaned siblings who try to stick together as a family (the eldest is twenty-four), but they decided to take a shot at it. Upon reading the script, the network greenlit the shooting of the pilot. "We got amazingly lucky with the cast," said Greenblatt, discovering soon-to-be stars like Scott Wolf, Neve Campbell, and Matthew Fox. Jennifer Love Hewitt would join them in the second season.

Sandy Grushow was the top executive pushing for the new hour series, and Lucie Salhany too was won over. "[Grushow] always believed in that, very, very strongly," recalled Salhany. "He screened it for the people at FOX, [and] not a person in the room had a dry eye."

Once *Party of Five* was set for the fall 1994 schedule, the question became where to put it. It was really an 8 P.M. show, but Salhany felt that FOX was not yet strong enough to launch a new drama with no big names as the opening of the evening's programming. In that case the only good fit was on Mondays at 9 P.M., following

Melrose Place, now starting its third successful season. This was one of the things Salhany and Murdoch had fought over, with Murdoch insisting that it could be moved elsewhere. "Of course we can change it. Where would you like to put it?" she shot back. Two months later Salhany was gone.

Fortunately Grushow was the one who felt pride of ownership in the show, and he kept it on the schedule. "It went on the air and did virtually no business," said Greenblatt. "There was a huge audience drop-off after *Melrose Place*. And part of the problem was that *Melrose* was a really campy, outrageous, comedic soap opera and *Party of Five* was a really dramatic, intense show. The audience never really made the shift until we moved it behind *90210*." With good reviews, and bad ratings, *Party of Five* seemed destined for the scrap heap. Grushow left FOX just after the premiere in September 1994 and was replaced by Matoian, and in the strange new world of FOX, *Party of Five* was a show he felt he understood. "He declared [to the other FOX executives] that he was going to support that show come hell or high water, and he did," remembered Greenblatt. At meetings there would be talk of canceling, but something odd happened. Everyone at the network loved the show. "We'd have these meetings at the end of the season where we'd be setting the fall schedule for the next year, and *everybody* supported it. Everybody. Sales loved it. Affiliates loved it. Business affairs. Everybody who watched the show and worked at the network loved it. It was just sheer willpower that we got it picked up for the first two years because it should have been canceled."

No one fought harder than John Matoian did to keep the series going. "My competitors at the other networks thought I was out of my mind. They were thanking me for letting *Party of Five* sit there as a soft spot on our schedule," Matoian said at the time. He shifted the show to Wednesdays—behind *90210*—in January 1995, but the increase in the program's ratings was agonizingly slow. Though it got generally favorable responses from reviewers, *Party of Five* ultimately succeeded by word of mouth: friends telling friends about this emotional drama they just *had* to watch. The pairing with the message-oriented *Beverly Hills 90210* was a much better fit than with the trashy, lurid *Melrose Place*. By the time the show seemed secure it was in its third season and John Matoian was gone from the network. Executive producer Lippman knew they were lucky to be in the right place at the right time. "We would not be on the air if we were not on FOX."

After winning the NFL (the first FOX kickoff was that fall of 1994) and closing the New World deal, FOX was on a campaign to close the gap in nationwide coverage between itself and the Big Three through a series of increasingly creative deals. The Savoy Pictures arrangement had raised eyebrows in the industry. The partnership was clearly an end run around the ownership cap by setting up a situation whereby FOX would not only gain new affiliates but have an equity interest in them, all the while skirting the FCC limitations by placing ostensible control in the hands of FOX's partners.

The complications raised by the network's dancing around the ownership restrictions crystallized in August 1994 when FOX purchased WHBQ in Memphis, Tennessee, the nation's forty-second TV market. It was believed to be the smallest market ever to have a network o-and-o, which were typically located in top-ten markets like New York, Los Angeles, and Chicago. That very same month SF Broadcasting—the FOX/Savoy partnership—bought stations in New Orleans; Honolulu; Green Bay, Wisconsin; and Mobile, Alabama. The New Orleans outlet had been with ABC; the other two had been affiliated with NBC. The next month FOX announced it was buying a Philadelphia station, WTXF, from entertainment giant Viacom, followed by the October repurchase of the Boston FOX affiliate, WFXT, from the Boston Celtics.

That same October FOX announced another partnership, this time with a $20 million investment in Blackstar Communications. In this minority-owned company, FOX would have no more than

20 percent ownership, though the goal of Blackstar was to buy up to eleven stations and convert them to FOX affiliates.

All this activity in buying up stations was a little too blatant to ignore. The FCC announced it would look into the SF Broadcasting operation to see if FOX was properly working within federal regulations, and that it would hold up the transfer of the Green Bay license for WLUK until it had done so. In November 1994 the FCC stated it would continue its investigation of SF Broadcasting but would allow the sale of the Green Bay station to proceed. Still, FOX had now exposed itself to attack. With so many TV stations changing hands, and every license transfer requiring FCC approval, each deal was a pressure point that could be used to question FOX's operations. NBC, about to lose several affiliates, asked the FCC to block some of the FOX purchases, using as its rationale two key issues. First, was SF Broadcasting a sham to allow FOX to control more TV stations than permitted by the FCC rules? Second, was FOX in fact a foreign-owned corporation? The NAACP complaint, dormant for most of a year, was suddenly back in play.

This was hardball, and if FOX lost it would mean the end of the fourth network, or at least Murdoch's control of it. Preston Padden, in his capacity as FOX's senior vice president of government relations, came out swinging. "NBC is simply using the FCC to thwart competition in the marketplace, and that is wrong," he said, noting that two could play at that game. FOX, he pointed out in an interview in November 1994, "could take out the catalogue of fraud convictions against NBC parent General Electric, but then we'd be no better than they are." (General Electric had been indicted and pled guilty in 1985 to padding time cards for employees working on government defense contracts. Federal auditors estimated that GE had added as much as $7.2 million to the expenses.)

Years later Padden, now chief Washington lobbyist for all the Disney operations, still smarts at how NBC tried to blindside FOX. "I was in the office—with Rupert—of Congressman John Linder [Republican of Georgia] when I was pulled out of the room by one of the congressman's aides. There was a reporter from the *New York Times* on the phone telling me that the next morning he was going to break the story of a major NBC/GE assault on News Corporation's foreign-ownership status. It was a comprehensive, orchestrated, coordinated campaign by NBC to try to hobble a competitor who was beginning to get the best of them. What happened is that NBC undertook this blitzkrieg which even included lobbyists from the GE government relations office, and they did their very best to throw as many monkey wrenches into the gears of the growth of FOX as they could."

The goal was clearly to hold up the license transfers of the TV stations to SF Broadcasting and tie FOX in knots in the process. FOX's problem was that they were as creative on the legal and business side as they had been on the programming side. They hadn't necessarily broken any laws—that's what the FCC would have to determine—but they had done a lot of stuff that hadn't been done before. Padden recalled that SF Broadcasting had originally been set up as a limited-liability corporation, an LLC, which would require different treatment under various laws than a standard corporation. "I'll never forget, counsel for one of the older networks said to me—he was huffing and puffing over this latest station move, and said, 'Why I've never even heard of an LLC.'

"This was counsel for one of the other networks. I laughed and I said, 'You know, I don't think there's an FCC rule that limits us to forms of business organization that you've heard of.'"

But FOX did have to admit that while Rupert Murdoch owned 76 percent of the interest in FOX's holding company, 99 percent of its money came from News Corp., an Australian company.

The start of 1995 looked rough for FOX, but no one anticipated where the next battle would be fought. The News Corp. chairman found himself caught up in a sideshow that might have been laughed off as a slapstick comedy of errors if wasn't for the fact that it was being played out on front pages and nightly newscasts across the United States.

In November 1994 the midterm congressional elections had brought a stunning defeat for the Democratic party and President Bill Clinton. The Republicans regained control not only of the Senate but—for the first time in forty years—of the House of Representatives. The new speaker of the House, Newt Gingrich, promised his new majority party a revolution in the way business was conducted in Washington, having campaigned on a "Contract with America" that would be voted on in the House, point by point, within a hundred days of the new Congress taking office.

Murdoch did not go out of his way to involve himself in partisan politics, but it was well known that he was of a conservative bent, and his media outlets were usually more favorable to Republicans. He could not have been displeased at the election results, though he may have been surprised when two Republicans and a Democrat introduced a bill to repeal the provision of the 1934 Communications Act limiting foreign ownership. Among its sponsors was Texan Republican Jack Fields, the new chairman of the telecommunications subcommittee. Peggy Binzel, who worked with Padden representing FOX's interests in Washington, dashed cold water on the idea. She noted that the network was already in compliance with the law as it was and didn't need such extra help.

Still, having friends in high places couldn't hurt, and shortly after the elections Padden proposed to Murdoch that they pay courtesy calls on Robert Dole, the new Senate majority leader, and Gingrich. Through outside counsel they made the appointments and arrived at Gingrich's old office, where he had served as minority whip. The suite was in chaos as his staff was preparing to pack up and move to their new location. Padden remembered the scene vividly, "There were people sitting all over the floor with stacks of pink phone messages piled to the ceiling. And Gingrich strode in from another meeting, made a remark about the mess and said, 'Let's go find someplace where we can sit down.' So we walked down the corridor and sat down on a bench, in a public hallway, in

front of God and the whole rest of the world and had a conversation about how speaker-designate Gingrich was going to remake
the world. And it was these two important leaders, Murdoch and
Gingrich, talking at a thirty-thousand-foot level about how the
world could be remade."

Padden was bemused by the high-flying rhetoric of both Gingrich and his boss, and thought he would try to bring it back to
Earth. Turning to Gingrich, he said, "By the way, General Electric and NBC have launched this campaign against us, filing all
this paper at the FCC, and we'd be grateful for any help you could
give us." The conversation stopped dead. Then, recalled Padden,
"He looked at me with a look that said, 'How could you, you
insignificant little thing, raise such a trivial matter when I'm in
the midst of such lofty thoughts?' and went right back to what he
was talking about."

There the matter might have rested, with Padden perhaps concerned that he might have muffed an opportunity with the new
speaker, when suddenly all hell broke loose. In December 1994 it
was announced that the publisher HarperCollins—a division of
News Corp.—had made a deal with Gingrich to write a book, *To
Renew America*, about his political prescription for the country.
Other politicians in office had written books: serious examinations
of public policy, campaign autobiographies, even spy fiction. The
difference here was the size of the author's advance. Gingrich was
to get $4.5 million. Both FOX's and Gingrich's enemies had reasons
to quickly connect the dots, whether they were there or not. FOX
had problems in Washington, Gingrich was a new power broker,
and Gingrich was receiving $4.5 million from Murdoch.

Padden was as surprised as anybody. He worked for FOX, not
HarperCollins, and had had no idea that any such book deal was in
the offing when he suggested and set up the meeting with Gingrich.
"I never talked to the people at HarperCollins books," said Padden.
"I'm pretty sure they didn't even know I existed."

What followed was farce turned into political scandal. In the wake of the HarperCollins announcement, both Gingrich and the publisher sought to justify it in terms of book industry practice. Other major publishers had bid on the project. Gingrich, not surprisingly, had taken the best offer. It might have been a one-day controversy until news leaked out about the November meeting between Murdoch and Gingrich. Now there was a new round of reporting, implying that there was a quid pro quo between the book deal and FOX's case before the FCC. Gingrich hadn't even been sworn in as speaker yet and was already under attack from all sides. In an effort to defuse the issue, he said he would still write the book but would take only one dollar as an advance against royalties. He said he would wait for royalties after publication to make his money on the book.

The controversy wasn't over yet. In an interview, Senator Dole remarked that of course the subject of FOX had come up in his conversation with Murdoch, so now it seemed that Gingrich was trying to hide what had really taken place. At this point Preston Padden got a phone call from Howard Rubenstein, Murdoch's personal publicist in New York. Padden recalled telling Rubenstein, "'Well, I *know* they didn't talk about the book deal in that meeting.'

"'How do you know?'

"'I was there.'

"'You were there?'

"'Yes.'

"'Let's get that out, that there's a third party who can swear that nothing was said about a book deal.'"

Unfortunately Rubenstein underestimated the Washington press corps' ability to see this not as exculpatory evidence but as further proof of the conspiracy. Now the headlines were not about Padden's "proof" that the book deal had not been discussed but about how Murdoch's people were finally admitting that a FOX lobbyist was present at the meeting with Gingrich. It was clearly not a great moment in public relations history.

After the dust from the Gingrich sideshow finally settled in late January, FOX had to get down to the serious business of beating back this challenge to the network's legitimacy in front of the FCC. In February 1995 Murdoch told the FCC he had done nothing wrong, in spite of the fact that the money he paid in 1985 for the Metromedia stations—the foundation for FOX—had come almost entirely from his Australian corporation News Corp. Said Murdoch, "If you listen to the tax lawyers, they run your whole life. I mean, you've got to decide what you're going to do and do it and pay your taxes. That's the philosophy I work under. Sorry."

That same month, in a surprise move, NBC withdrew its complaint. Apparently the network's attack on FOX had been seen among Washington officials as self-serving, as a way for NBC to sabotage a competitor. It was hurting NBC's interests more than it was helping the case against FOX. Not so coincidentally, NBC had other dealings with Murdoch. It wanted to launch new programming channels directed at Asia, and the means to doing that was getting space for the NBC signal on Murdoch's Star TV satellite. Robert Wright, president of NBC, said, "We believe it is now appropriate to seek withdrawals of our petitions and for us to cooperate with FOX on other matters of mutual interest."

Padden disputes that it was a direct payoff that influenced NBC. "They made a decision that they had done all the damage that they could reasonably hope to do, that any further pursuit of FOX would be pointless at best and maybe counterproductive at worst, and they decided to cease and desist. On their way out the door they got a berth for one of their program services on the Star service in Asia. But the appearance of a strong quid pro quo between those two is misleading, because I know for a fact that they were retreating from the playing fields anyway because of the feedback they were getting."

By spring 1995 FOX's situation was nonetheless growing serious. NBC may have withdrawn from the battle, but the NAACP complaint was still in play, and the FCC investigation was in full swing. David Honig, the Washington attorney who argued for the organization, said that the case—from his viewpoint—was never really about FOX at all. It was merely the most convenient target. "What FOX appeared to be doing was opening up a possible exception or reinterpretation of the foreign ownership rules," he said. "We were fearful that if FOX was permitted to retain ownership on the merits—if it had to be waived or interpreted or bent—you could have all foreign capital invested and still be a broadcaster. . . . It would add so much easily accessible capital to the mix that it would just drown minorities in their ability to bid for properties." Any citizen or group has the right to go before the FCC and challenge a license transfer or renewal, since the FCC regulates the *public* airwaves. The NAACP's New York chapter saw an opportunity here to make a point about the lack of opportunity for minority ownership of broadcast stations. Unfortunately for FOX, the status of News Corp. as an Australian corporation made the FOX deals the place where the NAACP chose to pitch its battle.

The longer the investigation continued, the worse off FOX would be, since they were facing closing deadlines on deals on various TV station purchases. If they didn't acquire the outlets by the established dates, the owners could offer them for sale to others, and at this point other groups were lining up for just that eventuality. In a March 1995 interview, Padden insisted that Murdoch "went to the FCC, disclosed everything, and then proceeded to make massive investments and take enormous risks. To have all of it second-guessed ten years later is grossly unfair and extremely troubling."

By April there were signs that the FCC was looking for a quick and easy way out of the continuing dilemma. The facts were no longer in dispute. Murdoch, a naturalized American citizen, owned 76 percent of the company that owned the network and the stations. News Corp., an Australian company, had put up 99 percent of the equity. Which factor would be more important in terms of deciding who owned FOX? (It wasn't going to be easy. On April 21, 1995, the FCC was closed down by a bomb scare. An unidentified FOX employee commented, "I'm sure they'll blame this on us too.")

A sign of which way the wind was blowing came in late April when the FCC ruled on the Green Bay transfer. The commission had allowed it to proceed, but there was a question as to whether it would be considered a FOX affiliate owned by SF Broadcasting, or a FOX o-and-o. In a victory for FOX, it was held to be an affiliate. Then came the judgment on the NAACP complaint. In a curiously split decision, the panel ruled that, on the one hand there had been a violation of the law because an Australian company had such an overwhelming equity interest in the FOX stations; but, on the other hand, there had been no deliberate attempt to deceive the FCC about the foreign financing involved. FCC commissioner James Quello, the only one still on the panel who had been in the room when Murdoch came before the commission in August 1985, argued forcefully to allow FOX's ownership to stand. In his opinion in the FCC decision, Commissioner Quello wrote, "I fully agree with the finding that FOX was not guilty of either misrepresentation or lack of candor in presenting its proposed ownership structure to the Commission ten years ago. . . . I was never in doubt about what FOX intended for one very simple reason: *I asked*. I asked, and FOX gave me what I considered then, and consider now, to be a perfectly frank response: that Rupert Murdoch, an American citizen, would control 76 percent of the voting stock of FOX. For that reason, it was, and still is, immaterial to me whether all, or part, of the equity ownership of the company resided with FOX's parent, News Corp. The item before us today finds that what I found to be true in 1985 continues to be true in 1995: Mr. Murdoch is, and has at all times been, in both *de facto* and *de jure* control of FOX."

A former broadcaster, Quello felt it was important that the fourth network, which had long been deemed an impossibility, now be allowed to continue. As to the specific issues involved, he was dismissive when discussing them in 1999: "Don't tell me that anything Murdoch has, he doesn't have control." He argued with his fellow commissioners at the time that since Murdoch had been upfront about the arrangements back in 1985, there was no need for any sort of waiver. But because of the ambiguities in the record, his colleagues felt such a waiver was necessary, and it was eventually granted in July.

From FOX's perspective, this was a victory. If FOX had been forced by an adverse FCC ruling to reorganize, it could have cost some $250 million in capital gains taxes. Instead the FCC decided that it was in the public interest to allow FOX to continue. An unnamed rival network executive, speaking to the *New York Times*, grumbled, "Again the commission seems to be saying that the rules that apply to everyone else don't apply to Rupert Murdoch."

Oddly, David Honig, the NAACP's lawyer at the time, did not consider the outcome a defeat, though he continued to pursue legal challenges against the network until the waiver was finally granted. "It was seen as a loss in the press because it was played as a battle of towering personalities," he remarked. "There was [also] a subtext that some of the press tried to suggest that because Murdoch is a conservative and the NAACP is liberal, this was an attempt to catch a conservative in an error and litigate. We did not care about politics. We kept it clean."

Instead the NAACP persuaded FOX to support what became the Emma L. Bowen Foundation for Minority Interests in the Media. FOX and the other networks sit on its board as well as make contributions, and it has provided scholarships and support for minority students interested in pursuing media careers. "We made peace with them," said Honig. "They have honored the settlement to the letter."

Padden too was pleased with the results, but for different reasons. "The bottom line was that the FCC concluded that there had been no misrepresentation, which was certainly the case," he said. "I think the reason it came out that way was, more than anything, the government did not want to punish FOX because FOX had done nothing wrong. In fact, FOX had done a lot of good. On the other hand, the government was very wary of creating a precedent that would enable other foreign corporations to gobble up American broadcasting assets."

The last word went to Commissioner Quello: "It is time to free FOX from costly litigation and unsubstantiated accusations and grant it the freedom and assurance to again devote all its resources to providing the public a strong, competitive, diverse, *American* fourth network."

Ten years before, in 1985, there had been a question whether the American marketplace could support four television networks. The marketplace could and did, and the FCC had pronounced that to be a good thing. Now there was a concern about whether it could support a *fifth* network. Two new entities were going to try to replicate the FOX formula and take advantage of the lessons learned from FOX. Each was headed by someone intimately familiar with how FOX worked. In January 1995 the WB was launched, with the Time-Warner-owned weblet gaining a big vote of confidence from Chicago-based Tribune Broadcasting, which affiliated a number of its stations with the start-up. Meanwhile Viacom, which now owned Paramount Pictures, had joined forces with Chris-Craft, which had several stations bail out on FOX a number of years before. They launched UPN, which stood for the United Paramount Network. It would offer the first network *Star Trek* show—*Voyager*—since the original had left NBC nearly thirty years before. (*Star Trek: The Next Generation* and *Star Trek: Deep Space Nine* had both thrived in syndication.)

WB was headed by founding FOX network president Jamie Kellner, who had left in 1993. UPN was being run by his successor at FOX, Lucie Salhany, who had lasted all of a year and a half. At the very moment that Salhany's successor, John Matoian, was trying to make FOX more respectable to viewers in order to attract a wider audience, its youth-oriented urban base was being attacked by not one but two upstart operations. It was a new world.

CHAPTER ELEVEN

"They finally got it"

[1 9 9 5 – 1 9 9 6]

THE FOX FALL PRIME-TIME SCHEDULE

	7:00	7:30	8:00	8:30	9:00	9:30
Sunday	Space: Above and Beyond		The Simpsons	Too Something	Married . . . with Children	Misery Loves Company
Monday			Melrose Place		Partners	Ned and Stacey
Tuesday			Movie			
Wednesday			Beverly Hills 90210		Party of Five	
Thursday			Living Single	The Crew	New York Undercover	
Friday			Strange Luck		The X-Files	
Saturday			Martin	Preston Episodes	COPS	America's Most Wanted

JOHN MATOIAN'S second season heading the network at FOX was as strained as his first had been. Once again many new shows premiered on the network in the fall of 1995 and throughout the year, but none would have a lasting impact. The action-oriented hour drama *Space: Above and Beyond* was FOX's bid to ride on the sci-fi bandwagon. It took the often-told story of a platoon of soldiers bonding together in battle and set the action in the middle of the twenty-first century. It was reported in the trade papers to be one of the most expensive shows on the air at $2 million per episode, but beyond a loyal core of viewers it just never caught on with the public. *Strange Luck*, starring D. B. Sweeney as an aircrash survivor who seems to have been born to beat the odds, was yet another attempt to create a Friday night lead-in to *The X-Files*, now in its third season. Unfortunately the fictional character proved luckier than the show, and it too went down in flames. It would be replaced by *Sliders*, which had the most curious fate of FOX's failures since *Alien Nation*. The series followed the adventures of a group "sliding" through a series of alternative Earths, trying to find their way back to their own. It had premiered in the spring of 1995 but left the schedule at the end of the summer. The show was brought back in 1996 for the Friday-night hour leading into *The X-Files*. After it was canceled in the spring of 1997, the series was picked up by cable's Sci-Fi Channel, which not only aired the reruns but commissioned new episodes. In spite of several changes in cast, it continued until 2000. The show would eventually be a success, but not for FOX. Matoian continued trying to put a hit show on the air, but he kept striking out.

"I don't think his taste was exactly what they needed at the time at the network," said industry reporter Brian Lowry.

Yet FOX could still surprise the competition. Darren Star had finally graduated from the Aaron Spelling School of TV Series where, with the veteran producer, he had created *Beverly Hills 90210* and *Melrose Place*. In the fall of 1995 he developed a show for CBS Entertainment Productions and gotten it on the CBS schedule. It was to be the Tiffany Network's answer to his FOX series. *Central Park West* was a glitzy adult soap starring Mariel Hemingway and a strong cast that included Lauren Hutton and Ron Leibman. When the show premiered on September 13, 1995, it was scheduled opposite the two-hour season premiere of *90210*. The following week the competition was *90210* and the heavily hyped one hundredth episode of *Melrose*. Star's new show never recovered from the competition. It was in fourth place in its time slot, and most potential viewers—having missed the first two episodes—never bothered to catch up. The ratings numbers told the story. Not only did *Melrose* top *Central Park* in the overall household ratings but in the adult (men and women) 18–49 demographic it nearly tripled the size of the audience that had tuned in for the CBS series. In that key demo—which Matoian had been charged with winning—*Melrose* was in second place for the time slot, behind only the sitcoms *Grace Under Fire* and *The Naked Truth* on ABC. FOX's strong showing in the ratings put CBS in fourth place overall, leading David Letterman to do a top-ten list on "Good things about being a fourth-place network." It included lines like "Can address all your viewers by name" and "Don't get that paranoid feeling people are watching you."

Yet knocking down CBS was not enough for FOX. John Matoian was supposed to be putting winners on the air, and he had yet to put on a single show that had become a FOX signature piece. The only one he could take partial credit for was *Party of Five*, and that was simply for renewing it for its current second season. Another FOX show, *The X-Files*, was being copycatted by CBS (with the supernatural *American Gothic*) and UPN (the paranoid thriller *Nowhere Man*). Yet flattery by imitation failed to win plaudits for Matoian because *The X-Files'* debut also predated him. In September 1995 he was quoted in the trade press about how FOX had matured: "Prior to this regime, there was a narrowcasting of content that said, 'No one over a certain age allowed.' When you begin to grow up, you need to give your audiences some grown-up choices." An executive at a rival network asked, "Can FOX be distinctive and different and alternative and also be the mainstream network? It's schizophrenic. I don't know if they know who they want to be."

By January 1996 Matoian was pleading with his industry critics to give him time: "Patience is really the only way we can hold the course." Time, however, was not on the side of the president of the Fox Entertainment Group.

Meanwhile Margaret Loesch and the FOX Kids Network continued to thrive with four hours of shows on Saturday mornings and three hours each day during the week. To her delight, network president Lucie Salhany had been even more supportive than Jamie Kellner had been. When Salhany left FOX in 1994, Loesch found that Matoian too appreciated her contribution to the overall network. "John was, perhaps, miscast in that role [of running the network], but he was a wonderful fellow," Loesch recalled. "The first thing John said was, 'Let's have a monthly meeting.'"

It was at those recurring meetings that she noticed an odd name for a project on Matoian's development list called *Goosebumps*. When she asked what it was, he told her that it was based on a series of horror books for young readers by R. L. Stine. Following the meeting Loesch went to a bookstore to see what the fuss was all about. She asked a clerk if they had any *Goosebumps* books and was told, "Yeah, see where all those kids are over there?" Loesch decided it was a project worth pursuing for FOX Kids. It would run for three years beginning in October 1995.

Overall Loesch had no problems working with Matoian, but she felt he never quite fit in at FOX. "It was just the environment in which John didn't flourish—the politics, the process. But I found him [to be] a love."

This would be the season of Loesch's greatest triumph as well as the beginning of the end of her time at FOX. In November 1995 a joint venture between FOX and Israeli producer Haim Saban was announced. Saban was the supplier of FOX Kids' biggest hit, *Mighty Morphin Power Rangers*, and Loesch had once suggested buying out Saban's company in order to control the show outright. Instead the two would now be partners in producing new shows. By the following September the company would be merged into FOX Kids, with Saban playing a leading role.

That was still in the future. In January 1996 Loesch went to the affiliates to keep a promise that had been made at the launch of FOX Kids back in the fall of 1990. As originally put together by station owner Harry Pappas and then FOX president Jamie Kellner, the affiliates would have an ownership stake in the Kids Network's programming and would receive a share of the eventual profits. Usually, under Hollywood's legendary creative accounting, many might have thought that day of profit would never come. But at the January FOX affiliate meeting in Las Vegas, Loesch had a surprise that Preston Padden, still running the network's affiliate relations, helped pull off. Rather than simply make the announcement and tell the affiliates that the check was in the mail, Loesch and Padden staged an elaborate event without telling them what it was all about. Loesch came out into the hall tossing play money into the crowd, and announced to the station executives that she had the real thing to hand out. She then proceeded to distribute $15 million in FOX Kids profits to the affiliates. "They were wild. We really bent over backwards to make the money work—in some cases it was a lot of money. We gave them the benefit of the doubt financially because they had ultimately been very supportive and very worried. They had done the right thing; they had turned over whole day parts to us. . . . They finally got it."

For a moment, everything seemed to be right at FOX. Kevin O'Brien, general manager at KTVU, recalled, "This giving out the check was a brilliant idea on Preston's part because the natives were restless and it really calmed everybody down. It was the right thing at the right time."

Now it was time for the financier Ron Perelman to enter into the life of FOX one last time. He had delayed Margaret Loesch going over to FOX in 1989. He had switched over his New World group of stations to FOX affiliation in 1994. Two years later he would personally close a deal with Rupert Murdoch that would shake the TV industry once again.

Perelman's New World stations had certainly increased the network's reach, but their independence from the network continued to rankle Murdoch. "What happened was that Murdoch, as the network got stronger, wanted to do other things," recalled New World's general counsel, Michael Diamond. "We had battles about ice skating. He wanted to do a morning news show. He wanted to do a post-morning show. . . . He couldn't do very much with us without our consent. That after-breakfast show? He couldn't impose [it] on us. He talked about a Sunday news show. Our guys weren't interested, and we had 15 percent of the network in terms of reach. . . ." With the New World stations having an effective veto over FOX's programming outside of prime time, the only solution was for FOX to take control of New World. But the FCC would never approve of such a sale, even if Perelman were willing to sell the stations to Murdoch, because it would put the FOX network over the limit of how many stations it could legally own.

That changed when, in January 1996, Congress passed the new Telecommunications Act, the first comprehensive rewriting of American communications law in decades. FOX executive Preston Padden, and especially his number two on the lobbying side, Peggy Binzel, worked tirelessly to ensure that the new ownership limit would be high enough to permit FOX to buy the New World stations. When the dust cleared, among the changes was a relaxing of the ownership cap for the networks. Now, instead a network of being limited to owning stations providing an aggregate of no more than 25 percent national coverage, that limit would be raised to 35 percent. Murdoch approached Perelman about buying the eight New World stations, but Perelman played hardball, telling Murdoch the deal would have to include the entire New World operation. Murdoch balked. He already had production and distribution entities far superior to anything New World could offer. Why would he pay good money for something he didn't need? It was Metromedia all over again—when, in 1985, John Kluge had tried to link his TV production and distribution operation to the sale of his stations to Murdoch. All Murdoch wanted were the stations, but they were being tied to other units that duplicated resources FOX already had. Still, Murdoch didn't give up on his goal. He just refused to take it on Perelman's terms.

By the spring of 1996, rumors of an imminent FOX/New World deal were reaching fever pitch. Michael Diamond, who also handled corporate communications for New World, kept insisting there was no deal. "It was very difficult. Employees were saying, 'We're going to FOX. We've got to get out of here.' And we were reassuring them that that was not going to happen. We had this big retreat and we said, 'We're not selling to anybody. We're expanding.' Because Murdoch had gone away; he had said, 'I'm not buying the company.'" From New World's perspective, the negotiations with FOX were over.

What Murdoch had under the 1994 affiliation agreements with New World were the tough contracts that favored the stations, not the network, and a 20 percent stake in the company, but with no voting stock. It was a position he didn't like to find himself in: someone else—Perelman—was calling the shots. When Murdoch balked at the New World offer, Perelman turned around and decided to expand his TV operations. He made an offer to buy King World, the distributor of such syndicated megahits as *Wheel of Fortune*, *Jeopardy*, and *The Oprah Winfrey Show*. This maneuver created a whole new problem for Murdoch. If New World absorbed King, buying out Perelman would be an even more expensive proposition. Something had to be done.

In July 1996 it looked like the union of New World and King World would be a done deal. Diamond kept fending off press inquiries with "No comment." On Friday afternoon, July 12, the *Wall Street Journal* reporter who covered the TV business called and asked Diamond, "If I go away this weekend, am I going to be surprised?" Knowing that the King World deal would not be announced until the following week, Diamond assured him he would not be.

Instead, not only was the *Wall Street Journal* reporter surprised, so was everyone else by what transpired over that weekend, Diamond included. He and the other top New World executives were on a plane to New York to finalize the deal when they got the call. They were not going to be buying King World, after all. They were selling out to FOX.

Here's what happened: Murdoch and Perelman were both attending a conference in Idaho. At dinner Murdoch approached Perelman directly about FOX purchasing New World. As he had so many times before, Murdoch had calculated that the loss of the stations would be a greater price to pay than any immediate cash problems. It was more important to own those stations and end those restrictive affiliation agreements that were hamstringing the network's ability to launch programming. Paying eighteen times the annual cash flow of the properties (instead of the industry standard of twelve or thirteen times cash flow), Murdoch and Perelman shook hands on a pact that would give FOX the stations in return for $2.5 billion.

"Going into the weekend we thought we were a buyer. Monday we turned out to be a seller," recalled Ken Ziffren, who was one of New World's outside counsel responsible for certain aspects of the FOX deal. Murdoch's strength, Ziffren said, was that he could move quickly where virtually anyone else might have let the deal get away. "He's a visionary and he can act on his own impulses. He doesn't have tons of committees around that study something to death."

FOX's deal was even more clever than many realized. Since UHF stations were presumed to have weaker broadcast signals, they were counted by the government regulators at only half their actual potential audience in determining a station group's aggregate reach. For example, VHF stations in Chicago have a potential reach of 3 percent of the country's TV viewing audience. Under the rules, however, FOX's Chicago affiliate, WFLD, counts for only half that, or 1.5 percent. This quirk in how the law measured UHF stations meant that a UHF-heavy station group like FOX's could actually go beyond 35 percent coverage that was the legal limit. Indeed, thanks to the boost provided by carriage of those UHF stations on cable outlets, FOX could now reach 40 percent of the country on stations it owned outright, more than any of the Big Three. For once, being the "coat-hanger network" was an advantage.

In a footnote to the deal, former NBC executive Brandon Tartikoff—author of the "coat-hanger" gibe about how viewers would need improvised antennas to pick up the FOX signal—resigned from his position as head of New World's entertainment division.

Although the network and the movie studio would remain the core of the larger Twentieth Century–Fox operation, much more was going on. As a result of the brouhaha a few years earlier over retransmission consent, FOX had parlayed the permission it granted cable companies to carry its broadcast stations into an agreement to launch FX, an entertainment-oriented cable channel. In 1992 Anne Sweeney was an executive at the Nickelodeon cable network and had just concluded a deal to carry the children's cable channel in England, on Rupert Murdoch's BskyB satellite. In the course of her dealings she met Murdoch but thought nothing of it in terms of her own future.

Then in May 1993 her husband graduated first in his class from Fordham Law School in Manhattan, and they spent Sunday evening celebrating. On Monday, still enjoying the family triumph, she received a call from Murdoch. "I'm in New York today. Are you free to have lunch with me?" They met and, Sweeney recalled, "We talked about, actually, everything except cable." It was an enjoyable business meal, but she was not expecting a follow-up call the next day. Murdoch invited her to meet for coffee, and when she arrived he offered her the job to head his start-up cable operation, the FX channel.

She started out with a $100 million programming budget and a mandate to be creative, including experimenting with live television, for which Murdoch had a great passion. FX built a studio on Fifth Avenue, near the historic Flatiron Building, in New York's old china and crystal district. When FX was finally launched in June 1994, it was available in eighteen million homes on various cable systems throughout the United States. The lineup was an eclectic mix of concepts, including a collectibles show, *Personal Effects*, which proved to be their biggest ratings winner. The program that attracted all the critical notice, however, was *Breakfast Time*.

It starred Tom Bergeron and Laurie Hibbard, and it was something that hadn't been seen on television in years—a quirky morning show that had comedy, interviews, and a wisecracking puppet. (Precedents went back to the 1950s, with examples like the arrival of chimpanzee J. Fred Muggs as a regular guest on NBC's *Today* in 1953 and the short-lived 1954 NBC series *Breakfast in Hollywood*.) It also had a set that was unbelievable. "We called it the FX apartment," said Sweeney. "Everything about the show was very mobile. There were a lot of hand-held cameras. We did segments from the bedroom, the library. We had a large space that we made into a ballroom. We used it for everything from large-scale demonstrations to exercise shows to bands. We had a kitchen area where we actually cooked breakfast. We had someone—one of the guys from the crew, actually, was a fabulous cook, and he cooked breakfast for guests who came on the show."

Bergeron was an affable Boston TV and radio personality who for a number of years had hosted a local daytime TV show called *People are Talking*. It had folded when the regional marketplace could no longer support the expense of a live daily talk show. So when he got the call to meet with people starting up a FOX cable network, he took it as a lark. "I felt it was a free day in New York. They're paying for it, I'll visit some friends, fine." Instead he met with Peter Faiman, director of the 1986 hit movie *Crocodile Dundee*, who had become a FOX production executive. "He had been a big star in Australian television as a producer and creator of shows, and we started talking about live television, and how rare a breed it is, and how wonderful it is to do live TV."

Bergeron was hooked on Faiman's notion for a show. For the next two years *Breakfast Time* was the sort of offbeat program that people loved to discover and then tell their friends. While Sweeney's charge was to build up FOX's cable operations, Bergeron said he and Faiman felt that FX was FOX's farm team, and that if their show succeeded they might go over to the broadcast network. In January 1996 rumors began that *Breakfast Time* would move to FOX and that FX would start emphasizing sports instead of Sweeney's quirky original programming. FOX would eventually develop separate sports cable operations, but it was becoming clear that FX was in transition away from its initial vision. That same month Anne Sweeney acquired the cable reruns rights to *The X-Files*. It followed the purchase several months earlier of the ABC hit drama *NYPD Blue* which, like *The X-Files*, was produced by Twentieth Century Television.

January 1996 was also the month when conservative Republican political consultant Roger Ailes departed from CNBC. He had landed there when his talk cable channel, America's Talking, had been acquired and turned into MSNBC, a joint venture of NBC and Microsoft. He denied reports that he was in negotiation with FOX, despite being seen heading into their Manhattan offices. Noting that News Corp.'s New York headquarters was located near NBC, he joked that "I get lost sometimes." Less than two weeks later Ailes was named the head of the new FOX News Channel, with a start-up budget of $80 million.

In late February 1996 FX announced that *Breakfast Time* was being canceled, though the show's final weekday episode would not run until that March. This was not goodbye, however. It was to give the show's team to a chance to retool. *Breakfast Time* was going to relaunch in August as *FOX After Breakfast*, the network's first attempt at morning programming. As a network show, it would be out of Anne Sweeney's hands.

"It was very inventive and had really been a fabulous laboratory for a lot of talent and a lot of good ideas," she said. "It was never as easy as 'let's just take that show and put it on the network,' because a network is a very different animal, a broadcast network is a different animal than a cable network. . . . It became a very different show when it moved over."

By spring, with FX focusing on showcasing reruns of network series instead of original programming, Sweeney decided it was time
to move on. She left to become the head of the Disney Channel and
eventually to oversee all its cable operations.

W ith so many prominent moves in play, the one area of network operations that couldn't seem to gain attention was
FOX's prime-time lineup. In April the network launched the dramatic series *Profit*, John Matoian's last best shot at getting credit for
a signature show for his network.

Matoian had appointed programming executive Bob Greenblatt to be the head of prime-time programming shortly after he
arrived in October 1994. He told Greenblatt, "I want to do shows
that are really unique." Greenblatt pulled out the pilot script for
Profit, and said, "Okay, read this script and tell me it's not unique."
The notion of a sociopath (to be played by Adrian Pasdar) who
ruthlessly runs a corporation by framing his rivals for murder or
having them committed to mental institutions was not exactly
original. J. R. Ewing had done much the same on CBS's *Dallas* in the
1970s and 1980s. But the execution of *Profit* was truly disturbing
since the ostensible hero of the show wasn't only greedy and ma-
nipulative, he was downright evil. Indeed, he was somewhat de-
ranged. This wealthy man had been so psychologically scarred in
his youth that his apartment included a large cardboard box where
he slept at night. The proposal had come from Stephen J. Cannell,
who had given FOX its first big hit in 1987 with *21 Jump Street*, but
when he had offered it to the network in 1993, Lucie Salhany and
Sandy Grushow couldn't buy it.

"They didn't get it conceptually," said Greenblatt. "And it sat on
the shelf."

Matoian got it. He told Greenblatt to order a pilot. (In a
strange twist of fate, another show that Greenblatt pitched around
that time came from writer David Chase. It was a quirky drama

about gangsters. "For some reason, and I don't know exactly why, the culture at FOX didn't really want to do a show about the Mafia," said Greenblatt of the series that would go on to be a hit on HBO in 1999 as *The Sopranos*. "Maybe it would have been the wrong network for it," he added, philosophically.)

By April 1996 *Profit* was on the air, Mondays at 8 P.M. It seemed to have been good counterprogramming, putting an hour drama opposite sitcoms like *Fresh Prince of Bel-Air* on NBC, *The Nanny* on CBS, and *Roseanne* on ABC, but the timing was wrong. It was just before the critical May ratings sweeps, and *Profit* was not the sort of fare that could become an overnight success. "If you're going to put on a show with a sociopath, it's going to take a while for it to catch on," said Cannell with hindsight. "It needed a full year on the air or they never even should have tried it." According to Cannell, they were trying for *Richard III*, Shakespeare's drama about the twisted British king who murders his way to the throne. People were supposed to be fascinated by the lead's villainy, not find it admirable.

Reviews were strong, but the ratings weren't. Jeff Jarvis, writing in *TV Guide*, described *Profit* as "*How to Succeed in Business Without Really Trying* reengineered with the deep-pit paranoia of an Oliver Stone film and the conspiratorial whiff of *The X-Files*." With May approaching, John Matoian got cold feet. He had hoped the show would create a quick buzz that would boost the May ratings. Instead *Profit* was pulled after four episodes. Several more installments were completed and never aired. Said Greenblatt, "I believe that, if given more time, it could have been an enormous hit show. It was really painful. But unlike *Party of Five*, within the company there was no upswing of support for it. Sales people were afraid of it because it was all too dark and immoral, and they were afraid of advertiser reaction. A lot of people, on first blush, didn't get it."

The show's supporters urged Matoian to give *Profit* another shot in the summer, but it never happened. To this day Cannell doesn't know why it didn't get a real chance to find its audience, but Matoian told him that he loved the show. Recalled Cannell, "[Matoian] said when he resigned that the darkest day he had in all that time he was at FOX was the day he canceled *Profit.*"

I t was a different cancellation that would be the darkest mark on Matoian's record at FOX. In May 1996 *America's Most Wanted* was finishing its ninth season on the network with a bang. Host John Walsh had invited all the missing children the show had helped to find, and their parents, and the people who helped to locate them, for a big party on the Washington Mall in the nation's capital where the show was based. The celebration would later appear on the show. Co–executive producer Phil Lerman recalled, "We were going to reunite every missing child we had recovered—which I think at the time was nineteen children, every tipster who had recovered them, and their families. Someone returns your missing child and you never got a chance to thank them. So we brought them all to Washington."

"It was a wonderful, wonderful weekend of everybody getting together and sharing their stories and helping each other along," said executive producer Lance Heflin. "It was really kind of a festive occasion for us."

It came time for the main ceremonies, which included remarks by Senator Diane Feinstein, but Walsh was out sitting in the car on the phone to Heflin. Heflin had just been notified by Chase Carey that there was no need for them to come to New York the next day for the network's annual upfront presentation to the advertisers. Said Heflin, "That meant only one thing: we were canceled." Walsh got out of the car and didn't say a word. The tribute to the recovered kids and their rescuers went off as planned. "People are singing 'Amazing Grace.' When they got to the line, 'I once was lost, but now I'm found,' everybody started crying," said Lerman. "It was the greatest and the worst day in the history of *America's Most Wanted.*"

So who canceled one of FOX's most successful, long-lasting shows? No one wanted to take credit for the deed, especially since

America's Most Wanted was still doing well in the ratings. Heflin's theory is that the sales people had never been comfortable selling spots on the show, considering it lurid and tabloid and somehow beneath them. They had been using it for "make goods," the extra time advertisers get when the ratings they are promised on another show they are advertising in don't pan out. For his part, Matoian insisted he backed the show. He told Heflin after the show wasn't renewed, "I really want to bring it back. It wasn't my idea to take it off the air. . . . Give me some time, I'll try to bring it back."

Then, as sometimes happens when a cancellation is announced or is in the offing, the network began hearing from viewers. FOX wasn't prepared for the onslaught that the axing of *America's Most Wanted* would bring. If a TV executive makes a decision based on ratings and sales figures, letters from viewers may not be enough to reverse the decision to pull the plug. But few shows generated the kind of public reaction this one did. The network and the show received boxes upon boxes of letters, including one with literally hundreds of signatures gathered by a North Carolina woman. A member of her family had been murdered, and *America's Most Wanted* was going to spotlight the case. When the show was canceled, she was informed that they would be unable to do so. She wanted the show renewed so they could tell the story of her family's tragedy. She attempted to deliver the petition personally to Rupert Murdoch on the FOX lot in Los Angeles, but settled for leaving it with a network spokesperson.

Depending on how close the call was on the show, the letters may or may not have made a difference. Letter campaigns had convinced NBC to keep *Star Trek* going in the 1960s and worked on CBS in the 1980s with *Beauty and the Beast*. Many more shows, however, had stayed canceled despite viewer write-in campaigns. Then the letters and petitions began coming in from members of Congress. Governors and state attorneys general communicated with FOX, urging them to keep the show on the air because of its proven track record in bringing criminals to justice. "Thirty-seven governors signed a petition to bring this back," recalled Lerman. "You know what it takes to get thirty-seven governors to agree what time of day it is?" The FBI, when asked, said it couldn't endorse a commercial television program, but several officials of the agency wrote individually to the network, praising the show's accomplishments.

Due to the timely nature of its content, *America's Most Wanted* didn't utilize reruns but continued doing new episodes throughout the summer. It could recycle material from old shows when an update was warranted, but airing a straight repeat would be like showing a rerun of the news from six months ago. Unlike dramatic series that are usually finished or near the end of production when the cancellation notice arrives, *America's Most Wanted* had to continue doing new shows for the more than three months that remained of the 1995–1996 season. When the fall rolled around, however, it was no longer on the schedule.

That same spring it was time for another executive shuffle at FOX. After the acquisition of NFL football broadcast rights in 1994, sports had become an important part of the FOX schedule. In November 1995 FOX made a $575 million dollar deal with major league baseball (MLB) to carry games for five years beginning in 1996, including the World Series in 1996, 1998, and 2000, and the All-Star Game in 1997 and 1999. FOX would also carry a regional Saturday afternoon game, five divisional playoffs, and one league championship. (NBC and ABC would also sign comprehensive deals with MLB.) David Hill, an Australian and the president of FOX Sports, was rewarded in midsummer by being named president and chief operating officer of FOX Television. Chase Carey, now chairman and CEO of FOX Television, would focus on deal making. As head of the FOX Entertainment Group, Matoian would no longer report to Carey but to Hill.

As it turned out, Matoian wouldn't be doing so much longer.

CHAPTER TWELVE

"Tom, you've got to script the ad-libs"

[1996–1997]

THE FOX FALL PRIME-TIME SCHEDULE

	7:00	7:30	8:00	8:30	9:00	9:30
Sunday	Big Deal		The Simpsons	Ned and Stacey	The X-Files	
Monday			Melrose Place		Party Girl	Lush Life
Tuesday			Movie			
Wednesday			Beverly Hills 90210		Party of Five	
Thursday			Martin	Living Single	New York Undercover	
Friday			Sliders		Millennium	
Saturday			COPS	COPS	Married . . . with Children	Love and Marriage

SHORTLY AFTER the start of the 1996–1997 television season that September, John Matoian was history at FOX. Although there were rumors that he'd leave, the official story was that Rupert Murdoch and Chase Carey had actually wanted to sign him for a three-year extension of his contract. It was reported in the trade papers that Matoian had turned it down because of a family illness that had kept him from the FOX lot in recent weeks. (He would end up leaving broadcast television altogether, signing on for a stint as president of HBO Pictures.) Whether he was pushed or left FOX of his own free will, his departure as head of the FOX Entertainment Group—and the person in charge of all network programming—continued the pattern begun after Barry Diller's resignation in February 1992. Journalist Brian Lowry, who had covered FOX for *Variety* and was now based at the *Los Angeles Times*, noted, "There's always been a tendency, and it was there every couple of years, to just grab someone else who was well regarded internally and stick them into that network job. I don't think it's been good for them in the long haul."

Into the breach stepped Peter Roth, who had been brought to FOX under Lucie Salhany's regime in 1993 and became head of the Twentieth Century Television production unit a year later. Roth had two priorities. First, he would continue Matoian's work in expanding the FOX audience to the 18–49 demographic. (Just a few weeks earlier, FOX had actually been number one in that demographic, but that was because the Big Three were committed to covering the Democratic National Convention.) Second, he would begin the process of rebuilding FOX's brand name.

The notion of the network being a brand name like Jell-o or Coca-Cola was one that all the networks would eventually adopt, putting their logo on screen throughout the broadcast day. FOX, however, was one of the first to realize it. Ratings analyst Andy Fessel was long gone from FOX by the time Roth arrived at the network, having moved into the new frontier of the internet and spending several years at Microsoft. But Fessel would have understood exactly what Roth was up to, because he used to preach about "FOX as brand name" to the network's sales team. "This FOX brand was a great array of descriptives: FOX was innovative, FOX was friendly, FOX was special, FOX was an underdog, FOX tried hard, FOX is younger . . ., FOX is intelligent," Fessel said he used to explain. "What was the image of the [Big Three] networks? The same old, boring, not for me, for older people, something my parents watched. The problem was the other networks were trying to be all things to all people."

John Matoian's background had been at one of those Big Three networks, CBS. With his mandate to broaden FOX's base, it was not surprising he turned to the Big Three model in programming the

network. He was following the dictate from above to capitalize on
the new viewers drawn to FOX by NFL football and, later, major
league baseball. Although the schedule still included past hits like
Married . . . with Children, *The Simpsons*, *Beverly Hills 90210*, *COPS*,
and *The X-Files*, Matoian had added nothing new to further define
the network. Building on past hits, Roth wanted the network to go
back to first principles. FOX, he felt, should be selling the idea to
viewers that the fourth network was "daring, distinctive, different,
unlike anything else you could find anywhere else on network television. That was my motto. That's my mantra."

Roth didn't waste time in moving FOX back to its earlier image
as a television maverick. Before the month was out he canceled two
poorly performing new sitcoms, *Lush Life* with Lori Petty and *Party
Girl* with Christine Taylor and Swoosie Kurtz. He replaced them
with a series of inexpensive reality specials that provided quick ratings jolts but led to negative comment in the press and in the industry. Shows like *When Animals Attack* and *The World's Scariest
Police Chases* led to many more such FOX specials whenever there
was a hole in the network's schedule that needed to be patched.
Barry Diller's wry comment several years back that one could attract viewers by showing car accidents had proven prescient. At the
same time Roth announced the return of one the most successful
series in the network's history.

D avid Hill, the FOX sports chief turned network executive, was
a fan of *America's Most Wanted*. When the letters and petitions
started pouring in, they were hard to miss, with many of them personally addressed to Rupert Murdoch. It had been a mistake to cancel the show, but networks make similar errors in judgment all the
time. Once shows are gone from the lineup, they rarely, if ever,
come back. Executive producer Lance Heflin recalled that the crew
had just finished taping the final episode of *America's Most Wanted*
in New Orleans. It had been a long week and a longer summer with

the knowledge that the program was going off the air. Heflin and Walsh were sitting by the pool at their New Orleans hotel that Friday when he received a call from Rick Jacobson, who had replaced Greg Meidel as the head of Twentieth Television. Jacobson told him, "I just got a call from David Hill. There's something going on here. You're back on the air."

"Excuse me. You don't understand. We just taped our last show."

"No," Jacobson replied, "I think you're back."

They tracked down Hill and asked him if it was true. He said it was. "Look, boys, I think it's a good show. I think we need to work on it a little bit. Take a month off and let's get back to it. It's a good show, and I think it could be better. So come on out and let's figure out how we're going to do that."

Recalled Heflin, "We hung up the phone and sort of looked at each other astounded. Well, that was the shortest canceled show in the history of television."

"I brought back *America's Most Wanted* with David Hill's endorsement, support, blessing," said Roth. "We thought we were doing a disservice to our viewers by taking off a show that was good, that moved them, that we thought had real value. Again, it was a habit that the audience really wanted to continue with."

While fortune—and the new FOX executives—smiled upon *America's Most Wanted*, other shows on the schedule that season were not as fortunate. By mid-October Roth had axed *Love and Marriage* and *Big Deal*, the latter a game show that had been intended for a limited run. *Big Deal*, a variation on the classic *Let's Make a Deal*, performed so poorly that even a political campaign ad by the eccentric Texas billionaire Ross Perot had beaten it in the ratings.

The cancellations signaled that Roth had a clear idea of what FOX was *not*—now they had to figure out what the FOX "brand" would represent. The network's first airing of the World Series in October 1996 under its five-year baseball contract brought home the schizophrenia of the FOX programming strategy. The baseball championship routinely gets high ratings, and whichever network has it uses it to promote itself and its other shows heavily. FOX's dilemma was that though the World Series drew large audiences, it also included a large number of older viewers who were unlikely to watch FOX under any other circumstances. As one advertising executive told *Variety*, "You can promote *The Simpsons* all day long, but if you're promoting to a sixty-year-old male, he's not gonna watch."

Roth had to get something on that people would want to watch and that put the network out on the edge again, attracting the younger viewers that had propelled such shows as *Melrose Place* and *In Living Color* to success. *Party of Five* would finally emerge as a hit in the 1996–1997 season, its third, but in the fall of 1996 FOX was seen as a network that hadn't produced a defining signature show since the premiere of *The X-Files* three years before. Roth needed a hit show.

If FOX's prime time was getting the full Roth treatment, the network's new venture into morning programming was suffering from not-so-benign neglect. *FOX After Breakfast* had premiered in August 1996, shortly before Matoian left. Roth had nothing invested in this new show. "I was involved in everything, but it was not my area of personal involvement. It was a lower priority for me. I wasn't part of that team," he said.

On the surface, the hour-long *FOX After Breakfast* on the broadcast network had a lot of similarities to *Breakfast Time* on the FX cable channel. Tom Bergeron, Laurie Hibbard, and the wisecracking puppet named Bob all made the transition, as did the apartment set and the use of hand-held cameras. But something had been lost in the translation. "There was a feeling that, well, we're going to network, we should clean it up just a little bit," said Bergeron. "Maybe instead of the funky riffs that opened the show, go for a theme song that—in retrospect—was an incredibly saccharine little number. So I think we went in not quite trusting the qualities that made the cable version the critical hit that it was."

The show aired weekdays from 9 to 10 A.M., competing with such syndicated hits as *Live with Regis and Kathie Lee*. But with John Matoian, Twentieth Television's Greg Meidel, and FX's Anne Sweeney all gone, *FOX After Breakfast* in the fall of 1996 was beginning its first season as a live, daily network show without a strong ally among the network's top executives. Changes were made without regard to what had worked on *Breakfast Time*, so Laurie Hibbard was let go, as was puppeteer Al Rosenberg. Bergeron was perceived as the "star" of the show and received continuing advice from the network that proved to him they just didn't get it. "My favorite line from David Hill was, 'Tom, you've got to script the ad-libs so the director knows when to take the shot.' I just thought, this is going to hell in a handbasket." There may have been skeptics back in the FX days, but Sweeney had insulated the talent and the staff from outside interference and had always fought for the show with the higher-ups.

Bergeron thinks the failure of *FOX After Breakfast* was somewhat due to the network but also places some of the blame on the people running the show—including himself—for being too cautious. "I think the failure of nerve was partly our fault on the creative end. . . . It would be nice if I could point fingers at the network and say it was all their fault, but in actual fact we didn't come in saying, 'This is our show.' We came in second-guessing ourselves a little bit, trying to make it more palatable. We were dulling our own edge, even as the network was sharpening its knives."

Roth might have become a champion of the morning show if he had cared to pay attention to it. The glib and easygoing Bergeron was trying to do a different kind of morning show. He has fond memories of one episode where his lineup included Beau Bridges, Martin Sheen, Emilio Estevez, Gladys Knight, and Garth Brooks—and Brooks confessed to being nervous singing in front of Knight. "It was incredible," said Bergeron. "We didn't have trouble booking the show. We had trouble convincing the network to support the show."

Over the course of the 1996–1997 season, *FOX After Breakfast* grew more and more conventional. "It was becoming the very show we had been created to counter. It was becoming this safe, pabulum-spewing daytime talk show, and I found that incredibly painful," said Bergeron. Finally, at the start of the summer of 1997, Bergeron couldn't take it any more. His mother-in-law was dying of cancer, he hadn't had a vacation in a year, and he was watching a program he cared about being transformed into something dull and ordinary. Officially his departure was described as by "mutual agreement." Unofficially he just walked away. He took the news that he had been replaced by Vicki Lawrence, a former talk-show host and onetime cast member of *The Carol Burnett Show*, as a sign that while FOX wanted to be edgy at night, in the morning they wanted a "safe, generic daytime show."

Bergeron would end up finding greater success later as host of the new *Hollywood Squares* with Whoopi Goldberg. He summed up his ten-month ordeal on *FOX After Breakfast* this way: "I can't imagine an experience that I'll treasure more than working with FX. And I can't imagine an experience I'll treasure less than working with FOX after that."

It goes without saying that the first year of tenure of any new TV network head is tough because it will take almost that long for any show he or she greenlights to get on the air. In October 1996 the supernatural police drama *Millennium* premiered. It was a new show from Chris Carter, of *X-Files* fame, and it was so scary and violent that viewers didn't know what to make of it. *Los Angeles Times* critic Howard Rosenberg called it "dark, brooding, melancholy and, unless profundity is in the wings, pointless." The hour-long series starred Lance Henriksen as a moody ex-FBI agent turned private detective who solves homicides through psychic impressions of the victims. "The concept is that we live in a culture where justice has been stolen from us," Carter told *Entertainment Weekly*.

"People have lost faith in the system. That's the madness and insecurity I'm trying to write about."

Programming executive Bob Greenblatt said the network decided that Carter had been so successful with *The X-Files* that they essentially gave him a blank check to develop a new series. "It was dark and grim, but he had a very strong vision for this kind of show. We basically said, you know more about having a hit show than just about anybody, so do whatever you want." The show hung on for three seasons but never achieved anything like the success of Carter's *X-Files*.

In January 1997 Roth finally got the new breakout hit he and the network needed. Although it was Matoian who had given the go-ahead for the show a year before, it was Roth who justly got the credit because he was the one who had initially sold it to FOX when he was head of Twentieth Century Television. Two years earlier Mike Judge, creator of MTV's animated *Beavis and Butt-Head* series, came to Roth and presented his idea for a new half-hour cartoon. Since FOX already had *The Simpsons*, which was still going strong, Roth saw this as something that could be promoted in conjunction with the established show. "In my office, on that very day, he pitched to me what became *King of the Hill*. He told me the funniest stories I'd ever heard about his own life in Austin, Texas, and about his neighbors. Literally, at that meeting, he pitched the voice of Hank Hill."

The show debuted strongly on Sundays at 8:30 P.M., even building on the lead-in audience of *The Simpsons*. *King of the Hill* accomplished what no show had done since the debut of *The Simpsons*: get people to tune into a prime-time animated series on a broadcast network. While cable produced the occasional hit like MTV's *Beavis and Butt-Head* or Comedy Central's *Dr. Katz, Professional Therapist*, there the stakes were much lower: cable still wasn't drawing audiences—or advertising revenue—comparable to the broadcast networks. The Big Three had tried to duplicate the success of *The Simpsons* several times, with such now forgotten entries as *Fish Police, Capitol Critters,* and *The Critic*, but they had all quickly failed. The success of *King of the Hill* was a lesson that Roth would not forget. Although the animation could still cause trouble, the economies of scale remained cheaper compared to a sitcom since the actors didn't have to record their voices all at the same time and the labor-intensive drawing process could be farmed out overseas.

Meanwhile the "branding" of FOX continued. Jim Cahill and Jim Atkinson, who had designed a new look for NBC back in 1994, were called in to create a new on-air image for the fourth network, something that would be distinctive and could be used in all promotion. By the February 1997 sweeps, the mood at the network was upbeat. Thanks to *The Simpsons*, *King of the Hill*, *The X-Files*, and another slate of reality specials, FOX's ratings were up. An analysis of their demographics provided good news as well. On Thursday nights, when NBC's powerhouse "must-see" lineup of *Friends*, *Seinfeld*, and *E.R.* had propelled the Peacock Network into first place for several years, FOX didn't even try to compete. Its Thursday schedule was squarely pitched at disfranchised African-American viewers, and it was paying off handsomely. While FOX Thursday-night shows ranked 100 or lower among all the week's prime-time shows for white viewers, *Living Single* had become the number one show among black viewers. The half-hour sitcom about African-American career women sharing an apartment, with a cast that included Queen Latifah and Kim Coles, had premiered in 1993. Other hits with black viewers included the multi-ethnic cop show *New York Undercover* that had bowed in 1994, and the sitcom *Martin* with stand-up comedian Martin Lawrence that had actually been airing since 1992. The lineup was classic counterprogramming. The strategy was the same one that the WB and UPN would use to get a foothold in the ratings for their fledgling networks.

Unfortunately it also foreshadowed the segregation of prime time into "white" shows and "black" shows on all the networks, which led to the eruption in the summer of 1999 against a new season that saw show after show premiere with all-white casts. Roth agrees that all the networks were guilty and thinks the public complaints have done more good than harm. "The NAACP is actually doing a service by forcing the networks to become aware again of the fact that they're ignoring African-American characters."

In the short run, Roth impressed the advertising community that FOX was breaking out of its slump both creatively and in terms of attracting viewers. "FOX's stuff is more identifiable than it was a year ago," one ad buyer told *Variety*. A snapshot of the season-to-date ratings in April 1997 tells the story. Advertisers seeking to reach women 18–49 faced the fact that the prime-time average on all the networks for such viewers was 28 percent of the audience. But on *Melrose Place* they made up 46 percent of the audience, as well as 45 percent of the viewership of *Party of Five* and 41 percent for *Beverly Hills 90210*. The prime-time average for men 18–49 was even lower at 21 percent, but sponsors targeting that demographic could buy time on *King of the Hill* knowing that 36 percent of its audience was in that range. For *The Simpsons* and *Married . . . with Children* it was 35 percent.

Of course all good things must come to an end, and in April it was announced that after ten seasons *Married . . . with Children* was finally calling it quits as of May 5, 1997. There would be no finale since the decision had been made after the last episode was already taped. Columbia Pictures Television had actually shopped an eleventh season of the series to UPN and the WB, but cast and other salaries had risen to the point where the cost per episode was now $1.5 million. When the final episode aired it ranked third in its time slot—but it came in first among both men and women 18–49. At the time it was the longest running sitcom on the air.

To take the sting out of the loss of their oldest (and, indeed, first) prime-time show, FOX received some surprising news. When the George Foster Peabody Awards were announced, *The Simpsons* and *The X-Files* received two of the four awards given to continuing series. The Peabodys are the most prestigious prizes given in broadcasting, and the recognition of two FOX shows indicated that

the network was now beginning to be recognized for the quality of
its programming, not just its success in drawing audiences and out-
maneuvering its rivals. *The Simpsons* was cited for its use of "biting
satire as social commentary" while the award to *The X-Files* com-
mended this "innovative and creative dramatic series which is reinvigorating the form."

Although John Matoian's departure and Peter Roth's arrival
were the biggest news at the network in the 1996–1997 season,
FOX was experiencing other executive shuffling as well. Some would
mark permanent changes while others would foreshadow shifts to
come. In October 1996 the FOX News Channel officially launched
its twenty-four-hour news service into seventeen million homes, directly challenging CNN for the cable news market. (They were soon
joined by the NBC/Microsoft hybrid MSNBC.) FOX News was derided
by some media critics as a "conservative" news channel, belying its
ongoing ad campaign that insisted it was simply reporting the facts
and "you decide." Still, when the distinguished TV journalist Brit
Hume left ABC after twenty-three years to become FOX News's chief
Washington correspondent and managing editor for political coverage, that had to be taken seriously.

That same month, one of the key behind-the-scenes players at
FOX began his exit. Preston Padden, who had alternately wrestled
with and cajoled both the affiliates and the FCC, decided it was time
to move on after nearly seven years. FOX had formed a partnership
with communications giant MCI to develop a domestic satellite TV
business, and Padden was put in charge. "I had told Rupert [Mur-
doch] that I was interested in running a business of my own for
him," said Padden. "So I left FOX to try to build this new corporation for FOX." Padden would be gone within a year and half when
his start-up was merged with another satellite operation, Echostar,
whose chief executive decided he didn't need a partner for day-
to-day operations. Padden moved on to ABC, briefly heading the

network, and then further up the food chain to become chief lobbyist for ABC's parent, the Walt Disney Company.

Padden's departure in October 1996 marked a turning point in the network's relationship with its affiliates, which would become more adversarial in the years ahead. Joe Young, who had run FOX's Indianapolis affiliate during the Padden years, said the relationship could sometimes be strained, but it was ultimately one of mutual respect. Padden had been nicknamed "the Enforcer" for coming down hard on affiliates whenever one of them preempted the FOX network's programming. But, as Young put it, "That was his job, and he was very good at it. He didn't care what he had to do, or what message or whatever he had to use, he got it done and he did it very, very well. . . . Was he very zealous about what he did and very passionate about what he did? Yes. Did he cross the line a few times? Absolutely. But he did a hell of a job."

Some would say Preston Padden was the consummate lawyer, cogently able to put forth whatever argument his employer required. But it was clear was that when the fight was over and an agreement was reached, Padden's word was his bond. "For the most part he's aggressive, but he was good for the network. He was an asset to the company," said Alabama FOX affiliate owner David Woods. "He would talk to you, he would tell you where you stand, but he told you to your face. You can deal with a man like that. . . . If you agree upon something with Preston, that was the deal."

In a sign of things to come, the department that had once been called "affiliate relations" was now known as "network distribution." Relations were about to get testy, and the absence of someone the affiliates respected would magnify an already tense situation.

In November 1996 Chase Carey, the "honorary Australian," continued his upward climb in the Murdoch media empire. While he was still chairman and CEO of the FOX Television Group, Carey was now the co–chief operating officer for the entire News Corp. operation. "He's a smart guy," commented Brian Lowry of the *Los Angeles Times*. "He gets stuff done, and he seems to be fairly content behind the scenes." Carey was not someone to second-guess what the people below him in the corporate organization were doing. When Greg Meidel was running Twentieth Television from 1992 to 1996, it was Meidel who insisted on checking in. "If I'd talk to Chase once a week it was only because I would go down and camp out in his office and demand that he talk to me. . . . Rupert had Chase on a fast track."

In January 1997 Peter Roth's old position at Twentieth Century Television was filled by none other than Sandy Grushow, who had been a FOX executive and even briefly ran the network between Lucie Salhany's departure in July 1994 and John Matoian's arrival that October. Grushow would prove to be a survivor at FOX by being able to take credit for the shows he provided FOX and not having to take the blame when the network stumbled. It didn't hurt that his unit was turning out successful series for other networks like ABC's *The Practice* and WB's *Buffy the Vampire Slayer*. With FOX now having so many outlets for its programming, a show like *Buffy* wasn't the one that got away. FOX made money by distributing the hit series. Then they sold it to their sister FX cable channel where it appeared in reruns as had *NYPD Blue* and *The X-Files*.

In June 1997 another FOX veteran departed when Bob Greenblatt left as head of prime-time programming. He had arrived in 1989 when Peter Chernin took Garth Ancier's place as the chief programming executive, and eventually succeeded to Chernin's old spot as his mentor moved up in the organization. Greenblatt had finally gotten fed up with the constant turnover in the executive ranks. "We were reeling from a presidential regime change every eighteen months. So every eighteen months there was a whole new vision and a whole new set of marching orders," he said. After eight years he was feeling burned out. "There were so many presidential changes in those last three years that it started to become very difficult to start completely over every year right when we were getting our footing." He left and formed a partnership with David Janollari, who had once worked on comedy development at FOX, and they've since produced a number of network shows, such as the ABC sitcom *The Hughleys* as well as the HBO smash *Six Feet Under*. In 2003 Greenblatt left production when he was named entertainment president of the Showtime premium cable channel.

One more change would not fully play itself out until the following season. Once more the curious duo of Pat Robertson and Rupert Murdoch found themselves doing business. In 1984 FOX had bought its Boston station WFXT from Robertson, who had originally launched it as an outlet for his Christian Broadcast Network. When that foundered, Robertson retreated to cable and the Family Channel, a safe haven for family-oriented programming. Now Robertson's media empire was in a cash crunch, and it was Murdoch who bailed him out. Murdoch now had FX, FOX News, the FOX Movie Channel, and FOX Sports (which included several regional channels and even a Spanish-language one), and he had been shopping for yet another cable outlet. For $1.9 million he became the proud owner of Robertson's Family Channel, which was soon rechristened the FOX Family Channel. That meant that Margaret Loesch, who had brought the FOX Kids Network to the pinnacle, would now be vice chairman of FOX's growing children and family division, including FOX Kids, FOX Family, and Saban Entertainment. The chairman, of course, was Haim Saban, who had retained his base of power when his company merged with FOX. Like Preston Padden, Loesch was about to learn what happened when you were asked to work with someone whom Rupert Murdoch needed but who in turn needed no additional partners in the operation beyond Murdoch himself.

CHAPTER THIRTEEN

"We're not *the establishment*"

[1997–1998]

	7:00	7:30	8:00	8:30	9:00	9:30
		THE FOX FALL PRIME-TIME SCHEDULE				
Sunday	World's Funniest Home Videos		The Simpsons	King of the Hill	The X-Files	
Monday			Melrose Place		Ally McBeal	
Tuesday			Movie			
Wednesday			Beverly Hills 90210		Party of Five	
Thursday			Living Single	Between Brothers	413 Hope St.	
Friday			The Visitor		Millennium	
Saturday			COPS	COPS	America's Most Wanted	

ENTERING the fall 1997 TV season, FOX Entertainment Group president Peter Roth had to be feeling nervous. He had launched several shows over the summer, arguing that part of FOX's image was in being unconventional and not doing what the Big Three did. "When are we going to stop this archaic system of not programming the third quarter?" he asked. "We are abdicating our control over the airwaves in the summer." Indeed, knowing that broadcasters typically used the summer months for reruns and to burn off unaired episodes of canceled series, cable outlets like HBO and the Comedy Channel planned their summer schedules to maximum advantage, using it to aggressively launch new programming. Roth pointed out that once upon a time FOX had done the same thing, using the summer to premiere shows that had gone on to be signature hits, like *Beverly Hills 90210* and *Melrose Place*. But because it ran against the grain of standard broadcasting practice—why pay for expensive new shows when the ratings indicated fewer people were staying home to watch television?—summer launches weren't done unless someone in authority, like Roth, insisted they be done.

FOX turned to Aaron Spelling to perform magic once again, even though his efforts after *Beverly Hills 90210* and *Melrose Place* on FOX had been misfires. Spelling's *Models, Inc.* was a spin-off from *Melrose*, starring Linda Gray and a bunch of beautiful unknowns, that launched in the summer of 1994. It was gone before the following spring. His *Kindred: The Embraced*, featuring C. Thomas Howell as a San Francisco police detective turned vampire hunter, had had a brief run in 1996. Now he was back with *Pacific Palisades*, a soap that had premiered in the spring and would continue running new episodes into the summer. Though it had been a weak performer in the spring, the hope was that it would catch on in the summer simply because it was new.

Also on the schedule was *Roar*, a medieval epic set in fifth century Ireland. The radio ads summed up the show as being about "hot Renaissance babes slapping each other around," getting both the time and the place wrong but attracting a lot of viewers for its July premiere. Roth's feeling was that dramatic serials like *90210*, *Melrose*, and *Party of Five* did not repeat well. By slotting new serials in the summer, FOX would have a schedule that was 40 percent original programming instead of nearly 100 percent reruns. David Hill said it was a risky strategy, but to do otherwise was to be "abdicating the summer to cable."

For Roth this scheduling of fresh programming in the summer was a matter of principle as well as a matter of personal vindication. "Frankly, to me, it extends back to when I was at ABC in 1980, when I was at a retreat and I was [then] the head of current programming," he would recall years later. He got up at one session when network president Frederick S. Pierce was taking questions and asked, "Why is it, sir, Mr. Pierce, that we're not doing original programming in the summer?"

Roth recalled being dismissed out of hand: "Because it's all economics. It's unaffordable to put on original programming in the summer because you can't make your money back in repeats. And original programming is expensive, young man, and therefore we won't do it."

While Roth agrees that reruns are a traditional part of the way the network gets its money's worth for the programs it buys, doing nothing but repeats in the summer months has turned into a recipe for disaster given the increased competition to broadcast television. Each year the networks suffer a smaller percentage of the total audience as viewers find increasingly more entertainment options ranging from cable to home video and DVD to the internet. Said Roth, "The shame of it is, the networks abdicated the airwaves in the summer. They allowed cable to flourish. The short-term economic gain is a long-term economic loss."

It was a great theory and, given the nature of the increasing competition in the business, a perfectly sound one. Unfortunately the shows Peter Roth had to offer didn't do the trick. *Pacific Palisades* flopped. *TV Guide* critic Jeff Jarvis lambasted it: "Soap mogul Aaron Spelling has blown it with his latest lathering, *Pacific Palisades*. . . . So far, it's just a show about a bunch of would-be young people who are either moral scumbuckets or pathetically clueless and who have nothing better to do than be nasty to one another." As the legendary movie producer Samuel Goldwyn is reputed to have said about a failed movie, people stayed away in droves. Another summer offering, *The Ruby Wax Show*, featuring a comic actress better known to British audiences for doing quirky celebrity interviews, came and went without a ripple. As for *Roar*, featuring newcomer Heath Ledger, it turned into the medieval counterpart of FOX's 1995–1996 *Space: Above and Beyond*. It attracted a cult following, but at a reported million dollars per one-hour episode, it wasn't worth the cost. None of FOX's new summer offerings survived to the fall schedule. The only bright spot was a four-hour miniseries based on the Dean Koontz novel *Intensity*, about a psychic woman (Molly Parker) on the trail of a serial killer (John McGinley). This suggested that original movies or miniseries might fare better in the summer when viewers didn't want to be locked into something every week. In spite of the failures, Roth continued to believe he was on the right track. "I'm a loud and ardent advocate of original programming year round."

The arrival of the fall must have been welcomed, but it got off to a rocky start. In late August 1997, two weeks before the network premiere of the half-hour sitcom *Rewind*, a new show starring Scott Baio, the show was yanked unceremoniously from the schedule. In an official statement, Roth said the series was "evolving"; reports indicated it might show up later in the season. It did not. It was replaced with the return of *Living Single* for its fifth season, preserving the Thursday lineup for counterprogramming by appealing to African-American viewers. Among the other Thursday offerings were *Between Brothers*, a sitcom starring Kelly Perine, Tommy Davidson (of *In Living Color*) and Kadeem Hardison (of the *Cosby* spin-off *A Different World*), and *413 Hope St.*, a one-hour drama created by Damon Wayans and featuring Richard Roundtree, who had played *Shaft* in the 1970s black action movie series. Neither clicked, but *Brothers* would eventually find a home on UPN.

The good news in the fall would be on Mondays, when FOX's third attempt at a lawyer show set in Boston would finally succeed.

D avid E. Kelley was a Massachusetts attorney who would rather be in show business. While still practicing in downtown Boston, he wrote a film script that was made into the 1987 movie *From the Hip*, with Judd Nelson. It wasn't a particularly good picture, but it did mark Kelley as a writer who knew his way around the courtroom. At the time, TV producer Steven Bochco was looking for scripters with legal backgrounds for his long-running NBC series *L.A. Law*. Kelley came on board as a writer, and by 1988 he had moved up to supervising producer. He would eventually succeed Bochco as executive producer of the series. Afterward he branched out on his own, and though his movie career has yet to take off, his TV track record is nothing short of remarkable, having created *Picket Fences* and *Chicago Hope* on CBS, and then *The Practice* on ABC. All mixed quirky comedy with serious drama, all touched on legal and ethical issues, with the latter focusing on a small but feisty Boston law firm.

When *The Practice*, starring Dylan McDermott, premiered in the spring of 1997, Kelley told interviewers that he was developing another lawyer show that would start that fall on FOX. It would be different from his previous efforts. No one at the time knew just how unique it would be.

Bob Greenblatt, then still at the FOX network as executive vice president of content programming, recalled, "We were fortunate enough to make a deal with David Kelley, and he wanted to do something very different from what he'd done before. He first pitched us . . . a show set in prison." FOX Group chairperson Peter Chernin, among others, thought it would be too grim. It wasn't what they were looking for in the time period. "Basically, Chernin and Roth said, Let's have David Kelley do his version of *Melrose Place*, because we targeted his show to be a companion to *Melrose*, which was on Monday nights at 8. We knew he wanted to do something different, but we wanted something adult, and romantic, and sexy."

He came back with *Ally McBeal*, yet another Boston lawyer show, but this one was quite different. The title character had fantasies about one of her male partners at the firm, but he happened to be married to someone else. The law offices had a unisex bathroom. Singer Vonda Shepard would appear as herself, doing songs that would comment on Ally and the action. (At least two soundtrack CDs would eventually be released.) Another partner, played by Peter MacNicol, was so eccentric his nickname was "the Biscuit." If Kelley was worried that his ideas were too weird for FOX, he needn't have concerned himself. Once the network executives saw the direction he was going in—quirky and eccentric, as opposed to dramatic—they let him have his head. "It was basically him going off and coming back to us and saying, 'Here's what I want to do.' And he basically did it," said Greenblatt.

Ally McBeal became a phenomenon. Here was a confused post-feminist woman who could succeed as a professional and yet still feel her life was empty without a man. People debated whether this was a good or bad thing, but for FOX the important thing was that people were not only talking about the show, they were watching it in increasing numbers. By the following June, the star Calista Flockhart was on the cover of *Time* magazine as Ally, sharing space with Susan B. Anthony, Betty Friedan, and Gloria Steinem, with the caption "Is Feminism Dead?" The attention was as welcome as it was laugh provoking. Said Kelley, "We never endeavored to create this role model for feminism or prototype for modern women. It's kind of amusing to see scholars taking our show a lot more seriously than we take it."

Then there was the gossip about the thirty-something Flockhart or, specifically, about her weight. Could anybody really be *that* thin? While undoubtedly annoying to the star, she could take solace in Oscar Wilde's epigram that the only thing worse than being talked about is *not* being talked about. *Ally McBeal* was hot and the second breakout hit for FOX since Roth's arrival the year before, following *King of the Hill.* FOX even gave the go-ahead for Kelley's most audacious move: a two-part episode that would start on *Ally* at 9 P.M. and conclude on *The Practice* at 10. Such crossovers between series had been arranged before, but this was different. FOX was, in effect, telling viewers to change the channel from their FOX station to continue the story on ABC, where *The Practice* aired. The two shows, which aired back to back on April 27, 1998, are so different in style that the stunt didn't quite work from a dramatic viewpoint. But it was a public relations bonanza, especially when some of the FOX affiliates threatened not to run *Ally* that night. Why, they argued, should they encourage people *not* to watch their 10 P.M. newscast and instead to change channels?

"I think it's terrible. The only people who will benefit will be ABC, its affiliates, and David E. Kelley," said Cullie Tarleton, general manager of FOX affiliate WCCB in Charlotte, North Carolina. "I'm disappointed that FOX didn't put up more of a fight, but they were trying to get as many original episodes as possible for the May sweeps, and this was one of Kelley's conditions." In the end, the stations carried *Ally*, but they weren't very happy about it.

It would not be the last time Kelley would suggest something unusual to FOX, nor the last time they would agree.

If the FOX affiliates were grumbling about a one-time programming stunt, it was related to their growing annoyance with the way the network was treating them. What was in the best interest of FOX was no longer perceived as in the best interest of the individual stations. The once-vaunted FOX Kids Network was still performing strongly, but now it had competition. ABC's retooled Saturday morning lineup was doing exceptionally well, but the real competition was coming from cable outlets like Nickelodeon, the Disney Channel, and the Cartoon Network. This came as no surprise to Margaret Loesch. She had lost rerun rights to *The Muppet Babies* cartoon series—which she had helped to create—to Nickelodeon, when it outbid FOX for airing them.

"From the very beginning we were looking over our shoulder," she said. Shortly after FOX Kids went on the air 1990, Nickelodeon commissioned its first original series, and Loesch saw the handwriting on the wall. "What I saw possibly could happen was that we would be outmuscled by cable just like we outmuscled the traditional networks."

By 1997 the stations were seeing it too as their numbers declined. The marketplace had changed again, and now FOX was behind the curve. The affiliates said the time had come to leave kids programming to cable and start programming for adults in the afternoon, which they felt would provide better lead-ins for the evening local and network shows. FOX Kids Worldwide, the new umbrella for all of the FOX family efforts, was looking at a far bigger picture, including international sales and its new FOX Family Channel. (In an unusual proviso, the purchase agreement for the Family Channel from Pat Robertson required Robertson's evangelical talk show, *The 700 Club*, to remain on the schedule.) In November 1997 it became clear to Loesch that she no longer had a real role to play in the operation that was increasingly being run by Haim Saban, and she resigned. She would spend some time at the Disney Channel (helping to develop a new generation of children's shows like *Bear in the Big Blue House*) before taking over as president and CEO of the Odyssey Channel in 1998, a family-oriented cable operation owned jointly by Jim Henson Productions and Hallmark Entertainment. She is currently in independent film production and launching a consulting business dealing with juvenile media properties. She calls her high-rolling years at FOX, from 1990 to 1997, "the most exciting time of my life."

After Loesch's departure it was decided that changes would be made in the way the FOX Kids Network operated. There was talk of selling off its inventory of old programming, which the stations owned jointly with FOX, and getting out of the kids broadcast business altogether, focusing instead on cable and international sales. Station owners foresaw another big check coming their way. They were also looking forward to starting to get some of the income for the FX channel, since that was part of their 1993 deal with FOX over retransmission consent. They had given FOX the right to negotiate on their behalf with the cable operators, and FOX had used that leverage to launch FX with the understanding that the stations would share in the resulting profits.

What happened, instead, was that the contract for NFL football came up for renewal in 1997. Suddenly FOX wasn't paying dividends but looking for every dime it could find. With four networks now fighting over TV rights to air the games—CBS was determined to get back in—it had become a seller's market. In the end, FOX, ABC, and CBS each got a piece of the action. The three networks also received a bill that, combined, totaled $18 billion. FOX's share of that was an estimated $4.5 billion. This time it was NBC that was left out in the cold, but instead of anger, NBC affiliate managers cheered NBC Sports president Dick Ebersol for not paying the record high prices being demanded by the NFL. FOX, ABC, and CBS responded to their increased costs by going to their affiliates and telling the stations they would have to help pay for football. Until then the Big Three affiliates had been used to receiving compensation for carrying network programming. FOX had dropped that tradition several years earlier, but it had never paid all that much compensation to begin with because it programmed far fewer hours per week for its affiliates than the Big Three did. Now, however, FOX and the other networks were expecting to be paid by the affiliates to help underwrite the cost of the NFL deal, and the affiliates balked.

What happened at FOX was unique in the industry because its relationship with its affiliates was unique. No other network had offered to engage in profit sharing from particular projects like cable channels or children's programming. Now FOX wanted it all back. Kevin O'Brien was one of the affiliate general managers who negotiated the deal on the FOX Kids Network. A former affiliate board president, he was looked at as one of the leaders among the stations and a tough adversary in disputes with FOX. Now he would try to carve out a fair deal, but it was one that would leave some with a bitter taste.

"One of the problems with the setup was, there was some feeling on the part of FOX that we didn't really own the [Kids] Network, that it wasn't really ours. That Rupert [Murdoch] had financed it, which he did, because when we had the chance . . . early on, at the very beginning, to ante up money, to truly own that network . . . nobody had the guts to want to do it," said O'Brien. "So the way I see it, is that we kind of took the easy way out. It's our idea, we'll own it, but we'll let Rupert finance it and then we'll pay him back, which we did, out of the profits."

The decision was made by the network to sell off the ownership rights to the previously aired FOX Kids Network shows, with the affiliates getting an appropriate share. The network handled the negotiations, and a deal was finally struck for $100 million—with the FOX Family Channel. Some station owners were outraged. "The whole FOX Kids Network was a rip-off. We owned it. It was owned by the affiliates, not the network," argued David Woods, owner of the Montgomery, Alabama FOX affiliate, WCOV, and an outspoken critic of the network's dealing with the affiliates. He felt they should have opened it up for competitive bidding. "When the deal was done we heard from Nickelodeon, we heard from the Cartoon Network. They would have paid twice as much for the library. Animation libraries are very scarce. . . . We've been told by the programming people at the cable networks that it was worth so much more than what they told us. You've got to figure it was an inside deal."

The stations never saw any profits from the sale. Instead they were applied to what was deemed to be the affiliates' share of the cost of airing football. Harry Pappas, the station owner who had come up with the idea for the Kids Network in 1989 and who was now helping Kevin O'Brien sell it off, felt it was the responsible thing to do. "It was only the FOX affiliates four years ago that were willing to step up to the line. ABC and CBS probably wouldn't be asking for help if they hadn't seen the FOX affiliates helping the last time." Ultimately Pappas, O'Brien, and some of the others felt they didn't have the best bargaining position, given the decline in ratings for children's programming on broadcast stations, and the nature of their ownership. "Legally, there was some question—I think we would have prevailed in the end—but there was some question as to who really owned this network, was it FOX or the affiliates?" said O'Brien. "We never got the money for it, and part of that was due to Hollywood bookkeeping. We got one check. We never determined where the hell the profits were going. There was a big stroke game going on."

The Kids Network deal looked settled, but the football compensation negotiations were far from over. Stations were adamant that they would *never* pay FOX for the privilege of being an affiliate and carrying the football games. "At this point, we're open-minded," said Murky Green, president of the affiliate board and general manager of WFLX, FOX's West Palm Beach, Florida affiliate. "We need to find a solution. It's not an 'us vs. them.'" Trade reports focused on battles among the ABC affiliates over network compensation for *Monday Night Football* and at NBC over the reported $13 million per episode the network would be paying for a new season of *E.R.* and which they hoped to pass off, in part, to their affiliates. The situation at FOX, by comparison, was supposed to be going smoothly, but when June 1997 rolled around and the affiliates arrived in Los Angeles for their annual meeting with no deal for affiliate payments to the network in place, it got ugly. FOX Group chairperson Peter Chernin told the attendees they were hurting the ability of the network to compete in the future. "The next time event programming becomes available, if FOX hesitates because of a worry about the financial consequences, it would be potentially disastrous for all of us."

In spite of the fact that the network had been hoping for a quick resolution, the fight over how the stations would help the network pay for its increased costs would spill over into the 1998–1999 season.

O ddly, in spite of these very real problems with the affiliates, the 1997–1998 season was probably the best in the history of the FOX network to that time. Only weeks before the affiliates meeting, FOX executives had gathered for an afternoon show and a big party on the other side of the country. This was its annual New York "upfront" presentation to the advertising community, where it would have ample opportunity to brag about the success of the past season and promote the next year's offerings.

It began with actress Jane Krakowski, dressed in a slinky white dress, vamping across the stage in front of a theater full of advertisers. Better known as secretary Elaine Bassell on *Ally McBeal*—the only breakout hit on *any* of the networks that season—she was now seducing the audience by promising that "the best is yet to come." Behind her, huge signs announced "Just One FOX," which might have been a comment on her performance but was actually the network's new battle cry. Krakowski drove the point home with a lyric written for the occasion, "FOX will blow your mind." The FOX presentation on May 21 was the last of the upfront sessions for potential sponsors, following CBS, ABC, NBC, UPN, and the WB. FOX had plenty to celebrate. Ratings for CBS's shows were continuing to skew toward older viewers while ABC was coming off one of its worst TV seasons in recent memory. Even first-place NBC—high off the much-hyped series finale of its smash-hit sitcom *Seinfeld*—would have to deal with the fact that next season it would be without both that comedy and NFL football.

As Krakowski finished her routine, the flamboyantly mustachioed Chase Carey, now chairperson and CEO of FOX Television, came out on stage. Carey exchanged an awkward embrace with Krakowski—she seemed unsure how to react to one of the distant "suits" who ran the network—and then proceeded to set the tone for the presentation that would follow. FOX no longer had to rely on promises that things would get better in the future. Now it would operate on its record, one that could withstand the scrutiny of the advertising community to whom he was playing. "The network business we find ourselves in today has changed immeasurably. All of the networks continue to contend with rising programming costs at the exact same time audiences are exercising a greater power of choice than ever before. These are the new economics of television, and it very clear they will continue to punish the ill equipped and unprepared," he told the audience. In addition to the people in the theater, he was also addressing advertisers in key cities around the country who were watching the presentation on closed-circuit television. Carey noted that the network had continued to build the identity of the FOX brand name and that their target audience had responded. "We stand on the cusp of a momentous achievement, which is to become the most popular network among adults aged 18–49."

Carey relinquished the podium to FOX Broadcasting Company president and CEO David Hill, who appeared to fancy himself a comedian. He quickly demonstrated why he was not doing stand-up professionally. "What we've experienced is very, very rare on FOX: yes, folks, we just cut away from the Chase," he announced, cueing the band for a rim shot, which came a few moments later. Hill soldiered on. "We know you've been in network limbo for the past four days, and you've seen more pilots than the human resources department at United Airlines," he quipped, requesting and receiving another rim shot. "I was going to tell a proctologist joke, but Peter Roth wouldn't let me." It was probably just as well.

The ebullient Australian, who seemed to be enjoying his material much more than his audience, finally got down to business, and here the FOX message came through loud and clear. "FOX got good news and bad news earlier this year. The good news is that the press has finally picked up on what you guys have known for years: that FOX is part of the Big Four. Now for the bad news. We have no intention of joining that establishment."

With that, the gigantic screen dominating the stage, which had been used for program clips and to identify the speakers, now lit up with a defiant message: "We're NOT the establishment." The signal to the advertisers was unambiguous. Having made it to the top of the heap through edgy, off-center, and sometimes controversial programming, FOX had no plan to change and go conventional. Hill went on. "At FOX we demand to be the alternative." (The TV screen agreed: "We're THE alternative.") "We've always liked being the underdog, the guy on the outside looking in. But now that, I guess,

we're perceived to be on the inside, we're going to make sure we
don't get comfortable." As he wound up and prepared to introduce
FOX Entertainment Group president Peter Roth, Hill's enthusiasm
got the best of him again. "There's a real urgency and excitement
that seems to have gripped our network, and it's almost intoxicated
the people who work there. Or maybe just simply they're getting
into the sherry again. Who knows?"

It was almost a relief when the comparatively sedate Roth began
speaking, even though one of the first things he shared with his audience was the notion that after a year on the job he was "still a little crazy" but enjoying running the network more than ever. His
task that day was to introduce the coming season's schedule, including mid-season replacements that wouldn't air until the following winter. His presentation would take more than an hour,
between lengthy clips and brief appearances by various FOX show
performers like Heather Locklear (Amanda from *Beverly Hills
90210*) and William B. Davis, Tom Braidwood, Dean Haglund, and
Bruce Harwood (the Cigarette Smoking Man and the Lone Gunmen, respectively, from *The X-Files*). But Roth was keenly aware of
what his captive audience really wanted to hear and he led off with
a triumphal review of the past season.

"Last night we finished what others might call the traditional
television season, and with it what can only be called a historic year
for our network. We've cruised past some real milestones, and we're
only getting started," he told them. For the first time FOX had
beaten ABC and CBS among adults 18–49 for the entire season. Since
that was the prime demographic revered by advertisers, this was
music to their ears and the room burst into applause. FOX had
clearly become a player. Second only to NBC in that demographic,
it had actually bested its top-rated rival in February 1997 when the
Peacock Network had ceded two weeks of the ratings period to CBS,
which was carrying the Winter Olympics. Roth went on. For the
first time, FOX had surpassed ABC in *total* viewers in a sweeps period.
Among adults 18–49, FOX was in first or second place five of the

seven nights of the week. What's more, he added, "even as our competition slid, our network grew on five of seven nights."

One bragging point failed to impress the advertisers, though it was a source of pride to Roth. Pointing to such FOX shows as *Ally McBeal, Party of Five, The Simpsons, King of the Hill,* and *The X-Files,* he said that "for the first time in our network's history [FOX's schedule] had led the prestigious Viewers for Quality Television to recommend a greater percentage of our lineup than any other network." Considering it was once the network primarily known for *Married . . . with Children,* that was quite a coup, but quality doesn't always translate into high ratings. The applause was brief and perfunctory.

After presenting the network's planned lineup for its 1998–1999 season, Roth concluded with a statement of the network's philosophy: "The key to keeping ahead of the scene is to be nimble, be opportunistic, and be aggressive. Our network is all that and much more. At FOX, we play one way and one way only. At FOX, we play to win."

Later Peter Roth would say that the 1997–1998 season had been "a fabulous year," the result of "a very clear strategy, a tremendous amount of hard work, and a lot of luck." While he was quick to share credit for FOX's triumph, no one could blame him if he wished to crow a bit. He had been brought in less than two years earlier to assist a network in trouble, and he had helped shepherd it to its greatest success to date. What no one at that May 1998 presentation could have guessed—least of all Roth—was that his moment of glory would prove to be the pinnacle of his career at the FOX network.

CHAPTER FOURTEEN

"They've run the numbers"

[1998–1999]

THE FOX FALL PRIME-TIME SCHEDULE

	7:00	7:30	8:00	8:30	9:00	9:30
Sunday	World's Funniest Home Videos	Holding the Baby	The Simpsons	That '70s Show	The X-Files	
Monday			Melrose Place		Ally McBeal	
Tuesday			King of the Hill	Costello	Brimstone	
Wednesday			Beverly Hills 90210		Party of Five	
Thursday			World's Wildest Police Videos		FOX Files	
Friday			Living in Captivity	Getting Personal	Millennium	
Saturday			COPS	COPS	America's Most Wanted	

"WE ARE in no way endorsing or glamorizing drugs," asserted Peter Roth at the July 1998 meeting of the Television Critics Association in Pasadena, California. The cause for his defensive declaration was a show that had been developed under the title of *Feelin' All Right* but had been renamed *That '70s Show*. The series had come from *3rd Rock from the Sun* creators Bonnie and Terry Turner, who had also been involved in the surprise 1995 hit movie version of *The Brady Bunch*. Although *That '70s Show* was not as knowingly campy as the big-screen *Brady Bunch*, the two efforts shared an arch attitude toward the 1970s as simultaneously a more innocent era and a time of fashion atrocities. In many ways it hoped to do in the 1990s what the 1950s throwback *Happy Days* had done in the 1970s: use the past to comment upon present. The problem for some of the critics was that this new program had not sufficiently cleaned up the past.

In the pilot episode Eric Forman (Topher Grace) and his friends smoke marijuana in his basement hangout, and when he goes upstairs to talk to his straitlaced parents (Kurtwood Smith, Debra Jo Rupp), the wallpaper in the kitchen appears to be sliding up the wall behind them. It was a great visual gag and one that would have been greeted with howls of laughter in the 1970s. It got laughs in the 1990s too, but now the show was accused of making drug use look like fun. Roth refused to back down. "We're not lying about it. We're not saying we didn't inhale," he told the assembled TV reviewers, and then noted that the scene had been shot so that the actual drug use was not shown on-camera. "How come you all knew what was going on? This is something that only those who personally recognize it will appreciate." Terry Turner added that doing a show about teenagers in the 1970s without acknowledging marijuana use "would be like doing *The Untouchables* without ever mentioning Prohibition." When anti-drug groups began criticizing the show, which had yet to air, Roth and the Turners discussed showing the consequences of drug use, but that was ultimately abandoned as a show guideline. "We're not going to turn this into an *ABC After-School Special*," Turner insisted.

Roth stood by *That '70s Show* and even set it as one of the first premieres of the new season on FOX, where it made its debut on August 23, 1998. Once again he had prevailed in programming original shows during the summer months, including scheduling several new episodes of *Melrose Place*. The network also had July premieres for *Guinness World Records* and *FOX Files*, the latter an attempt at a FOX-style newsmagazine show. Unlike the preceding summer, when the hot weather tryouts didn't last past the first autumn frost, both of these shows eventually found spots on the network's schedule, filling in gaps as other entries were canceled. *FOX Files* were needed rather quickly when problems developed with *Hollyweird*. Developed by horror director Wes Craven (*Nightmare on Elm Street*, *Scream*) and actor-turned-producer Shaun Cassidy (who had done the highly regarded CBS misfire *American Gothic*), the show was to follow a couple in their early twenties who solve bizarre crimes in Los Angeles while shooting material for their hometown public-access cable channel back in Ohio. There was dissatisfaction with the pilot, and the series was reconceived as centering on struggling artists in L.A. The original cast was told they would have to reaudition for the re-vamped pilot. In late August 1998 Shaun Cassidy had had enough. "After having spent much of the last year trying to fix something I never viewed as broken in the first place, I am withdrawing from the process of deconstructing *Hollyweird*," he declared.

Hollyweird never made it to the air. It was one of several development problems that arose that summer. For undisclosed reasons, executive producer Michael Cernuchin quit the supernatural drama *Brimstone* before its premiere. Then comedian David Chappelle and executive producer Peter Tolan pulled the plug on a show being developed for Chappelle, claiming the network was trying to make it less black oriented. Roth said he had wanted to broaden the appeal of the sitcom but denied that the argument was over adding white characters to the cast.

As the 1998–1999 fall season began, the trade paper *Variety* noted a troubling trend in television. In a corporate hierarchy with multiple chiefs, the job of president of network entertainment just wasn't as important as it used to be. CBS had just appointed Nancy Tellem as the second woman at a Big Three network to win the post, but she no more had the power to set the network's schedule than did ABC's Jamie Tarses. Lest sexism thought to be at play, it was noted that at FOX Peter Roth had a lot of power to develop shows, but executives such as FOX chairman and CEO David Hill, News Corp. president and chief operating officer Peter Chernin, FOX TV chairman Chase Carey, and ultimately News Corp. chairman Rupert Murdoch were there when the fall schedule was set. One would think this shared decision-making would lead to shared responsibility for the successes and failures of that schedule, but that was not the case.

FOX was about to launch one of its poorest fall lineups in years. *That '70s Show* started strong, sputtered, but ultimately hung on. It wouldn't truly catch on until the summer reruns. Meanwhile the other new shows began dropping like flies. The worst of them was *Holding the Baby*, which took the hoary sitcom plot of the single dad and the nanny, and then did almost nothing with it. The reviews were scathing. "How does FOX plan to fight [CBS's] *60 Minutes* this fall?" asked one. "Well, it doesn't—at least not from 7:30–8 P.M. on Sundays, where the web has all but tossed in the towel with this glaringly unoriginal new comedy. . . ." Another review called the concept "well-worn, and the writing is, more often than not, pedestrian."

By early October 1998 the FOX schedule was a shambles. The move of *King of the Hill* to Tuesdays at 8 P.M. had been a traditional TV chess move: take a hit show from one night and use it to lead off another evening. FOX had successfully done it years before with *The Simpsons*. This time viewers were not following. Worse, the effort that was supposed to build on *King*'s lead-in, the South Boston–set crude comedy *Costello*, was pronounced dead on arrival. It was canceled after only three episodes, with the fourth and final installment airing October 13. It was the first new show of the season to be axed on any of the networks. It was replaced by reruns of *King* through the November sweeps period. The attempt to create a Friday night sitcom block with the new *Living in Captivity*, a satire about suburbia from veteran *Murphy Brown* producers Diane English and Joel Shukovsky, and the second season of the workplace comedy *Getting Personal*, fared no better and were soon off the schedule.

Next up was *Brimstone*, about a good cop (Peter Horton) who is sent to Hell for avenging his wife's murder and now has the chance to redeem himself by recapturing escapees from the afterlife. John Glover played the Devil with relish. Since there were 113 souls involved in the hellish jailbreak, there was theoretically enough mate-

rial available for several seasons of episodes. Unfortunately *Brimstone*
had to compete with sitcom hits like ABC's *Spin City* and NBC's *Just
Shoot Me*, as well as a new WB show called *Felicity*. *Brimstone* was soon
sent back to the netherworld, but it was emblematic of what FOX was
now facing. Ten years earlier FOX had been the guerrilla network going up against the stuffy Big Three. Now the four, in turn, had competition from upstarts like UPN and the WB, the latter under the
control of FOX alumni Jamie Kellner and Garth Ancier. "I don't particularly look at us as one giant audience anymore," said Kellner
about WB's strategy. "I look at us as groups of viewers that have to try
to be satisfied." With *Felicity*, the WB lucked on to what became one
of the cult successes of the season, the ongoing story of an attractive
young woman (Keri Russell) attending college and making it on her
own in the Big Apple. *Brimstone* never had a chance.

Both the WB and UPN declared that they were targeting the
18–34 demographic exclusively, and had no intention of going for a
broader audience, as FOX had by shifting its focus to adults 18–49.
The distinction between 18–34 and 18–49 might seem to be relatively insignificant, but for advertisers and programmers it's the difference between, for example, who watches MTV and who watches
The X-Files. There's overlap to be sure, but since advertisers pay on
the basis of how many people are estimated to be tuned in to a given
show, a studio promoting a twenty-something movie that advertises
it on *X-Files* would be paying for viewers it didn't need and who
wouldn't be responding to the ad anyway. General media reporting
on the TV ratings inevitably ignored the demos and relied on the
general audience "household" figure, rather than try to make sense
of the literally dozens of ways the audience can be dissected and an-
alyzed. In this instance the TV journalists were way behind the industry in their understanding of what ratings really matter.

With the failure of *Brimstone*, FOX's hopes were left hanging on
the new season of *The X-Files*. Now in its sixth season, the show
still did well, but the premiere was down in the ratings from the
previous season. Critics wondered whether the show had peaked.

The X-Files movie had been released by Twentieth Century–Fox that summer to okay results; it wasn't a blockbuster hit, but it wasn't a resounding flop either. But some *X-Files* fans might have been feeling cheated when the movie advanced but did not resolve the mysteries making up the core premises of the show. Was series creator Chris Carter unwilling—or unable—to do so? Although *The X-Files* remained a mainstay of the FOX schedule, it was pointed to, along with *Melrose Place*, *Beverly Hills 90210*, and even *The Simpsons*, as a series that may have overstayed its welcome. *Melrose* would indeed wrap up in the spring, and the joke about *90210* was that in the already extenuated plotline they'd eventually have to hold the class reunion at a senior citizens home.

This was supposed to be the season when FOX would surpass NBC in the vital 18–49 demographic. Instead it was battling neck and neck with CBS, a network that continued to be considered a place for older viewers. The World Series in October 1998 provided a welcome ratings shot in the arm, as would the Super Bowl in January 1999, but a network's bread and butter are the regular series, not the special events.

Finally, in November 1998, Peter Roth was informed that there would be a corporate restructuring. This would allow him to resign since the change constituted a technical breach of his contract. In an interview a year later, Roth said he felt he was being blamed for the fact that most new shows each season fail on all the networks. "It is a truism that if you go back to 1990, at any and every network there's an 84 percent failure rate," he said, pointing out that the previous year, deemed a smashing success, had produced only one major hit for FOX, *Ally McBeal*. After he left, three more shows that Roth had announced for the schedule would premiere—*The PJs*, *Family Guy*, and *Futurama*—and all would do well enough to be renewed for a second season, as would *That '70s Show*. "The success ratio of the year I lost my job was actually greater than the previous year, which is counted as one of the great years of all time," he said.

Roth was quick to accept blame for what went wrong. "There was failure, no question about it," he said. "*Costello* failed. For that I take responsibility. *That '70s Show* worked. For *that* I take responsibility. And that's how it works."

Having compiled an impressive track record, why would his mistakes in the fall of 1998—made with the knowledge if not the total complicity of Rupert Murdoch, Chase Carey, David Hill, and Peter Chernin—have been cause for dismissal? First, many of the season's new entries came from producers with track records on the Big Three. In addition to pedigreed series like *That '70s Show* and *Living in Captivity*, *Costello* had come from Wind Dancer Productions, which was responsible for the huge ABC success *Home Improvement*. There was some feeling in the executive suite that it was time for FOX to move in a different direction than Roth had been going.

Still, the middle of the November sweeps is an odd time to announce a major shakeup at a network. Something else was on the minds of the News Corp. executives that fall, and that was the initial public stock offering for the FOX Entertainment Group. It gave investors a chance to own an entity that would include the FOX network, Twentieth Century–Fox's movie and TV production companies, the FOX o-and-o station group, and the growing number of FOX cable channels (though only a partial stake in FX and FOX Family Channel). The offering of 85 million shares was snapped up quickly (at $21 to $24 per share), even though the new company would own less than one-seventh of all the FOX operations. News Corp. would continue to retain control over everything. It almost didn't matter. The demand for stock was so great that FOX ended up expanding the offering to 124.8 million shares. As a result, News Corp. was flush with $2.8 billion in new cash. Seen in that light, the firing (or, officially, the resignation) of Roth can be taken as a reassurance to Wall Street that the FOX network did and would remain under Murdoch's firm control.

Although Roth was given a face-saving production deal (Hill even went so far as to state that he hoped FOX would be Roth's first and only stop for any new TV shows he developed), he would go on to become president of Warner Bros. Television, the production arm of that corporation. There he did the same thing he had done at Twentieth Century Television: produce product for all the networks.

Peter Roth would not depart until January 1999, but attention in the industry immediately focused on his replacement. Doug Herzog was not a broadcasting executive but a cable guy. He had first made his mark at MTV, then moved over to run Comedy Central. He refocused the comedy channel to target young men, scoring its biggest hit with the animated *South Park*. It was a half-hour show about little kids in a Rocky Mountain town. The material was so outrageous that Herzog would schedule it only for late evening so that he wouldn't repeat the controversy MTV had endured when a youngster set a fire in imitation of a sequence on MTV's *Beavis and Butt-Head*.

"I want to take risks," Herzog told reporters in November 1998. "FOX is committed to breaking the rules. I have doubts as to whether *South Park* could air in its current form on broadcast TV, but hell yeah, I'd love to try to get it on." David Hill touted Herzog as "the breath of the future," but others were skeptical. An unnamed executive at a competitor took a shot, telling *Variety*, "Herzog's hire is for Madison Avenue. They are saying, 'We have a comedy problem. Hire someone from Comedy Central.'"

Herzog had first been approached by Peter Chernin, and he had no idea why he was being wooed by FOX. Initially he thought they might be offering him the FX channel, even though Peter Liguori had recently been brought on board. Maybe they were having second thoughts? He was stunned when it was the FOX network post he was offered instead. Herzog wasn't sure he was up to it. "I was a complete interloper," he would later recall. "I had not spent one minute in the network television business before arriving at FOX. The only scripted show I'd ever done in my life was *South Park*. And I had a hell of a lot to learn and a short time to do it."

Herzog's problem, of course, was that he was coming into FOX in January 1999, in the middle of the TV season. He could move the pieces around, but the game was already in motion. Not until the following fall could he begin to put his own stamp on FOX. In the short run that gave him some freedom to operate since he couldn't be justifiably blamed for decisions that were made before he arrived. "I was literally thrown in the deep end of the pool here and told to swim, and I've just jumped in with both feet," he told the trade publication *Broadcasting & Cable* that September. While he would have to touch base with Murdoch, Chernin, and—for a while at least—David Hill, he was left alone. "No one is standing right over me. And people are always saying to me that it must be terrible, and there are all these people looking over your shoulder. No, it's actually kind of cool. The biggest disappointment has clearly been the cafeteria, which hasn't changed its menu since Barry Diller was here."

Still, Herzog knew it was better to lower expectations if he had any hopes of surviving in a tough job where no one since the Diller days ended in 1992 had lasted more than a couple of seasons. He declared he would have a lot to learn: "I'm sure a lot of people are going to think I'm an idiot for the first six months."

While Herzog began learning, as well as relocating his family from New York to Los Angeles, the shows that Peter Roth had already put in the pipeline as mid-season replacements began appearing on the air. In a cruel twist of fate, the man who was fired because he couldn't get a half-hour comedy to succeed on the air in the fall scored three times with half-hour comedies in the winter and spring. The only difference was that they were all animated.

All three got their turn in the treasured Sunday 8:30 P.M. slot, right behind *The Simpsons*. First up was *The PJs*, an odd collaboration between comedian Eddie Murphy and the Will Vinton Studios, best known for the TV commercials featuring the "California Raisins." Rather than traditional cel animation, which is how most cartoons are produced, Vinton preferred a process called Claymation, which involved photographing three-dimensional clay models.

Murphy provided the voice of the lead character, Thurgood Stubbs, the superintendent at a housing project who mixes into the lives of the neighbors. The program generated a storm of controversy before the first show aired, when black activists blasted the show for stereotypes and for making light of serious problems like poverty, alcoholism, and drug abuse. Even film director Spike Lee piled on Murphy, saying, "I kind of scratch my head why Eddie Murphy's doing this, because it shows no love for black people. I'm not saying we're above being made fun of and stuff like that, but it's really hateful, I think, toward black people. Plain and simple."

Larry Wilmore, co-creator of the series with Murphy and Steve Tompkins, wasn't phased by the attacks. "We tried to shrug it off as much as possible," he recalled. "We thought we were having fun with individual people and not with that whole thing. And also it was a satirical show. We were being respectful at the same time, but part of irreverence is going out on a limb."

Next up was *Family Guy*, a seeming clone of *The Simpsons* in that it was a cartoon about a loving but comically dysfunctional family. Yet it had its own seriously bent humor, courtesy of twenty-five-year-old creator Seth MacFarlane. The dog was the family intellectual, while baby Stewie was an evil genius who was constantly building death rays to make the world safe for people who hate broccoli. *Family Guy* premiered in the favored slot right after the Super Bowl but wouldn't begin its regular run until April 1999 where, to the surprise of many, it was given the prime post-*Simpsons* position.

It was surprising because the third animated offering was *Futurama*, the long-awaited new project from Matt Groening, who had created *The Simpsons*. Set a thousand years in the future, it followed the adventures of a pizza delivery boy who was accidentally frozen and then revived ten centuries later. Although it failed to reach the comic brilliance of *The Simpsons*, critics and viewers understood that—as with the earlier show—that would take time. When it began its run in March behind *The Simpsons*, the lineup was such a natural that people couldn't figure out why *Futurama* was then switched to Tuesdays, in a new animation block that would include *King of the Hill* and *The PJs*. To go from Groening's *Simpsons* to Groening's science fiction spoof to *The X-Files* would seem to be the prime illustration of the concept of audience flowthrough. Instead *Futurama*'s ratings dropped when it aired on Tuesdays, as did the previously successful *King of the Hill*.

All three shows would be renewed for the 1999–2000 season, meaning that Roth had put four shows on the schedule that season that would survive. *Futurama* would be returned to Sunday. Meanwhile problems would continue to dog *The PJs* and *Family Guy*. *The PJs* was renewed for a full season of episodes but then not placed on the upcoming fall schedule. Eddie Murphy was so angry at the treatment that he walked off the show, and actor Phil Morris was called in to voice Thurgood for a few episodes. But FOX made it clear that it liked the show and that it would be on the schedule, and apologized for any real or perceived slight. *The PJs* would eventually move to the WB for its third and last season. *Family Guy* would also struggle through a few seasons and then find a devoted cult audience on the Cartoon Network and on DVD.

Animation proved to be a problem elsewhere on the 1998–1999 schedule. The FOX Kids Network had seen its glory days, but now like everyone else in broadcasting, it was having more and more difficulty competing with cable's Nickelodeon, the Disney Channel, and the Cartoon Network. *Mighty Morphin Power Rangers* had been a huge hit in the mid-1990s, but its original fans had outgrown it, and the next group of youngsters was already on to something else. Even renaming the series *Power Rangers Turbo* couldn't halt the decline in ratings. Haim Saban, who had brought the show to FOX Kids and was now in total control of its parent, FOX Family Worldwide, might have been expected to take an interest, but his attention was focused elsewhere. Saban and Rupert Murdoch were instead putting their efforts into the reinvention of the FOX Family Channel, and launching it into other markets around the world.

In February 1999 FOX and its affiliates made a deal that would involve the network dropping its low-rated hour of cartoons on weekday mornings in return for FOX claiming some of the affiliates' ad time for itself during the two-hour kids' block in the afternoon. As part of the new arrangement, the afternoon programs and the four-hour FOX Kids block on Saturday mornings would now include promos urging kids to watch FOX Family Channel. It made sense from FOX's perspective, but it was a bitter pill for the affiliates, who saw their stations being used to promote what they saw as competition. "As far as the FOX Kids Network deal, we have to promote the FOX Family Channel every day, six days a week—Saturday mornings included—for ten years. The value of that promotional time is more than the price they paid for the entire Kids Network," grumbled affiliate owner David Woods in Alabama. "If you watch FOX Kids Afternoon, every twenty minutes you'll see a promotion for the FOX Family Channel." (By 2001 the Family Channel was no longer FOX's problem. They had sold it to ABC.)

The relationship between the network and the affiliates had clearly changed. Stations traditionally complained about the heavy-handed methods used by the networks, but at least they saw they had a common interest. Now some affiliate owners and managers were arguing that FOX had forgotten they had ever been partners in creating the network. (The FOX-owned station group was not affected by any of this since everyone there was a FOX employee. What was good for the network was considered good for the station.)

Tribune's Patrick Mullen, one of the moderates among the FOX affiliates, recalled that in the old days "if they gave us a reason as a group to say this isn't working, we're out of here. So they had to make it work. They didn't have the leverage. . . . Now they've built a network which they feel that we as stations would be in huge financial trouble if we were to say we're no longer going to support it, we're going to walk away, we're going to retreat to our independent days. They've run the numbers. They know what kind of revenue the network generates for the station, and I think they've calculated exactly how much our profits would be if we were to walk away from the network, and they're willing to use that leverage accordingly. The leverage has shifted."

Kevin O'Brien of KTVU was another station executive fiercely loyal to the network, though he had been a thorn in the side to more than one FOX official. He also sensed a shift in the past few years. "The FOX executives that are initiating this now were not involved in the dark days, back in the failure days, and have no appreciation for the loyalty and dedication that the affiliates who stuck with it really exhibited during those difficult days of constant failures, of loss of income. . . . What disturbs me is that the folks at FOX have a very short memory about what I consider to be the true heroes of this incredible dynasty now, and that were the original affiliates that made FOX what it is today. . . . Instead of reaping those rewards as we should and the respect that we should have gotten, basically we're treated like cattle, in a lot of cases, by very difficult demands placed upon us by FOX executives."

The blowup occurred in April 1999 when FOX demanded nearly one-quarter of the local commercial availabilities in prime time to be returned to the network. That meant less prime-time ad spots to sell locally, and an estimated loss of up to $175 million in revenue to the stations annually. The network was desperate for new sources of revenue to cover the rising costs of new shows, sports acquisitions, and other ventures. With local stations running at high profit margins, they were an obvious target. In practical terms this meant that FOX was reducing the number of thirty-second spots available for sale by local stations during prime time from ninety to seventy. The fact that FOX had given its affiliates more spots per half hour in the early days of the network, as a way of making up for the paltry network compensation, didn't matter. The affiliates had grown used to the arrangement and resented the unilateral way FOX was now acting. Instead of approaching the affiliates and asking for help, which would at least have softened the blow, the bad news was announced by network president Larry Jacobson during a monthly conference call with the affiliate board. Chase Carey personally called some of the more important station group owners. "It is necessary to make an adjustment to the economic relationship between the network and the FOX affiliates to take into account the ever-widening imbalance in profits between us," Jacobson later wrote in a letter to the affiliates.

The other TV networks too were playing hardball with their affiliates. ABC had gone so far as to stop negotiating with its affiliate board over how the affiliates would contribute financially for *Monday Night Football*. The network announced it would now deal with stations and station groups individually. At least FOX and its affiliate board were still talking, if only barely. Quipped WCOV owner David Woods, "They don't call it affiliate relations, they call it network distribution. You know why they call it network distribution? Because they don't relate to their affiliates."

The network's motives were further questioned when FOX offered a compromise. They would now allow the stations to "buy back" the twenty spots at below-market rates, permitting them to sell the time locally and keep the difference. Most of the affiliates refused even to dignify the offer with a response, and there was a suggestion that the matter could end up in court, with some stations claiming that FOX's action violated the current affiliation agreement. The proposed FOX plan would also allow the stations to get fifteen more prime-time spots on top of that, at a cost of 25 percent of what they sold them for. Explained KJTV station owner Brad Moran, "What they were doing is tapping into the local station's ability to sell for a higher cost per thousand [viewers] than the network would get in the national marketplace to sell an ad."

A compromise was finally worked out in May 1999: FOX resold the twenty spots back to the stations for a flat fee, and sold them an additional fifteen spots for the same flat fee. In some markets it would be a wash—the additional income from the fifteen new avails would cover the cost of the payment to FOX for the thirty-five spots. For the network it was a victory in the sense that it would reap an estimated $50 to $75 million per year from the deal—but that turned out to be far short of the $175 million envisioned originally.

In June FOX told the affiliates they could renegotiate their own retransmission deals with cable operators when the contracts came up for renewal that summer. It was an easy concession since FOX had already used the leverage of the original retransmission negotiations to trade the rights to carry FOX stations on local cable outlets to launch the FX cable channel in 1994. In the original agreement, stations would share in the profits of FX, but the network had long since reclaimed any such payments in order to pay for NFL football. FOX also could dispense with the added leverage since it now had several cable channels up and running. The network did reserve the right to a share in any money the stations received for the retransmission rights, but since none was expected to change hands, that was strictly hypothetical.

I n a show of who held the real power at the network, FOX chairman and CEO David Hill did not follow Peter Roth out the door because of the disastrous fall 1998–1999 season. While Hill had been placed in charge of the entire network at the time Roth arrived, he was rewarded in June 1999 with a promotion to the post of chairman and CEO of the new FOX Sports Television Group. He would be in charge of all FOX sports operations worldwide.

That was good news for Hill but bad news for Doug Herzog. The planning for the 1999–2000 season was already well under way when Herzog arrived, with development deals and pilot orders mostly in place. "There were certainly decisions to be made, but I didn't necessarily get to come in and put my imprimatur on everything because of the timing. I got there in January, and we were announcing a fall schedule in May. So, in network parlance, there was not a hell of a lot of time to conjure things up," he recalled.

Herzog also faced the situation without much of a support network. Hill, he said, "was one of my few bigger, vocal supporters." Now, with little experience, Herzog was expected to swim on his own among the network sharks. Particularly troubling were rumors that he was just marking time and that all television operations would soon be consolidated under Sandy Grushow, who was then running the television studio operation. Herzog was assured that, as at Comedy Central, he would remain his own boss. But it was also made clear that he would have a limited time to prove himself.

If Herzog had reason to be nervous, so did many affiliate station owners. Many feared that the network would be happier not having to deal with affiliates and would rather go it alone. They could not have been reassured by the news from Washington, D.C.: that same month FOX and all twenty-two members of its station group resigned from the National Association of Broadcasters (NAB), the industry's trade and lobbying organization. NAB had been fighting any increase in the FCC's cap on the number of stations any one group could own, while FOX—which already had 40 percent coverage of the country on its own stations—wanted them raised or repealed. "Our view was that to pay money for a trade organization to lobby against us was not a smart thing to do," said Peggy Binzel, who had succeeded Preston Padden as FOX's official lobbyist.

What was significant about the problems with the affiliates and FOX's resignation from NAB was just how much had changed. In a world where FOX had once needed all the friends it could get, the network was now making it clear that it no longer needed anyone else.

CHAPTER FIFTEEN

"I never got a real at bat"

[1999–2000]

	7:00	7:30	8:00	8:30	9:00	9:30
Sunday	The World's Funniest!	King of the Hill	The Simpsons	Futurama	The X-Files	
Monday			Time of Your Life		Ally McBeal	
Tuesday			Ally	That '70s Show	Party of Five	
Wednesday			Beverly Hills 90210		Get Real	
Thursday			World's Wildest Police Videos		Family Guy	Action
Friday			Ryan Caulfield: Year One		Harsh Realm	
Saturday			COPS	COPS	America's Most Wanted	

THE FOX FALL PRIME-TIME SCHEDULE

NOW DOUG HERZOG would have a chance to put his own stamp on the network. Most shows were already in the pipeline when he had arrived in January, but the scheduling and promotion of the new season would be in his hands. The show he hoped would make his reputation was *Action*.

"The idea of doing conventional sitcoms made me ill, especially where I made a career out of not doing such things," he would later recall. "I decided to hang my hat on *Action*, probably wrongly, because it's a tough show to put over on a network."

Action was a satiric half-hour sitcom set at a movie studio. Comedian Jay Mohr was cast as a profane executive who screws over anyone in his path as he desperately tries to achieve the material success by which he is measured by everyone from fellow producers to the maitre d's at the trendiest restaurants. Several real-life film stars, like Keanu Reeves and Sandra Bullock, appeared in episodes as themselves, adding a neat twist to the satire. What caught everyone's attention was that the scripts would not use euphemisms for the profanities that still could not be heard on broadcast television. The key word was "heard," since the show's gimmick was that while Mohr and others would utter the words, but they would be bleeped out before hitting the airwaves. The problem was that *Action* was paired with *Family Guy* on Thursdays in the killer time slot of 9–10 P.M., which was still owned by NBC's blockbuster "Must See TV" lineup. *Action* generated a lot of buzz, but it never found its audience and was canceled before all its episodes had aired.

Action proved to be only the most obvious of FOX's problems that fall. Several FOX signature shows were either gone or near the ends of their runs—including *Melrose Place*, *Party of Five*, *Beverly Hills 90210*, and *The X-Files*—so Herzog's prime job was to create some new hits. Instead a number of shows were quickly cycled through the schedule, with one of them never making it to the air at all. *Manchester Prep* was pushed back to a December launch and then canceled. It was inspired by the 1999 teen movie *Cruel Intentions*, which was in turn inspired by the novel and movie *Dangerous Liaisons*. With teenagers using sexual blackmail and engaging in other depraved behavior in *Cruel Intentions*, the proposed TV series was shut down as those involved tried to figure out just how far they could go on air and what sorts of story arcs they ought to be developing.

"It wasn't working," said Herzog. "It kind of veered on camp."

Then there were the shows Herzog inherited whether he wanted them or not. "Nothing is done till it's done, but we were going to do the Chris Carter show, and we were going to do the Jennifer Love Hewitt show, come hell or high water, for a lot of different reasons," he said. "Chris Carter had a big commitment, and obviously *The X-Files* was a very valued member of the News Corp. team. And Jennifer Love Hewitt was coming off *Party of Five* and was kind of a big deal. And everybody was like, 'Of course we'll do a show with Jennifer Love Hewitt on FOX. That's perfect. Whatever it is, we'll do it.'"

Harsh Realm was the new project from Carter, taking the place of Carter's canceled *Millennium* on Fridays. It involved a soldier (Scott Bairstow) entering a virtual-reality war game and then realizing he is stuck inside its universe. Unfortunately the show premiered in early October. The obvious way to reach potential viewers would have been by heavily promoting it on Carter's *The X-Files*, which wouldn't begin its new season until November. By that time *Harsh Realm* was already gone. (All nine episodes that had been shot for the series, including ones that didn't air, were eventually shown on the FX cable channel.) It didn't help that no one at the network would champion Carter's show until it could gain some traction—assuming it ever did.

It was further complicated because Fox and Carter were involved in an ugly lawsuit over *The X-Files* that had been brought by star David Duchovny. The actor was suing the studio, claiming that in syndicating reruns of the show to FX cable and to broadcast stations (including the FOX o-and-o's) they had lowered the price to the other FOX units in order to reduce the profits of which Duchovny was entitled to a percentage. Although Carter was not a party to the suit, Duchovny alleged that Carter knew what was going on and was paid to go along with it. Could part of that supposed payment have been the greenlighting of *Harsh Realm*?

Duchovny's complaint was brutal: "FOX sits at both sides of the bargaining table in any negotiation for the distribution rights to [the show], thereby enabling it to manipulate negotiations in any way that serves its corporate interests." Nevertheless Duchovny was still agreeing to appear on *The X-Files*, though cutting back his participation. By May he settled for an undisclosed amount and agreed to several appearances in what would prove to be the final 2000–2001 season of the show.

For his part, Herzog had nothing whatsoever to do with the lawsuit, and the scheduling of *Harsh Realm* was also beyond his control.

When the show tanked, however, he pulled the plug as he did on several other series that fall. Chris Carter did not take the cancellation lightly. He told the trade press, "I have a feeling we're part of a much bigger problem [at FOX]."

Meanwhile another public failure was also laid at Herzog's doorstep. Once again it was a matter of having to go along with one of the major players on its schedule, David E. Kelley, creator of *Ally McBeal*. Like its lost opportunity in failing to premiere *Harsh Realm* before *X-Files*, FOX debuted the *Ally McBeal* spin-off *Ally* before the original show started its third season. Perhaps nothing could have saved this bizarre effort at recycling. The prolific Kelley proposed a half-hour sitcom that would be made up of material from *McBeal*'s first two seasons mixed in with previously unseen outtakes.

At first Herzog thought Kelley was proposing changing his hour show into a half-hour sitcom. Talking with the producer on his car phone while driving to work, Herzog recalled, "I literally almost had a heart attack and drove off the road." Perhaps he should have tried to talk Kelley out of it, but the producer was more in demand than ever, having won Peabody Awards for two of his shows: ABC's *The Practice* and FOX's *McBeal. Ally* was a flop. It was unceremoniously yanked off the schedule before the November sweeps and subsequently canceled.

In a season of admitted disasters, Herzog felt that *Ally* may have been merely ahead of its time. "Everybody fell in love with David's idea," he recalled. "Mr. Chernin was a big supporter of that. You know, it was an interesting idea, a noble failure. Look at how repurposing has become a staple of network television." Certainly running shows on broadcast and on cable to boost the audience invested in a program has caught on, but thus far the reformatting of an hour dramatic series—even a quirky one—into a half-hour show has yet to succeed.

Now, though, the clock was ticking, and Herzog was in trouble on two fronts. First came the announcement in November 1999 that Sandy Grushow's rehabilitation at FOX was complete. After several years of exile after briefly filling in for Lucy Salhany after she had departed, Grushow had been running the television studio. Now he would be the chairman of the FOX Television Entertainment Group, where he would oversee not only the studio but the network as well. He would become, in effect, Herzog's boss. For Herzog, the handwriting was on the wall.

"I was no longer the guy in charge," he said. Now all of his actions were subject to Grushow's stamp of approval. "Sandy came in, and Sandy's a hands-on guy. The dynamic had changed."

For his part, Peter Chernin tried to put the best face on it. He said Grushow's promotion shouldn't be taken as an attack on Herzog or a reflection of FOX's dreadful fall. "A guy who comes in in the middle of January isn't responsible for this. To the degree there are problems at FOX, they're years in the making. To blame Doug for this year is stupid."

Nonetheless Herzog still had a schedule to fill, and the network was running out of shows. *Ryan Caulfield: Year One* was canceled, and young-skewing hour-long dramas like *Get Real* and the *Party of Five* spin-off *Time of Your Life*, with Jennifer Love Hewitt and Jonathan Saech, started off weakly in the ratings. Herzog had very little to put on in their stead.

During his first six months at the network, Herzog was still living in New York City and commuting back and forth to Los Angeles. Every Friday he'd catch a flight back east, with a pile of scripts to read. "Somebody on my comedy staff said, 'I think you should read this script. I think you'll really like it,'" recalled Herzog, remembering it as "the funniest thing I had read since I got there." He arrived home at 1 A.M. and was so excited about the script he woke up his wife and started reading her passages from it. It was the pilot episode of *Malcolm in the Middle*.

The show about the brainy middle child of a suburban family had been in development at UPN. The programming executives there passed on the script, which is often the end of the show. Who wants to develop someone else's rejects? But Herzog fell in love with *Malcolm*. He contacted Gail Berman of Regency Television and told her, "Hey, get this out of UPN. We'll make this."

Peter Chernin had told his new hire that the network needed a live-action comedy. *That '70s Show* was on the air, but it was still in its first season and had not yet become a hit. So when the *Malcolm* script came up, Herzog felt he was doing his job by pushing it through. In many ways this would be his one triumph at FOX, made sweeter by the fact that no one else wanted to do it. The other executives had plenty of reasons why the show would fail: it was a single-camera comedy, shot like a movie, instead of a three-camera sitcom shot with a studio audience. It starred a kid. It had no laugh track.

Herzog recalled someone in marketing condescendingly wishing him luck. "It was like 'Good luck, kid. You don't have a fucking clue what you're doing, but good luck.' It was my pet project. Nobody cared about it."

When they started to prep the pilot for production, Herzog could not have been reassured. He went to the table read where the cast members first read the script aloud. Bryan Cranston had just been cast as the father. The kids (including Frankie Muniz as Malcolm) had little experience doing a table read. It was a disaster. One of Herzog's people tried to console him that it had been a valiant effort. Herzog was nervous but kept the faith. The pilot would go on to win Emmy Awards for Linwood Boomer's script and Todd Holland's direction.

The naysayers, however, remained skeptical. It was deemed a Nickelodeon show (a kid's cable channel that featured some original sitcoms) rather than FOX material. Worse, it was produced by Linwood Boomer, a relative nobody. Herzog didn't see the problem.

"He's not an A-list guy," he was told.

Here's where Herzog coming from outside the world of network television helped. "I'd look at the front of the script and not know anybody's name. The only names I knew were David Kelley and [*E.R.* writer-producer] John Wells and Chris Carter," he said. "So Linwood Boomer didn't mean anything to me either way." When Herzog put the show on the schedule, he was told Boomer couldn't be the show runner—the guy who oversees the show week to week—but Herzog stood fast. "What do you mean? He *is* the show," he replied. Boomer had some producer credits on the NBC sitcoms *Night Court* and *3rd Rock from the Sun*, but this would be the first show he had created. As far as most people were concerned, he had no track record.

Malcolm in the Middle was announced for FOX's fall schedule, but that was a bluff. It was to get the buzz going since it was set for Sunday evening and FOX's Sunday schedule was beholden to NFL football until January. It was described as "a live-action *Simpsons*" by *TV Guide*, which named it a "fall preview favorite." "We're just sorry we have to wait until football is over to see it," wrote the magazine's editors. The show bowed on January 9 and pulled in the best premiere numbers for FOX since *The Simpsons* a decade earlier. Herzog had finally gotten his hit, but it was already too late.

F OX had decided to drop the reality-based specials that Peter Roth had once used to punch up the schedule. They had been inexpensive ratings winners but had been ridiculed by the critics and even by stand-up comics. The feeling was that these specials had run their course and had eventually tarnished the network. "FOX was coming off a period where Peter and David Hill and Mike Darnell had put on a lot of that first generation of reality stuff. *The World's Worst . . . The World's Craziest . . .* That kind of stuff. Police chases. We very much wanted to get away from that. FOX would do very well in the sweeps, but that's all they would be running." Now, however, a reality show—which could be produced fairly quickly and relatively cheaply—started to look good.

ABC had found a ratings bonanza in the nighttime quiz show *Who Wants to Be a Millionaire?* With host Regis Philbin and a variety of gimmicks, the show had captured the public imagination and was soon appearing several nights a week during sweeps periods. FOX tried its hand at the quiz show with a short-lived series called *Greed*, but its next attempt forever changed the face of reality television, and it started with the man responsible for specials and "alternative" programming at FOX.

"Mike Darnell was so totally vexed by the success of *Who Wants to Be a Millionaire?*" remembered Herzog. "It just plagued him all summer. And one day late in the summer he came running into my office one morning. He had just come in from home with his cup of coffee saying, 'I got it!'

"I said, 'What is it?'

"He said, '*Who Wants to Marry a Millionaire?*'

"I said, 'That's great. What is it?'

"He said, 'I don't know.'

"I said, "Well, go figure it out. That sounds great.'"

It would eventually go on the air as *Who Wants to Marry a Multimillionaire?* and quickly become one of the most celebrated successes and notorious failures in the short history of reality television. On Tuesday, February 15, FOX offered the show as a two-hour special. It was every bit as audacious as viewers and critics both hoped and feared. For two hours, fifty women competed in both bathing suits and wedding gowns to impress Rick Rockwell, forty-two, a former stand-up comedian turned real estate operator. At the end of the show he selected Darva Conger, thirty-four, an emergency room technician, as the winner and his bride. The couple then proceeded to marry on the air.

The show was outrageous in its sexist premise that marriage could be reduced to a game-show prize, but it also proved to be irresistible television. Nearly 23 million viewers tuned in, with the ratings growing over the course of the two hours. In the key 18–49 demographic the network was number one for the night, even beating ABC and its previously invincible *Who Wants to Be a Millionaire?* FOX quickly announced not only a follow-up special for the May sweeps period but a hastily planned one-hour edited version of the show for the following Tuesday night. In the wake of the show, talk about it ran from the office water cooler to the editorial pages of the news media. Patricia Ireland, president of the National Organization for Women, reflected the jaw-dropping reaction of many when she commented, "It took something like this to make the Miss America pageant look good to me."

Things soon turned ugly. An internet site revealed that Rockwell had been accused of hitting and threatening a former girl friend and that a restraining order had been issued against him, which made the dashing prince seem a less than desirable catch. Rockwell's criminal record had been investigated, but because he was never convicted of anything the restraining order from 1991 didn't come up.

Then questions were raised as to whether he really was a "multimillionaire." The network insisted he was worth at least $2 million. As for Conger, who was billed as a "Gulf War veteran," it appeared that while she had been on active duty as a military nurse during the Gulf War, she had not served in that theater of operations. Follow-up news reports indicated that Rockwell and Conger were back from their ostensible honeymoon—where they stayed in separate rooms—and were continuing to live apart. Plans for the condensed version of the show quickly vanished. In spite of the hokiness of the show's premise, audiences had watched trusting that some things were indeed real. But if the "multimillionaire" really wasn't, and the on-air marriage was treated as a contrivance that was quickly annulled (Conger filed for an annulment a month later), the whole point of the show was lost.

In one final bit of irony, largely overlooked in accounts of the debacle, the man responsible for allowing the show to go on the air in the first place escaped all blame. "I'm the guy who greenlit *Who Wants to Marry a Multimillionaire?*" said Herzog. "It hit the air, it caused a furor, it did very well. And then the shit hit the fan." At that point Herzog was already packing his bags at FOX. He decided that he had been hired to run the network—to be "the guy," in his words—but now was merely an underling to Grushow. It was less a personality conflict than the realization that there would be only one boss at the network, and it was no longer him.

The easy, cynical thing to do was for Grushow or Chernin to fire Herzog—or allow him a face-saving resignation—while putting out the word that it was all his fault that the scandalous *Multimillionaire* had ever aired. Instead his name didn't come up in the public discussion at all. Grushow used the opportunity to issue a public *mea culpa* in which he took responsibility for the show and promised it would not be repeated. Even as late as July, when the show was old news and Herzog's replacement—Gail Berman of Regency Television, which produced *Malcolm in the Middle*—was already in place, Grushow was still at it. At the summer press tour for the Television Critics Association, he was still apologizing.

"You've got to balance a desire to win with a desire to do it with some honor, integrity, and dignity," Grushow told the press. "When looking at some of these reality ideas, never are those two impulses colliding more. At the end of the day, you're certainly playing with fire." He promised that PricewaterhouseCoopers would now be investigating and vetting the participants for future FOX reality shows.

By taking responsibility, Grushow had made it clear to the world that he was in charge. Herzog? He was yesterday's news. Blaming him would be giving him credit for having more of an impact at FOX than he had actually had. Although he had had some noble failures and an unqualified success with *Malcolm in the Middle*, Herzog had never been fully in control.

Herzog returned to cable, first as president of USA Networks and then, in 2004, going back to his old stomping grounds at Comedy Central. He admits to making a number of rookie mistakes during his brief time at FOX, but adds, "The truth of the matter is, I never got a real at bat."

PART III

21st Century Fox

CHAPTER SIXTEEN

"It was the perfect fit at the right time"

[2000 AND BEYOND]

IT WAS A HEADLINE that would not have been imaginable just three years earlier. The August 11, 2003, issue of weekly *Variety* had a series of articles about Rupert Murdoch's empire, and the banner for the TV section story was, "It's Fox's Dream Team—Stability in top exec ranks lead to ratings jump." Stability? At FOX?

It was true. When the dust settled after Doug Herzog's departure, Gail Berman was brought over from Regency Television to take the job of president of FOX Entertainment. Now into her fourth year, she has served longer in that position than anyone since the Diller/Kellner era. Peter Chernin, who came aboard in 1989 to handle programming and has outlasted everyone else, is now chief operating officer and overseeing not only News Corp.'s television operations but movies and publishing. Perhaps most amazing is the rise to power of Sandy Grushow. His history at FOX goes back to 1988, but his rise to the top was brief, serving as little more than a placeholder between Lucy Salhany and John Matoian, before he departed in 1994.

Three years later he was back running the television production arm, before being installed as Herzog's boss in 1999 as chairman of the new FOX TV Entertainment Group. Whatever the problem was back in 1994, Grushow now apparently had Murdoch's complete confidence. Actually, as the *Variety* story made clear, it was more than confidence. History was being rewritten so that Grushow was now being depicted as the savior of the network. "The revolving door stopped and you now have got a number of people who've been here a while," Grushow was quoted as saying. This allowed FOX to engage in long-range planning. Of course the fact that it was Murdoch and Chernin—as well as other top executives such as Chase Carey and David Hill—who were undercutting and replacing their top television programmer every other season was a big part of the reason for the instability.

Grushow was cited for retaining programming executive Mike Darnell after the *Who Wants to Marry a Multimillionaire?* fiasco as well as for hiring Berman. In a bit of selective editing that suggests the network was rudderless until Grushow assumed his post, he was even given credit for the one big hit of the Herzog era. Wrote Josef Adelian in *Variety*, "Chernin in late 1999 turned to Grushow to whip things back into shape at the network. Grushow immediately got his hands dirty, helping cut promos for shows like *Malcolm in the Middle*—the same job he did when he first joined FOX in 1988." To complete the illusion that in the TV industry the only place for network history is a nostalgia-laden special scheduled during a sweeps period, the current regime got credit for the innovation of programming year round, including launching new series in the summer.

In fact, as this book has tried to demonstrate, the history of FOX can be divided into three parts. In the first part, from the launch of *The Late Show with Joan Rivers* in October 1986 to early 1992, Fox, Inc., chairman Barry Diller received the credit for everything. Murdoch was a presence at the network and was kept fully informed, but Diller was the public face of FOX and had more or less a free hand to operate his domain. As has been recounted in these pages, other executives contributed greatly to the venture's success. It's important that people like Jamie Kellner, Preston Padden, Margaret Loesch, and Andrew Fessel, among others, get their due.

The second part of FOX's history began in February 1992, after Diller left, when Rupert Murdoch took a more hands-on approach, either directly or through designated representatives like Carey, Chernin, and Hill. As the executives came and went, some had more success than others. The network still benefits from decisions made under Lucy Salhany and Peter Roth, while John Matoian and Doug Herzog had more troubled reigns.

Part three is still unfolding, and while FOX is positioned as never before to be a broadcast powerhouse, that is still to be determined by the decisions being made today and in the months and years ahead. It remans to be seen if the surprise resignation of Grushow in January 2004 will have an impact. (Grushow, apparently seeing no room for advancement, opted to form Phase Two, an independent production company based at the studio.) Meanwhile, Fox exercised an option on Gail Berman's services through June 2005.

At the start of the twenty-first century, tastes change, as do viewership habits. Today's oddball hit is tomorrow's flop. FOX continues to have notable failures, like *Skin*—a teen romantic drama set against the backdrop of the porn industry—which was canceled after three episodes in the fall of 2003. It still produces shows that never make it to the air, like the Randy Quaid sitcom *The Grubbs*, or that are so second-guessed that they fizzle when they finally do, like *Firefly*, a western/science fiction hybrid from Joss Whedon, creator of *Buffy the Vampire Slayer*. Launched in the fall of 2002, FOX executives shelved the pilot, which explained the backgrounds of the characters and their situation, and had Whedon do a new premiere episode. It attracted a loyal but small following and was gone by mid-season.

Yet when they get it right, and remember to take chances that their rivals avoid, they can still have spectacular successes and leave everyone else playing catch up.

Nowhere is FOX's ability to set the bar for American television more obvious than in the area of so-called "reality TV." In the 2000–2001 season FOX chugged along, rebounding from the previous year. David E. Kelley had a hit with *Boston Public*, an hour drama set at a high school, while Chris Carter had his third flop in a row with the *The X-Files* spin-off *The Lone Gunmen*. It featured Bruce Harwood, Tom Braidwood, and Dean Haglund as the three computer hackers who had made several popular guest appearances on *The X-Files*. But they were unable to sustain a series on their own. Movie director James Cameron created a splash with his first TV series, *Dark Angel*, making a star out of Jessica Alba and generating good ratings, at least in the short run.

The show that raised eyebrows and showed the network still had the capacity to shock was *Temptation Island*. Like CBS's *Survivor* or MTV's *The Real World*, it featured a group of strangers thrown together in a highly artificial situation, with many cameras around to record the results. It was what was coming to be known as an "unscripted" drama, in that there were characters and stories for viewers to follow, but the show was about actual people engaging in actions with potentially real consequences. *Temptation Island* took that idea a step further by bringing together four unmarried couples as well as more than two dozen attractive and flirting singles, putting them up in an exotic location in Belize, and then separating the couples. Would they remain faithful or would the partners succumb to temptation?

It was either a brilliant stroke or a new low for broadcast television, but viewers tuned in. Although the couples were separated, they could see what their significant others were doing via video, and that simply added to the melodramatics. It was salacious, and FOX made no apologies for it. But when ads for the show began popping up on programs that kids might be watching, like *The Simpsons* and *Malcolm in the Middle*, complaints appeared, including one from the FCC. The network quickly announced that it would promote the show only before appropriate audiences.

How important was it to the network's bottom line? At season's end, the success of *Temptation Island* had made a big difference. Add in the fact that *That '70s Show* was finally taking off, and the freshman successes of *Boston Public* and *Dark Angel*, and the story was that FOX had rebounded. Although in overall viewers FOX was in fourth place among the networks, it was second in adults 18–49 and first in adults 18–34. "We had our most competitive season ever. We truly believe that in spite of all the noise that the other networks are making, the real story is the emergence of FOX as a real player and contender for prime-time leadership," said a triumphant Sandy Grushow.

He wasn't wrong. Even as broadcasters have seen their audiences shrink with the rise of cable, the internet, and other entertainment alternatives, they still represent the best way for advertisers to target large audiences. The lesson of *Temptation Island* is not that sleaze sold, but that if FOX was going to compete in the new era of reality TV, it had to remember to give it a uniquely FOX spin. *Temptation Island* didn't even bother offering prizes. If a couple stayed together after this two-week "vacation," they won. (The two weeks were then transformed into six hour-long episodes.) When the second season launched, and the ratings went down, another lesson would be taught as well: novelty sells . . . once. It was a lesson that, alas, would soon be forgotten.

After an uneven 2001–2002 season, FOX broke new ground again in June 2002 with the launch of *American Idol.* This was one of the hoariest of TV formats: the talent show. From *Ted Mack's Original Amateur Hour* to *The Gong Show* to *Star Search*, it's the last thing anyone might have thought of as grist for the FOX mill. One innovation was to run episodes on consecutive nights, so that when audiences voted for their favorites, they got immediate gratification the next evening. Rick Kissell, reporting on the week's ratings in *Variety* noted, "Initial episodes of *Idol* delivered the week's top two scores for entertainment programs in both adults 18–49 and 18–34, boosting FOX to second for the week in those categories." By late July, against meager competition to be sure, FOX had won the night for seven consecutive Tuesdays.

What was the appeal? Part of it was the talented young singers and the chance to root for a favorite and directly participate in their being the last one standing. Part of it was also waiting to see how the judges would react. One of them, singer/dancer/choreographer Paula Abdul, added glamour and sex appeal no doubt, but the new celebrity born on the show was Simon Cowell, an acerbic Brit who didn't pull his punches in assessing the talent (or lack thereof) of the contestants. What's more, audiences continued to love the new stars even after the season was over. Kelly Clarkson (first-season winner) and Ruben Studdard (second-season winner) went on from the show to work on eagerly anticipated albums. Whether they will have long careers in the notoriously fickle music business remains to be seen, but for viewers it was obviously a chance to see a potential star being born.

Viewers could also identify with the pressures and agonies of those who didn't make it. There was certainly plenty of backstage drama. Vocal coach Debra Byrd told *TV Guide* that in the first season "every one of the finalists either went to the hospital or had to have a doctor come to them." The audiences kept growing, attracting the younger viewers (teens and adults) who were supposed to be leaving network audiences in droves. The second season premiere of *American Idol* in January 2003 drew 26.5 million viewers, including an incredible 40 share among teens. That meant nearly half of all teenagers watching TV at that time were tuned to *American Idol*. It was actually up 16 percent over the first-season finale, where viewership would have expected to peak.

Having these mid-season blockbusters would prove crucial for FOX. The traditional fall kickoff to the networks' new season was problematic since FOX was now carrying the major league baseball postseason of playoffs or World Series or some combination thereof. That meant that if the network kicked off in September with everyone else, the shows would be preempted for several weeks and lose momentum. Instead FOX was now launching its series in late October, just in time for the November sweeps, and holding its reality shows in reserve for the winter and spring. "We weren't playing with a full hand," explained Gail Berman. "Everyone else had their big unscripted guns in the fourth quarter. We didn't."

In January 2003 FOX launched its most audacious reality show yet: *Joe Millionaire*. A platoon of beautiful women vied for the attention of handsome Evan Marriott, an eligible bachelor supposedly worth $50 million. The network had learned its lesson and promised no on-screen wedding. The catch was that Marriott wasn't even a millionaire. The audience knew that all his trappings of wealth were being provided by the show, so the gimmick was not only watching the women compete to win the millionaire in the name of love, but seeing what would happen to the "winner" when she found out he wasn't a millionaire. Was this about love or the money?

In spite of, or perhaps because of, the hokiness of this contrived premise, the ratings went through the roof. By the February sweeps FOX was the number one network. *American Idol* and *Joe Millionaire* not only delivered the numbers but boosted overall FOX viewership. The dramatic series *24* benefited greatly from the lead-in from *Idol*. Said Grushow, "If you use reality properly, it infuses energy into the entire network." During the February sweeps the two reality shows comprised nearly a quarter of the network's prime-time programs. (Of course it still programmed seven hours less than the Big Three because the network schedule went only to 10 P.M.) By season's end, the two reality shows were two of the most popular shows on the air, sharing the top-three spot with NBC's *Friends* among adults 18–49 and CBS's *CSI* among adults overall.

Clearly reality TV would remain a big part of FOX's future, though a second season of *Joe Millionaire* fizzled in the fall of 2003, suggesting that it was more like *Temptation Island* than *American Idol*. Once the gimmick had run once, that was enough. As for *Idol*, the phenomenal success of its second season suggests that as long as FOX can come up with unknowns who can win over viewers with talent and heart, the show may be in for a long run.

"Our goal is to have a balanced schedule that uses unscripted shows to help scripted series," declared Gail Berman in early 2003. "FOX had great successes with shows like *90210* and *Party of Five*, and we want to speak to that tradition."

It's in the area of series development that a network lives and dies. A good sitcom or dramatic series can run for years and provide a network with an identity. FOX is still the place to take risk with oddball shows, even if they go down in flames. When *Ally McBeal* ended its run, David E. Kelley pitched a new series about women attorneys in Boston called *Girls Club*. The reviews were brutal, and the ratings followed suit. It left the air quickly. A quirky sitcom set behind the scenes of a television show and starring comic movie actors Eugene Levy (*American Pie*, *Best in Show*) and Seth Green (*Austin Powers: International Man of Mystery*) might have seemed like a safe bet. But the main characters on *Greg the Bunny* were hand puppets. Original? It was certainly different for a prime-time series, perhaps a little too different. It too did a fast fade.

Two well-reviewed shows that were successful with viewers demonstrate the still schizophrenic nature of network program development. Either the network can give the creative team room to be creative, or it can interfere and second-guess, attempting to fix what only it perceives as broken.

The fall of 2001 was a risky time to introduce a new series that had to do with international terrorists. In the days and weeks after the September 11 attacks on the World Trade Center in New York and the Pentagon in Washington, D.C., there was a lot of talk about what the American public would or would not accept in their entertainment. The Arnold Schwarzenegger thriller *Collateral Damage*, in which he seeks vengeance after losing family in a terrorist attack, was shelved, and the movie wasn't released until the following year. Syndicated episodes of the nineties sitcom *Seinfeld*—set in New York City—were reportedly edited to remove shots of the twin towers. Meanwhile FOX was anxiously waiting to launch one of the most original concepts for a dramatic series in some time: *24*.

The premise for the series is that the entire season takes place on a single day, and each episode constitutes one hour of real time. Thus the premiere covered midnight to 1 A.M. The convoluted plot centered on an assassination attempt on a presidential candidate (Dennis Haysbert) and the counterterrorism operative (Kiefer Sutherland) who is trying to foil the plan. The problem for FOX was that a key plot point involved one of the conspirators covering her tracks by jumping off a plane, which then blew up. Given the four planes that had been hijacked on 9/11, with all lives aboard lost, it was something that could quickly turn off an audience. When the show premiered on November 6, 2001, most of the explosion was edited out and remained only by implication.

That was the least of the network's problems and was easily fixed. The real problem was that the show required the viewer to make a commitment. It was appointment television. If you missed a couple of episodes you might never catch up, given the twists and turns of the plot. *24* launched with great reviews and a *TV Guide* cover, but it was up against a two-hour special episode of *NYPD Blue* on ABC and was clobbered in the ratings. (Ironically, *Blue* is produced by Twentieth Century–Fox Television, the company's production arm.) Gail Berman tried to be upbeat: "We can't control the expectation bandwagon. We're where we expected to be once *NYPD Blue* was put in the time period. We had to play the hand that we were dealt. It's sweeps; everyone threw their goods at us."

FOX couldn't complain about this type of counterprogramming. They had done it themselves. Now they were considered serious competitors and were on the receiving end. But in the new television environment, FOX did have another card to play, and that was "re-purposing." With the entertainment cable channel FX at hand, FOX announced that each week's episode of *24* would repeat on FX. This was not a new idea, as premium channels like HBO routinely gave several runs to each episode of their original series. It was catching on among broadcasters as well. The WB was second-running *Charmed* on sister cable channel TNT. Lifetime re-aired episodes of ABC's *Once and Again*. NBC got a second run of its game show *The Weakest Link* on PAX.

Repurposing would prove controversial. Does the talent get paid extra for the show's additional runs? Should affiliates resent the fact that their viewers will now be able to view some of their network offerings on competitors? For FOX it proved to be a mixed blessing. *24* got the boost in viewership, hung on through the first season, and finally emerged a hit. By its second season it was one of FOX's upscale shows, attracting the kinds of viewers who might not tune in to *Joe Millionaire*. But FX was trying to develop its own audience, and viewers who were using it merely to catch the *24* episodes they had missed weren't sticking around. Grushow told *Variety*, "We'll have to reassess repurposing as a business." The plan was to drop the FX repeats, but by October they had reassessed again.

What had changed? The agreement to repeat second-season episodes kept the episodes out of prime time, so that they would neither affect the show's ratings nor compete with the FOX affiliate's prime-time fare. This time change also allowed FX to pay less to air the episodes. The third factor may have been the most important: TNT had inquired after the "repurposing" rights for the second season. FOX executives decided that if outsiders thought it was a valuable commodity, perhaps they shouldn't be so fast to sell it to someone else. When a first-season marathon of all twenty-four episodes ran on Labor Day and attracted notice and viewers for FX, the deal was sealed. So *24* would become one of FOX's signature shows, where the executives focused their creativity on scheduling the show and making it easier for viewers to commit to watching an entire season of episodes.

Meanwhile, as *24* was struggling that first season to get people to tune in, another show premiered on FOX to rave reviews and solid numbers, becoming FOX's unquestioned series hit of the 2001–2002 season. For some reason, though, *The Bernie Mac Show* would become a target of network tinkering that would continue to make its path bumpy.

Comedian Bernie Mac had been developing a growing reputation in movies and television when he appeared in Spike Lee's 2000 *The Original Kings of Comedy*, a concert film in which Mac was one of four featured comedians. One of the people who saw the movie was TV writer-producer Larry Wilmore, whose credits included work on *In Living Color*, *The Fresh Prince of Bel Air*, and *The PJs*. "I had a conceptual idea of doing a TV show that borrowed a lot from reality, where it felt like we were eavesdropping on the action, where the character was confessing his sins to us," he recalled. "When I saw Bernie's bit I thought, 'Boy, that whole thing about his sister and crack and the kids is such an emotional story, but it's funny, too.'" Wilmore took the idea of doing a sitcom built around Mac to Peter Aronson (who had succeeded Gail Berman at Regency Television). The two of them pitched it to Mac. With him on board, the show was offered to FOX.

"They were hungry for live-action sitcoms. At the time I pitched it, *That '70s Show* wasn't the hit it would eventually become," said Wilmore. The success of *Malcolm in the Middle* helped, given that it was also a quirky, single-camera, family-oriented sitcom with no laugh track. "I know Gail Berman really wanted to do a really good black family show. . . . She just thought it was the perfect fit at the right time."

The network let Mac, Wilmore, and the rest of the creative team have their heads. The show was launched in November 2001, and not only received good reviews—as had *24*—but attracted viewers from the start. By the following January the news was that *Bernie Mac* was a crossover show. Too many black comedies played primarily to black audiences while white viewers looked elsewhere. There was something about the cleverness of the writing and Mac's engaging performance that clicked with a larger audience. David Nevins, FOX executive vice president of programming, was pleased. "It's definitely a reminder that if you have the right person, it doesn't matter about race." Wilmore was more blunt: "The only color that counts in the end is green."

Bernie Mac might have been nurtured as another *Malcolm in the Middle*, a show to be treasured for its success and what it brought to the network. Instead the network thought it needed improving.

"They always kept comparing it to what it should be, and I always insisted that it's *The Bernie Mac Show* and should only be compared to itself," said Wilmore. Suggestions to make it more like *Malcolm* or more like *Roseanne* left the writers bewildered. It was almost as if the network executives didn't understand the show. "It was a big struggle at the network. They did not believe in the show they had. They kept wanting something different. They were very afraid they were going to lose the audience. They didn't think the show was funny enough. They didn't think the writing was good enough." The ratings were strong, but then the show was shifted to compete against ABC's *My Wife and Kids*, a sitcom featuring a black comedian—Damon Wayans—and his quirky take on domestic life. What it did was divide the audience. *Bernie Mac* suffered, then rebounded when it was moved back and had *American Idol* as a lead-in.

In the fall of 2003 *Bernie Mac*'s fate was far from certain. At the last minute FOX delayed the show's fall premiere—in a favored spot following the ever-popular *Simpsons*—to after the November sweeps. It was replaced by *Simpsons* reruns. That's not exactly a vote of confidence, especially after Wilmore was ousted from the show in March 2003. Wilmore said the news was delivered to him by Regency, not the network, but there's no doubt who gave the order. As to what the problem was, he remains mystified and the network isn't talking. "We had great ratings and great reviews. The audience loved us. I think it was a personal issue to be honest. For some reason they were more interested in proving themselves right, that I was somehow wrong about the show being good," said Wilmore, who ended up with a production deal at NBC.

Networks have been accused of sabotaging hits and potential hits for years by the people connected with the shows, and it may simply be the nature of the industry that requires collaboration but leaves some of the collaborators with more authority than others. However original FOX may be in its programming, in some ways it's still business as usual. For the viewer, though, what counts is that FOX has succeeded in creating an identifiable "brand" that should continue to serve it for some time to come. With the 2003–2004 season seeing the final seasons of long-running hits on rival networks, like *Friends* and *Frasier*, FOX is well positioned to grab time periods where viewers will have no predetermined loyalties.

As Gail Berman declared, "Our brand is alive and well. People know it, they recognize shows that should be on our air."

The other pressure point for FOX is its relationship with its affiliates. In November 1999 the network formally petitioned the FCC to raise the ownership cap, which signaled that FOX wants to own outright as many of the broadcast stations carrying the network as it possibly can. It may succeed. The business and regulatory climate has undergone a dramatic shift in recent years, with the growing consolidation of media properties like the Disney/ABC merger, the CBS/Viacom merger, and the AOL/Time Warner merger. In addition, the FCC changed its rules and decided that it would now permit "duopolies" (meaning that for the first time one company would be allowed to own more than one TV station in a market).

At this writing FOX and other media giants have prevailed before the FCC, and the ownership cap has been raised. The battle has shifted to Congress and, possibly, the courts. Opponents of this move aren't the other networks, all of which are also moving to expand their ownership of TV outlets, but the individual station groups and owners. How much easier—from a business perspective—if instead of a huge affiliate group FOX had to deal only with a few major station group owners, like Hearst/Argyle and Tribune, to fill in the gaps of their coverage.

Contrary to popular belief, it is more lucrative to own several TV stations than the network. Former FOX syndication chief Greg Meidel once pointed to Mitch Stern, head of the FOX o-and-o station group, as the real unsung power in the organization. "Mitch Stern is the cash cow of the FOX organization. Those stations generate approximately $650 million a year in cash. Think about it. That's on billings of $1.2 billion or $1.3 billion. He has over [a] 50 percent [profit] margin. That's the first call Rupert makes, I think, every day. One individual, one division, generates more cash, year in and year out, than anybody else. Period."

If that's what FOX was making with only twenty-two stations—when Meidel was speaking—how much is it earning on its current thirty-five-station group? What could it earn if it was allowed to own fifty or one hundred stations? Stern continues to be a major player on the FOX team who remains largely unknown to the general public. He describes his relationship with Murdoch as close: "There's a sense of trust or understanding that builds up over time, and everything becomes like shorthand. That's why this company moves very, very quickly."

One such move was in 2001 when Chris-Craft decided to sell off its TV stations. UPN desperately wanted them to build up its outlets, but FOX beat it to the punch. "The Chris-Craft acquisition was very important because it made us a very, very important player in the arena of TV stations, and what you can build off of TV stations is enormous," said Stern. Today FOX has coverage of nearly 45 percent of the country on stations that it owns itself, including "duopolies" in New York, Los Angeles, and Chicago, the nation's three top markets. Now syndicators who have shows that are passed on by the FOX stations find that it's a real struggle to get sufficient coverage across the country if the other big station group owned by Tribune passes as well. "There are still some people trying to play by the old rules," Stern told *Variety*. "This business has changed so much. It's always been competitive, now it's unbelievably competitive."

FOX now has leverage not only over the syndicators but over its remaining affiliates. It's no secret to the station owners, who saw the battles over prime-time availabilities as a bald attempt by the network to take a cut of local stations' profit margins. Said former

KTVU general manager Kevin O'Brien, "The networks find it difficult to manage their own business. They look elsewhere for help, rather than clean up their own acts and wash their own dirty laundry. They turn and blame it all on us." The affiliates—of all the networks, not just FOX—are coming to view their relationship with their network as less of a partnership and more like extortion. Added O'Brien, "They don't do a good job of managing their own businesses, and so they look outside themselves for help, and they see us as the bad guys who are making all the money. And the reality is, we're simply better broadcasters and better business people. So why should we be punished? That's the nature of the game right now."

Alabama broadcaster and the owner of FOX affiliate WCOV, David Woods, is bitter about the changes. He recalled the early days in the 1980s when Murdoch talked about the wonderful "marriage" between the fledgling network and its new affiliates. In 1994, in the wake of the New World deal when FOX dropped longtime UHF affiliates in favor of association with several VHF stations, the tune was changed. Now FOX and its affiliates were merely "dating" and might change partners from time to time. "You remember how Murdoch gave us both those speeches? Well, let me give you the sequel to that: today, they're charging us. They're prostitutes. . . . They said, 'I'm no longer going to give you the programming for free, I'm going to charge you for it.' They redefined themselves that they're selling their services. FOX is a hooker."

If Murdoch was right back in 1986, that this was a marriage, today the ties between the network and its affiliates clearly need mending. The world of television has changed since FOX debuted, and there are alternatives—in some markets at least—for stations that want a divorce from FOX. The coming battles may be over the notion of just how important affiliates are to a TV network. For most of broadcast history they have been crucial, not only carrying the network's shows but also providing a local face for the network in the community. The networks, though, seem to think they can do without affiliates, either by buying stations outright or through the even more radical notion of leaving broadcasting altogether. More than one network has floated the idea of ceasing operations via broadcasting and becoming a purely cable-delivered service. FOX, NBC, and Disney/ABC already have several cable outlets apiece. If one day the accountants discover it's more profitable to deliver new programming on cable—as is already done on myriad cable channels from CNN and Lifetime to the Food Network and American Movie Classics—American network broadcasting as it has been known over the past half-century may cease to exist.

P redicting the future is always chancy, but it is especially risky today in the field of television because we are on the verge of a revolution that could be as important as the launch of commercially broadcast television was in 1948. Network radio as it was known until that time was gone within a decade as television became the major mass entertainment medium. People often think the future will be like the present, only with more gadgets. Certainly it's easy to foretell that satellite TV, with the higher multiple of channels offered over cable, will expand. Likewise, cable is likely to grow, especially as it upgrades from copper cable to fiber optic delivery systems. The arrival of companies like RCN, which exist not to wire new communities but to compete with existing cable companies, suggests that more homes will purchase cable service and that geographic competition—once thought impossible in cable—could become the norm. Some even suggest that the growth of the internet and the ever-increasing speeds with which data can be transmitted mean that someday we will get movies, concerts, and other entertainment material direct from the web.

One additional industry alternative is only starting to be noticed by the general public. The coming of digital broadcasting, usually referred to as High Definition Television (HDTV), is commonly portrayed as providing a bigger, better picture and improved sound. That is certainly true. But as the equipment has become commercially available, and stations under a federal mandate to broadcast a digital signal have begun doing so, it turns out that most people are not willing to spend a lot more money to get the same thing they're already getting, only "prettier." Stations could broadcast separate programs on their digital channels while they make the transition from the current, or analog, system, but why would networks spend a lot of money creating programming few people could receive?

No, the real change coming is something called "multiplexing." The digital signal will itself be bigger than the analog signal, and broadcasters will have the option of running several programming streams at once rather than a single HDTV channel. Thus someone able to receive the digital signal may find that—even without cable —they can receive three or four FOX channels rather than one. None will be HDTV, but all will be crisper than the current analog broadcast, and a savvy programmer can appeal to four different audiences simultaneously. FOX could, for example, put the equivalent of the current FOX network on FOX-1, FOX Kids on FOX-2, FOX Sports on FOX-3, and FOX News on FOX-4. Viewers would be able to press a button and access closed captions or a Spanish-language soundtrack. For a special event like the Super Bowl or a blockbuster movie, a network could switch to a single HDTV broadcast, then resume the multiplexing afterward. When that practice becomes widely accepted, we will be that much closer to the mythical "500 channel universe" that has been promised for years, especially for viewers with access to all the cable channels.

FOX is well positioned to take advantage of the coming technological and industry changes. But it's far too early to say whether the network will be seen as a cutting-edge alternative, as it has been for much of its broadcast history, or simply another content provider, no different from all the other myriad choices. It was easy for FOX to be different when it was being compared only to the tried-and-true methods of the established Big Three networks. When it is just one voice—or even several voices—among hundreds, what will make it stand out?

The history of broadcast television for the past two decades has been, in many ways, the history of FOX. FOX helped define what the old order was by programming against it. The Big Three, in turn, were eventually forced to respond. FOX's signature shows—from *Married . . . with Children* to *The X-Files* to *Ally McBeal*—became models that others copied. FOX alumni began turning up in other key industry posts, often bringing the FOX sensibility along: Scott Sassa and Garth Ancier at NBC, Barry Diller and Stephen Chao at USA, Jamie Kellner and Ancier at WB, Lucie Salhany at UPN, Preston Padden at ABC. When FOX succeeded and additional networks were launched in the mid-1990s, the FOX model was used as the basis for comparison. FOX, quite simply, redefined the world of American broadcast television.

Now that phase of American television is drawing to a close. Sometime in the twenty-first century, the way the TV industry works will change so radically that today's world, already so different from the so-called "Golden Age of Television" of the 1950s, may be looked upon as another quaint, historical period. FOX's current troubles with its affiliates and with its programming may seem, in retrospect, to be mere growing pains during the transition. Or they may be seen as the beginning of the end. It would be foolish to predict either with any degree of certainty.

This we do know: Rupert Murdoch foresaw the possibility of a fourth TV network in the United States when the experts and the conventional wisdom deemed it a near impossible task. He was right. With the help of many talented executives and a good many stations around the country, he succeeded in ways he might not have been able to fully imagine himself. These days Murdoch is not spending a lot of time in Los Angeles worrying about where to place *The Simpsons* on the schedule. Instead he's in China or France or Latin America, making deals to bring FOX programming there, launching FOX TV channels, and forging international partnerships. Will FOX turn into one of the first truly global television networks? No one can say.

But stay tuned.

Notes

PROLOGUE

page

6 "We were in the process . . . with partners." Interview with Bob Bennett, August 16, 1999.

6 "No sooner than we did that . . . on the junk bonds." Bennett interview.

6 "Milken had a party . . . all these big money guys." Bennett interview.

10 "I just thought it was crazy." Alex Ben Block, *Outfoxed* (New York, 1990), p. 102.

10 "I didn't want . . . going to cancel the deal." Bennett interview.

10 He recalls once dickering . . . Murdoch paid it. Bennett interview.

11 "He was very straightforward . . . with the guy." Interview with James Quello, March 11, 1999.

12 Diller said . . . anticipation of our future." *Variety*, October 16, 1985, p. 5.

13 "The FCC is treating . . . assume to be political." *Variety*, November 13, 1985, p. 110.

CHAPTER ONE: 1985–1986

17 "I was thirty-eight . . . sort of the ultimate challenge." Block, *Outfoxed*, p. 117.

18 "I told him why he would fail . . . good answers." Block, *Outfoxed*, p. 128.

19 "I'd been at NBC six and a half years . . . a once in a lifetime kind of thing to try out.'" Interview with Garth Ancier, September 10, 1999.

19 "It was certainly intensified . . . UHF stations?" Ancier interview.

19 "I will never put a fourth column . . . only be three." Ancier interview.

19 "My very best friend at NBC . . . a couple of years older than I am." Interview with Kevin Wendle, August 5, 1999.

20 "Garth and I left NBC the same day . . . it's competitive." Wendle interview.

22 "We're taking these independent stations . . . competitive to the networks." Interview with Andrew Fessel, August 10, 1999.

22 "What we found was a tremendous vacuum . . . the consumers were indicating to us that they had." Fessel interview.

23 At its peak, *The Tonight Show* . . . the network's entire profits. Bill Carter, *The Late Shift* (New York, 1994), p. 17.

25 "Then a friend—a real friend . . . I almost died." *Still Talking*, by Joan Rivers, with Richard Merryman, *Still Talking* (New York, 1991), p. 177.

26 "Okay, make it a zoo, make it a circus." Rivers, *Still Talking*, p. 187.

26 "I said, 'I can't comment.' . . . he was on the phone with Brandon." Ancier interview.

26 "I consider Joan Rivers to be . . . 'Oh, that's a pre-established hit.'" Ancier interview.

27 "It was more of a lark for us, the downside was minimal." Interview with Brad Moran, June 13, 1999.

27 "Early on they didn't have the manpower . . . top seventy-five at the inception." Interview with David Woods, June 9, 1999.

27 "The guy was smart . . . you've got to give me Indianapolis.'" Interview with Joe Young, June 25, 1999.

27 "Basically, we all sat around a room . . . decided to call it FBC, like NBC." Ancier interview.

28 "They had announced and walked up on stage . . . And the room erupted." Interview with Rob Kenneally, August 15, 1999.

CHAPTER TWO: 1986–1987

32 "It's self-evidently correct . . . signing with the FBC network." *Variety*, August 27, 1986, p. 65.

33 "On Sunday night . . . movie would be effective." Fessel interview.

34 "My recommendation . . . see what happened?" Fessel interview.

34 "Nobody in the drama . . . makes no sense to me." Rivers, *Still Talking*, p. 175.

34 At the meeting with Diller . . . "Shut up!" Rivers, *Still Talking*, p. 185.

36 "Now that I've been nice, can I have my guards?" Rivers, *Still Talking*, p. 203.

36 "Oh, I knew so quickly . . . I didn't tell anybody, but I knew." Block, *Outfoxed*, p. 157.

36 "Ultimately it was our first and only show . . . could have grown into being more successful." Wendle interview.

36 Programming head Garth Ancier . . . but [the network is] partners in it." Ancier interview.

36 "It was a shame . . . came between her and Fox." Wendle interview.

37 "Did it get petty? . . . an armed camp separate from us." Ancier interview.

37 "Do you realize what you are fighting about? People would buy tickets to see this." Rivers, *Still Talking*, p. 222.

37 "You're a tinhorn dictator . . . Go fuck yourself." Rivers, *Still Talking*, p. 233.

38 "We're trying to say . . . the first week as sort of open house." *Variety*, December 24, 1986, p. 77.

38 "You're ignoring a brand . . . as your signature." Ancier interview.

39 "They were extraordinarily lavish . . . really young and really gorgeous." Interview with Brian Lowry, July 14, 1999.

39 "Everyone was in on that decision . . . as much sampling as possible." Ancier interview.

40 "It's not young enough . . .We want really, really young." Interview with Stephen J. Cannell, June 23, 1999.

40 "I hadn't even talked this over . . . he went, 'I love it.'" Cannell interview.

40 "He thought it might feel like it was going to be religious or something." Cannell interview.

41 "I always hate to do that to an actor . . . We need to do it." Cannell interview.

42 "But still I was staggered . . . my show was a failure." Rivers, *Still Talking*, p. 238.

42 "You just don't make a change like that . . . wouldn't have done it." *Variety*, July 15, 1987, p. 41.

43 "FOX had given us a legitimate prime-time atmosphere on the weekend." *Variety*, July 15, 1987, p. 41.

44 "They were threatening to boycott the Emmys . . . just a ragtag lineup of stations." Lowry interview.

CHAPTER THREE: 1987–1988

45 "Why are some of these stations . . .We'll run an analysis of it." Fessel interview.

46 "What does UHF mean? . . . cable can also change channel numbers." Fessel interview.

47 "This FOX cable report is actually very historical . . . where they stood with cable." Interview with Paul McCarthy, April 16, 1999.

48 "Many FOX affiliates hadn't done that . . . Why should I buy you?" McCarthy interview.

49 "It improved their ratings, marginally, almost overnight." McCarthy interview.

49 "We actually ran the numbers . . . which was a really good improvement." Fessel interview.

49 "They're clinging to the notion . . . right next to the other network affiliates." McCarthy interview.

50 "We would bring in . . . really want to see." Fessel interview.

50 "Don't get too close to those guys . . . they're dangerous." Interview with Jamie Kellner, September 2, 1999.

51 "Sunday night was literally . . . a pretty easy thing to do, very honestly." Interview with Patrick Mullen, August 12, 1999.

52 "We couldn't continue with the situation . . . *Mr. President* at 8 was getting only a 3." *Variety*, December 23, 1987, p. 48.

52 "We're in the business to make money . . . ratings on Saturday night." *Variety*, December 30, 1987, p. 23.

53 "We made a choice early on . . . it made Sunday night a much more viable night." Ancier interview.

54 On December 15, 1987, Massachusetts Senator Edward Kennedy . . . enforce the cross-ownership rule for everyone. William Shawcross, *Murdoch: The Making of a Media Empire* (New York, 1997), p. 260.

55 "The Hollings amendment strikes at Murdoch with the precision of a laser beam." Shawcross, *Murdoch*, p. 264.

55 "The Appeals Court, in a split decision . . . the culprit has gone free." *Variety*, April 6, 1988, p. 35.

56 "We have every intention . . . better than anticipated." *Variety*, June 29, 1988, p. 56.

CHAPTER FOUR: 1988–1989

58 "I take issue with people . . . substantial use of docudrama." *Washington Times*, April 21, 1988, p. E-2.

58 "We've never really—to a lot of people—arrived . . . our reenactments are all assiduously researched." Interview with Lance Heflin, September 2, 1999.

59 "In the beginning . . . too much for most people." Heflin interview.

59 "We had to sever it . . . the project for the network." Interview with Bob Mariano, July 23, 1999.

60 "We just weren't willing to accept half a marriage." *Variety*, July 27, 1988, p. 39.

60 A mix of news, comedy skits, and interviews . . . the late-night slot in FOX's schedule." Alex McNeil, *Total Television*, 4th ed. (New York, 1996), p. 916.

60 "We didn't understand . . . Had that show been on CBS, maybe." Ancier interview.

61 "I don't want to leave . . . have a say about programming." Wendle interview.

61 Ancier, who later calls Diller a "friend" . . . I don't respond to that kind of sibling rivalry situation very well." Ancier interview.

62 "I think for the six months . . . It wasn't through bad management." Wendle interview.

62 "Barry played games with Garth . . . upbraid Ancier for failing to act. George Mair, *The Barry Diller Story* (New York, 1997), pp. 159–160.

62 "It wasn't a great situation . . . People can get bruised." Wendle interview.

63 Diller told him . . . "We're going to give him his chance." Block, *Outfoxed*, p. 261.

63 "What you need is two people . . . which was pretty reprehensible." Ancier interview.

63 "It was weird . . . I really had no choice." Wendle interview.

64 "So I left his office . . . he goes, 'Well?'" Kenneally interview.

64 "I wasn't sure which way to go . . . sort of self-conscious in either office to the other one." Kenneally interview.

64 "It was clear to an outsider . . . hopefully our mixed agendas would produce results." Kenneally interview.

64 "Some of the best shows on FOX . . . we probably would have grown even faster." Ancier interview.

65 "When I say it was awkward . . . but we worked together as a threesome." Kenneally interview.

65 "I think it became clear to me that Peter wanted to bring in his own people." Wendle interview.

65 "I've said to Kevin that I would probably never work with him again." Ancier interview.

66 When *Married . . . *was selected . . . that the public hasn't seen yet." Wendle interview.

67 "You told us to be free. Now you tell us not to be free. Which is it?" Block, *Outfoxed*, p. 220.

67 *"Married . . . with Children* could have stayed or gone . . . It did not have national awareness." Kenneally interview.

67 Rakolta had tuned in . . . that's when I have to get involved." *Variety*, March 8, 1989, p. 44.

67 "She was [exercising] on a treadmill . . . You found it that disgusting?'" Interview with Kevin O'Brien, July 22, 1999.

68 The Gillette Company announced . . . "not a desirable vehicle for [our] advertising." *Hollywood Reporter*, February 3, 1995, p. S-23.

68 "All the while we were getting phone calls from FOX saying that we had to tone it down." Mair, *Diller*, p. 164.

68 Tribune's Patrick Mullen . . . a very successful show for FOX." Mullen interview.

69 "That was the best thing . . . put on different kinds of programming." Young interview.

69 "The spike in our ratings . . . in the lobby of the FOX network at one time." Kenneally interview.

CHAPTER FIVE: 1989–1990

72 "They'd force their way into the room . . . everybody could be heard." Fessel interview.

72 "A woman in the accounting department . . . how they're treated on *Married . . . with Children?*" Mariano interview.

73 "I think the idea of having everyone . . . we need honest feedback." Ancier interview.

73 "Why do you fight for this show? . . . Do you suggest we program those?" Kenneally interview.

74 "Basically, the movie business is a weekend business . . . the same timetable, which as weekly." Fessel interview.

74 "We would turn around on Wednesday . . . we'd start all over again." Fessel interview.

75 "We would have been better off if we stayed where we were." Cannell interview.

75 "People wanted him to go . . . And then we *were* canceled." Cannell interview.

76 "What happened to *Jump Street?* . . . but we want the show." Cannell interview.

76 "It was great . . . why did you cancel *Jump Street?*' but I never did that." Cannell interview.

76 "Look, Barry [Diller] decided . . . I want it to be two hours." Interview with Ken Johnson, July 20, 1999.

77 "They kept thinking it was *Lethal Weapon* . . . not what I wanted to do." Johnson interview.

77 "I remember Ken Johnson . . . other science fiction shows up to that point." Interview with Paul Stupin, July 21, 1999.

78 "Because of the breakout success . . . we were in breakout mentality then." Kenneally interview.

78 "Barry did not think . . . I don't know." Johnson interview.

79 "We all felt it was like a gift . . . everybody just flocked back to do it." Johnson interview.

79 "He called us . . . hocus pocus." Fessel interview.

80 "I designed *The Simpsons* . . . getting people's attention would not do it." Mair, *Diller*, p. 170.

80 "It should fit well into the FOX lineup . . . this initial effort." *Variety*, December 20, 1989, p. 48.

81 Tracey Ullman called it quits . . . a network that didn't exist." *Variety*, May 23, 1990, p. 74.

81 "It's going to be a long month." Mariano interview.

82 "That was a must-have . . . sell to all the cereal advertisers." Interview with Brad Moran, June 13, 1999.

83 "The syndicators that were clearing . . . a huge source of revenue for all of us at that point." Mullen interview.

83 "Why don't you do for us in kids what you're doing for us in prime time?" Kellner interview.

83 "I basically used Harry . . . than network ideas." Kellner interview.

84 Calling it a "historic arrangement" . . . from advertising revenues." *Variety*, February 28, 1990, p. 37.

84 "Well, what about you?" Interview with Margaret Loesch, July 22, 1999.

84 "I'm very intimidated by Barry . . . I would buffer you." Loesch interview.

85 "I didn't know Peter. I had met him, but had no relationship." Loesch interview.

85 "I wanted to be as independent as possible . . . Jamie was surprised but pleased by my request." Loesch interview.

85 Kellner had a request . . . "one of the most painful years of my career." Loesch interview.

85 "What Margaret didn't understand . . . all my affiliates' shelf space." Kellner interview.

86 FOX countered . . . "ready to proceed on schedule." *Variety*, January 17, 1990, p. 44.

86 General manager Kevin O'Brien . . . (i.e., run the shows at the times Disney demanded). *Variety*, January 24, 1990, p. 166.

86 In February 1990 he warned . . . a house that has only four rooms." *Variety*, February 14, 1990, p. 57.

86 O'Brien lashed out . . . with their two-hour kids block." *Variety*, February 28, 1990, p. 37.

87 Loesch recalled receiving . . . well that was really [some] Belgians." Loesch interview.

88 NBC argued, "There is absolutely no basis . . . effective competition to the networks." *Variety*, July 27, 1988, p. 38.

88 "We can't wait any longer without stopping the growth of the fourth network." *Variety*, January 31, 1990, p. 66.

89 One day Kellner was walking . . . I said, 'That's the guy.'" Kellner interview.

89 They had a drink . . . you're just the guy to fill it." Interview with Preston Padden, March 9, 1999.

89 "And so we were literally all alone . . . Failure was not an option." Padden interview.

90 "Foreign ownership is not a particularly relevant issue." *Variety*, February 7, 1990, p. 147.

91 "The mentality of the show . . . it was young urban." Interview with Eric Gold, October 8, 1999.

91 "When I came along . . . it was something different." Kristal Brent Zook, *Color by FOX* (New York, 1999), p. 105.

91 "I don't need to meet with them . . . what's out of bounds." Gold interview.

91 "Nobody knew . . . we would just rue the day we ever saw the show through." Kenneally interview.

92 "What happened was like *South Park* . . . a must-see tape that everybody watched." Gold interview.

92 Programming executive . . . a new positive cachet in the creative community. Kenneally interview.

92 Series producer Gold recalled . . . from his stations which were not that sure yet." Gold interview.

93 "What might have been . . . by being funny." *Variety*, April 25, 1990, p. 108.

93 "I can't tell you how many . . . We had a lot of people watching that show." Young interview.

CHAPTER SIX: 1990–1991

94 An ABC executive there . . . young boys all over America." *Variety*, September 17, 1990, p. 30.

96 "Sure there was trepidation . . . the more excited we got." *Variety*, June 6, 1990, p. 39.

96 "My recollection is that Barry . . . discussion and subsequent excitement." Stupin interview.

96 "We have no illusions about that . . . the other two networks aren't really hitting." *Variety*, June 6, 1990, p. 39.

96 "You're doing great . . . work twice as hard." Interview with Phil Lerman, September 1, 1999.

96 "Boy, that's an amazing move." *Variety*, May 30, 1990, p. 1.

96 "I looked in the mirror . . . except to get into the programming business." Interview with Gerry Walsh, February 11, 1999.

98 "If you create a satellite-delivered service . . . Would a kiss be too demonstrative?" Padden interview.

98 "There was a little bit of fear there . . . and they got a rash." Kellner interview.

99 "He had been a cable basher . . . Well, I changed jobs." Fessel interview.

99 "We had noticed that . . . the value that an affiliate brings to a broadcast network." Padden interview.

100 "We closed the rating gap . . . by about half." Padden interview.

100 "It was another place to sell . . . there were other opportunities." Loesch interview.

101 "I think we need something . . . that would work better for us." Loesch interview.

101 "I don't know how to do sixty-five half hours in six months." Loesch interview.

101 "We . . . had a series . . . took twenty-eight weeks." Loesch interview.

102 Years later, KTVU general manager . . . "a disaster, it was a bomb." O'Brien interview.

102 "Okay, you'll fix it. You'll do something else." Kellner interview.

102 "We told everybody . . . what made the whole thing work." Kellner interview.

102 "Saturday morning on the networks . . . They could not see it." Loesch interview.

103 "I built a reputation . . . It was a joke." Loesch interview.

103 "It's a huge undertaking . . . But then some harsh economic realities set in." *Variety*, March 18, 1991, p. 27.

104 "Very few 100+ markets . . . as there is at 10." Woods interview.

104 "It's a very, very expensive thing to do . . . people have to do it." Mullen interview.

105 "Of all the shows I've done . . . You have two teenage kids, and you live in Beverly Hills.'" Aaron Spelling with Jefferson Graham, *Aaron Spelling: A Prime-Time Life* (New York, 1996), pp. 172–173.

105 "I went over to Aaron Spelling's office . . . I didn't come to you." Kenneally interview.

105 "CAA went to war with us . . . one of the major talent agencies had cut the supply line." Kenneally interview.

106 "So even before I officially moved . . . we had developed almost completely internally." Stupin interview.

107 "Maybe the best thing to do . . . of that audience." Kenneally interview.

107 "Aaron and Darren met . . . any of our creative ideas that were interesting." Interview with Bob Greenblatt, July 23, 1999.

107 "Aaron and Darren would do versions of the script . . . and had his own creative thoughts." Greenblatt interview.

108 "I remember to this day . . . and we shot the pilot." Stupin interview.

108 "What is this *90210*? . . . Never heard of it." Mariano interview.

108 "It struggled a lot . . . like almost every show on FOX at that time." Greenblatt interview.

110 "The big lesson . . . we must continue to act that way." *Variety*, January 21, 1991, p. 1.

110 "Rob?" said Diller. "*DEA*—D." Kenneally interview.

CHAPTER SEVEN: 1991–1992

112 Calling the charge "bird-brained" . . . to sell to the three networks." *Variety*, August 19, 1991, p. 21.

112 "Actually, FOXification was the word . . . drop it and go FOX19." Mariano interview.

113 "People come up to me . . . you are much better.'" *Variety*, October 14, 1991, p. 63.

113 "Compensation from us is not a major part of our affiliates' revenue." *Variety*, August 26, 1991, p. 1.

114 "Let's knock off NBC . . . take the kids away." Loesch interview.

114 "I thought this guy was a lunatic . . . He was absolutely right." Loesch interview.

115 "It is time to put this conflict . . . statesmanlike decision." *Variety*, February 3, 1992, p. 26.

117 "At the same time that CBS . . . They were a unique generation." Fessel interview.

117 "From the movie industry's point of view . . . without a lot of work." *Variety*, August 10, 1992, p. 17.

117 Fessel would gleefully point out . . . Demos are really the key to us." *Variety*, December 23, 1991, p. 26.

118 "We found that the African-American audience . . . generating ratings points." Fessel interview.

119 "The highest ratings we've ever had . . . those shows from FOX." Woods interview.

119 "I saw a survey . . . we didn't have the eyeballs." Walsh interview.

119 "FOX changed the course . . . make alternative programming." Zook, *Color by FOX*, p.105.

120 "It wasn't my store . . . but it wasn't mine." Gail Sheehy, *Understanding Men's Passages* (New York, 1998), p. 112.

120 "He told me . . . in this company only one principal.'" Shawcross, *Murdoch*, p. 390.

120 "They think I'm an idiot . . . prove them wrong." *Variety*, March 2, 1992, p. 1.

120 "Let's put it this way . . . That's liberal bullshit." *Variety*, March 2, 1992, p. 1.

121 "This is completely amicable . . . could not be found—anywhere." FOX press release, February 1992.

121 "When Barry left we were throwing . . . six offices to get champagne." Interview, name withheld upon request.

121 One employee, formerly at CBS . . . not by shouting obscenities. Interview, name withheld upon request.

122 "The reality is that there were not many ideas . . . with people like Barry Diller." Interview, name withheld upon request.

122 "I did not like his . . . I don't respect that kind of management." Interview, name withheld upon request.

122 "I think one of the real humorous . . . He gets far too much credit." Interview, name withheld upon request.

122 "I think Barry Diller was . . . Kellner was the one who was making the program decisions . . ." Mullen interview.

123 "Rupert had the money . . . like the Celtics replacing Larry Bird." Walsh interview.

123 "He's certainly a tireless executive . . . from Diller, the head of Fox, Inc. Interview with Tom Allen, August 26, 1999.

123 "He was the most brilliant . . . and he will totally respect it." Mariano interview.

123 Trade reporter Brian Lowry . . . they were part of the landscape." Lowry interview.

124 "When you pitched a project to FOX . . . what sensibility to orient projects towards." *Variety*, March 2, 1992, p. 1.

125 "The idea is to spotlight . . . develop those people as personalities." *Variety*, May 11, 1992, p. 60.

126 "Rupert really wanted to . . . encouraged to huddle up." Interview with Greg Meidel, July 20, 1999.

126 "First of all, Chao's . . . credit for the speech." Meidel interview.

127 "No way . . . not going to have a stripper." Meidel interview.

127 "You never heard such nervous laughter through an entire room." Meidel interview.

127 "It's a terrible thing to see . . . that there are limits." Shawcross, *Murdoch*, p. 395.

CHAPTER EIGHT: 1992–1993

132 "We can't just allow animation . . . that real-life characters can't do." *Variety*, February 24, 1992, p. 86.

133 "There were three areas we wanted . . . *Melrose Place* was born." Kenneally interview.

133 "FOX wanted a *90210* spin-off . . . as big a hit as *90210*." Spelling, *Spelling*, p. 185.

133 "Aaron was very reticent . . . probably be a good idea." Greenblatt interview.

133 "We figured, why don't we try . . . worked pretty easily." Greenblatt interview.

134 "You know what . . . a big, outrageous soap." Greenblatt interview.

134 "Amanda set off a rather powerful . . . girls started popping up *everywhere*." David Wild, *The Official Melrose Place Companion* (New York, 1995), p. 25.

134 Greenblatt said if it hadn't been . . . off the air pretty quickly." Greenblatt interview.

135 "The book we all read . . . after a point Jamie had had enough." Gold interview.

136 Financial officer Tom Allen remembers . . . "Our standards department approved all three." Allen interview.

136 The laughter stopped dead . . . how Jamie manages people." Allen interview.

136 "And Keenen went crazy . . . Our audience is out partying." Gold interview.

137 "Lucie and I got into a big fight . . . Don't you understand?'" Gold interview.

138 "He was furious . . . Peter Chernin's decision." Interview with Lucie Salhany, June 29, 1999.

139 "I think like most businesses . . . helped it survive and blossom." Kellner interview.

139 She recalled, going in . . . he could be "very difficult." Salhany interview.

140 In April 1993 the trades were reporting . . . get back to you in a couple of days." *Variety*, April 12, 1993, p. 1.

140 Padden took the opportunity . . . their old independent ways." *Variety*, February 1, 1993, p. 35.

140 "I had said to Jamie . . . he thought it was a good idea." Loesch interview.

141 "I felt very alone . . . Salhany became my biggest cheerleader." Loesch, ibid.
142 "The way that worked was cable operators . . . for their retransmission consent." Padden interview.
143 "I think that the decision . . . got actual cash out of the deal." O'Brien interview.
144 "Honestly? No." *Variety*, June 14, 1993, p. 23.
144 Executive producer James L. Brooks . . . classification is defying us." *Variety*, August 2, 1993, p. 23.
144 Series creator Matt Groening . . . beating *Garfield* every year." *Variety*, August 2, 1993, p. 23.

CHAPTER NINE: 1993–1994

146 "Chevy is the most recognized . . . he will be out there in late night." *Variety*, September 9, 1993, p. 19.
147 "Lucie brought a programming angle . . . a late-night show." Interview with Bob Leider, September 24, 1998.
148 "I don't think any of the affiliates . . . doing an interview show." Interview, name withheld upon request.
148 "I should have known . . . there was no hope." Salhany interview.
149 "We'll all be there watching . . . ground zero." *Variety*, September 9, 1993, p. 19.
149 "We acknowledge that . . . with our rhythm." *Variety*, September 20, 1993, p. 19.
150 "Twentieth Television was producing . . . 'Okay, guys, I'll be here.'" Salhany interview.
150 "The shows weren't very good . . . on the air." *Variety*, October 8, 1993, p. 46.
151 "What are you going to do? . . . I don't want you to go alone." Salhany interview.
151 "Everybody thought Rupert was horrified . . . don't look back." Salhany interview.
152 "Every time there's a problem . . . 'strip mining' is the perfect term.'" *Variety*, November 1, 1993, p. 28.
152 "You have to realize . . . our best interest to be hanging out there." Gold interview.
152 Ultimately they settled . . . we're over it now." Gold interview.
152 "The person that I guess we blame . . . she was very bad people." Gold interview.
153 "I always felt we had a good relationship . . . very, very different style." Allen interview.
153 "There were negotiations . . . but it was never serious." Salhany interview.
154 "They wanted the time back . . . didn't want to give the time back." Walsh interview.
154 "The typical affiliate owns . . . half those availabilities to sell." Leider interview.
154 "Had we come up with a good show . . . would have taken it." Salhany interview.
154 "I would find it hard to believe . . . a very scary proposition." O'Brien interview.
155 "When I had first shown . . . that I had to follow." Loesch interview.
156 "In many ways she was . . . very smart." Loesch interview.
156 "I really agonized the night before . . . It's horrible. It's cheesy." Loesch interview.

156 Saban had cagily held onto . . . *Power Rangers* as a marketing tie-in. *Jerusalem Report*, August 17, 1998, p. 45.

157 "Yeah, it was . . . Thank you, *Power Rangers.*" Allen interview.

157 "We all thought the show . . . a little tongue-in-cheek humor." Greenblatt interview.

158 Violence had been defined as . . . 117 violent incidents." *Variety*, December 27, 1993, p. 42.

158 It was followed . . . "a little sci-fi cult show." Greenblatt interview.

159 Roth liked the idea . . . to series and eventual success. Interview with Peter Roth, July 19, 1999.

159 "The irony of that . . . singular and not commercial." Roth interview.

159 "Everybody will take credit . . . Grushow did not want the show." Salhany interview.

160 Roth wouldn't pin the blame . . . in the value of *The X-Files*. Roth interview.

160 "If we hadn't been patient . . . it would take time." *Variety*, April 25, 1994, p. 1.

161 "It's created in-house . . . what a show should achieve, that is it." Meidel interview.

162 "First of all you have to give . . . anyone of the new regime." Salhany interview.

162 "The league's perspective was . . . whether they were qualified." Interview with Ken Ziffren, July 20, 1999.

162 "I didn't know that . . . the NFC that was stronger." Salhany interview.

163 "I went through all of the ratings . . . had no idea about this." Salhany interview.

163 "I remember we had . . . considered on the merits." Ziffren interview.

163 "That's how we built the whole campaign . . . here we are growing?" Salhany interview.

163 Indeed, at the time the median age . . . on ABC it was 56.2. *Variety*, February 14, 1994, p. 68.

163 "When Rupert took over . . . I'm willing to pay for it.'" Salhany interview.

164 "Everybody was on pins . . . pacing the floor." Meidel interview.

164 "Rupert was, 'Let's get it . . . they had lost it." Meidel interview.

164 "I think the number . . . wouldn't have been as effective." Meidel interview.

166 "Chase [Carey] was the guy who . . . make the network stronger." Salhany interview.

167 "New World had stations . . .what could we get?" Interview with Michael H. Diamond, July 21, 1999.

167 "We're going over to FOX . . . Miami that had done that." Diamond interview.

167 "We can do it . . . you can get out of the affiliations." Diamond interview.

168 "So we went in . . . the stations that we had." Diamond interview.

168 "It happened in five days . . . a legal deal putting it together." Salhany interview.

168 Diamond recalls that one issue . . . ice-skating are major sports." Diamond interview.

169 The deal covered every . . . "Get this done." Diamond interview.

169 "You can't do that . . .We really can." Diamond interview.

169 "I thought it was so badly . . . Rupert [Murdoch] didn't." Salhany interview.

170 "The argument we made . . . ABC, CBS, or NBC affiliation." Padden interview.

170 "You know, listen, life goes on." Leider interview.
170 "It was of particular concern . . . That became the goal." Interview with Ed Ansin, September 24, 1998.
170 "The miracle here . . . one of the then major networks." Padden interview.
171 "We don't want it, no matter what it is." *Variety*, June 27, 1994, p. 104.
171 "I kept saying to the board . . . in the middle of our relationship." Padden interview.
171 "At the time . . . our affiliation was threatened." Young.
172 "The only disappointing note . . . team that you're on." *Variety*, June 27, 1994, p. 104.
172 "There were a lot of stations . . . what he wanted to do." Young interview.
172 "How come you make my mommy cry all the time?" Salhany interview.
173 "He was caught short . . . Sandy took over." Salhany interview.
173 Fox Entertainment Group chairman . . . encountered anything like that." Salhany interview.
173 At the close of the affiliate . . . interested in what she had to say. Salhany interview.

CHAPTER TEN: 1994–1995

176 "We probably sided with them . . . where it was done." *Variety*, May 2, 1994, p. 1.
177 "Those ownership issues . . . in the NAACP filing." *Variety*, December 6, 1993, p. 20.
177 "Everywhere in the world . . . a struggling, emerging operation." *Variety*, May 2, 1994, p. 1.
177 The network was owned . . . rules to the limit." *Variety*, May 30, 1994, p. 24.
179 Matoian was a former . . . little old ladies." *Variety*, October 10, 1994, p. 33.
179 "Matoian is a class act . . . a little higher brow." *Variety*, November 14, 1994, p. 23.
179 "We always were guided . . . no medical shows." Greenblatt interview.
180 He called Matoian . . . different as one could ask for." Roth interview.
180 "I think that the brand . . . had been uniquely FOX." Roth interview.
181 "We had the idea . . . the parents were gone?" Greenblatt interview.
181 "We got amazingly lucky with the cast." Greenblatt interview.
181 "[Grushow] always . . . had a dry eye." Salhany interview.
182 "Of course we . . . like to put it?" Salhany interview.
182 "It went on the air . . . moved it behind *90210*." Greenblatt interview.
182 "He declared . . . it should have been canceled." Greenblatt interview.
182 "My competitors . . . on our schedule." Brenda Scott Royce, *Party of Five: The Unofficial Companion* (Los Angeles, 1997), p. 42.
183 "We would not be on the air if we were not on FOX." Royce, *Party of Five*, p. 42.
184 "NBC is simply . . . no better than they are." *Variety*, November 28, 1994, p. 108.
184 General Electric had been . . . $7.2 million to the expenses. Thomas F. Boyle, *At Any Cost* (New York, 1998), pp. 257–258.

184 "I was in the office . . . growth of FOX as they could." Padden interview.

185 "I'll never forget counsel . . . that you've heard of.'" Padden interview.

186 The suite was in chaos . . . how the world could be remade." Padden interview.

187 "By the way, General Electric . . . he was talking about." Padden interview.

187 "I never talked to the people . . . didn't even know I existed." Padden interview.

188 "Well, I *know* they didn't . . . about a book deal.'" Padden interview.

189 "If you listen to the . . . philosophy I work under. Sorry." *Variety*, February 13, 1995, p. 29.

189 "We believe it is now . . . of mutual interest." *Variety*, February 20, 1995, p. 200.

189 "They made a decision . . . the feedback they were getting." Padden interview.

190 "What FOX appeared . . . to bid for properties." Interview with David Honig, April 6, 1999.

190 In a March 1995 interview . . . extremely troubling." *Variety*, March 20, 1995, p. 23.

190 "I'm sure they'll blame this on us, too." *Variety*, April 24, 1995, p. 19.

191 "I fully agree with . . . *de jure* control of FOX." Concurring statement of Commissioner James H. Quello, May 4, 1995, pp. 1–2.

191 "Don't tell me that anything Murdoch has, he doesn't have control." Interview with James H. Quello, March 11, 1999.

192 "Again the commission seems . . . to Rupert Murdoch." *New York Times*, May 8, 1995, p. D8.

192 "It was seen as a loss . . . We kept it clean." Honig interview.

192 "We made peace . . . to the letter." Honig interview.

192 "The bottom line was . . . gobble up American broadcasting assets." Padden interview.

193 "It is time to free FOX . . . *American* fourth network." Quello, concurring statement, p. 6.

CHAPTER ELEVEN: 1995–1996

195 "I don't think his taste . . . the network." Lowry interview.

196 "Good things about . . . people are watching you." *Variety*, September 25, 1995, p. 31.

196 "Prior to this regime . . . some grown-up choices." *Variety*, September 4, 1995, p. 33.

196 "Can FOX be distinctive . . . who they want to be." *Variety*, February 12, 1996, p. 1.

196 "Patience is really . . . hold the course." *Variety*, January 22, 1996, p. 34.

197 "John was, perhaps, miscast . . . a monthly meeting.'" Loesch interview.

197 It was at those recurring . . . those kids are over there?" Loesch, ibid.

197 "It was just the environment . . . [to be] a love." Loesch interview.

198 Loesch came out into the hall . . . They finally got it." Loesch interview.

198 "This giving out the check . . . at the right time." O'Brien interview.

198 "What happened was that Murdoch . . . in terms of reach. . . ." Diamond interview.

200 "It was very difficult . . . not buying the company.'" Diamond interview.

200 Diamond kept fending off . . . assured him he would not be. Diamond interview.

201 "Going into the weekend . . . study something to death." Ziffren interview.

202 Then in May of 1993 . . . the FX channel. Interview with Anne Sweeney, September 10, 1999.

203 "We called it the FX apartment . . . guests who came on the show." Sweeney interview.

203 "I felt it was a free day . . . to do live TV." Interview with Tom Bergeron, October 1, 1999.

204 "I get lost sometimes." *Variety*, January 22, 1996, p. 28.

204 "It was very inventive . . . when it moved over." Sweeney interview.

205 He told Greenblatt . . . tell me it's not unique." Greenblatt interview.

205 "They didn't get it conceptually . . . And it sat on the shelf." Greenblatt interview.

206 "For some reason . . . the wrong network for it." Greenblatt interview.

206 "If you're going to put on . . . not find it admirable." Cannell interview.

206 "*How to Succeed* . . . whiff of *The X-Files*." *TV Guide*, April 6, 1996, p. 12.

206 "I believe that, if given more . . . didn't get it." Greenblatt interview.

206 "[Matoian] said when he resigned . . . the day he canceled *Profit*." Cannell interview

207 "We were going to reunite . . . them all to Washington." Lerman interview.

207 "It was a wonderful . . . festive occasion for us." Heflin interview.

207 "That meant only one thing: we were canceled." Heflin interview.

207 "People are singing . . . *America's Most Wanted*." Lerman interview.

208 "I really want to . . . bring it back." Heflin interview.

208 "Thirty-seven governors . . . what time of day it is?" Lerman interview.

CHAPTER TWELVE: 1996–1997

211 "There's always been a tendency . . . in the long haul." Lowry interview.

211 But Fessel would have understood . . . all things to all people." Fessel interview.

212 FOX, he felt, should be selling . . . my mantra." Roth interview.

213 Heflin and Walsh were sitting . . . in the history of television." Heflin interview.

213 "I brought back *America's* . . . wanted to continue with." Roth interview.

214 "You can promote *The Simpsons* . . . he's not gonna watch." *Variety*, October 21, 1996, p. 201.

214 "I was involved in everything . . . I wasn't part of that team." Roth interview.

214 "There was a feeling that . . . critical hit that it was." Bergeron interview.

215 "My favorite line from David Hill . . . hell in a handbasket." Bergeron interview.

215 "I think the failure of nerve . . . was sharpening its knives." Bergeron interview.

215 He has fond memories . . . network to support the show." Bergeron interview.

216 "It was becoming the very show . . . incredibly painful." Bergeron interview.

216 Officially his departure was . . . by "mutual agreement." *Variety*, July 14, 1997.

216 Unofficially, he just walked . . . "safe, generic daytime show." Bergeron interview.

216 "I can't imagine . . . working with FOX after that." Bergeron interview.

216 *Los Angeles Times* critic . . . in the wings, pointless." *Los Angeles Times*, October 25, 1996, p. F1.

216 "The concept is . . . trying to write about." *Entertainment Weekly*, October 18, 1996, p. 47.

217 "It was dark and grim . . . do whatever you want." Greenblatt interview.

217 "In my office . . . he pitched the voice of Hank Hill." Roth interview.

219 "The NAACP is actually . . . ignoring African-American characters." Roth interview.

219 "FOX's stuff is more . . . than it was a year ago." *Variety*, March 31, 1997, p. 35.

219 A snapshot of the season-to-date . . . was 35 percent. *Variety*, April 21, 1997, p. 28.

220 *The Simpsons* was cited . . . reinvigorating the form." *Variety*, April 7, 1997, p. 53.

220 "I had told Rupert . . . new corporation for FOX." Padden interview.

221 "That was his job . . . a hell of a job." Young interview.

221 "For the most part . . . that was the deal." Woods interview.

221 "He's a smart guy . . . behind the scenes." Lowry interview.

222 "If I'd talk to Chase . . . Rupert had Chase on a fast track." Meidel interview.

222 "We were reeling . . . we were getting our footing." Greenblatt interview.

CHAPTER THIRTEEN: 1997–1998

224 "When are we going . . . the airwaves in the summer." *Variety*, April 21, 1997, p. 1.

225 The radio ads . . . for its July premiere. *Variety*, July 21, 1997. p. 17.

225 David Hill said . . . "abdicating the summer to cable." *Variety*, May 5, 1997, p. 225.

225 "Because it's all economics . . . therefore we won't do it." Roth interview.

226 "The shame of it is . . . long-term economic loss." Roth interview.

226 "Soap mogul Aaron Spelling . . . nasty to one another." *TV Guide*, May 10, 1997, p. 16.

227 "I'm a loud and ardent advocate of original programming year round." Roth interview.

227 In an official statement . . . later in the season. *Variety*, September 1, 1997, p. 24.

228 "We were fortunate enough . . . romantic, and sexy." Greenblatt interview.

229 "It was basically him . . . And he basically did it." Greenblatt interview.

229 "Is Feminism Dead?" *Time*, June 29, 1998, cover.

229 "We never endeavored . . . a lot more seriously than we take it." *Los Angeles Times*, September 9, 1998, p. F9.

230 "I think it's terrible . . . one of Kelley's conditions." *Variety*, March 30, 1998, p. 83.

230 "From the very beginning . . . we outmuscled the traditional networks." Loesch interview.

231 She calls her . . . "the most exciting time of my life." Loesch interview.

232 "One of the problems . . . out of the profits." O'Brien interview.

233 "The whole FOX Kids Network . . . was an inside deal." Woods interview.

233 "It was only the FOX . . . helping the last time." *Variety*, February 9, 1998, p. 35.

233 "Legally, there was some question . . . a big stroke game going on." O'Brien interview.

234 "At this point, we're open . . . not an 'us vs. them.'" *Variety*, March 9, 1998, p. 30.

234 "The next time . . . disastrous for all of us." *Variety*, June 8, 1998, p. 19.

235 It began with actress . . . At FOX, we play to win." All quotations from the "up-front" presentation are from a videotape of the event.

238 Later Peter Roth would say . . . a lot of luck." Roth interview.

CHAPTER FOURTEEN: 1998–1999

239 "We are in no way endorsing or glamorizing drugs." *Variety*, July 27, 1999, p. 24.

240 "We're not lying about it . . . will appreciate." *Variety*, July 27, 1999, p. 24.

240 Terry Turner added that . . . without ever mentioning Prohibition." *Boston Globe*, July 23, 1998, p. D8.

240 "We're not going to turn this into an *ABC After-School Special*." *Los Angeles Times*, June 20, 1998, F1.

241 "After having spent much . . . of deconstructing *Hollyweird*." *Hollywood Reporter*, August 20, 1998, p. 3.

241 As the 1998–1999 fall . . . when the fall schedule was set. *Variety*, August 24, 1998, p. 1.

242 "How does FOX plan . . . glaringly unoriginal new comedy. . . ." *Variety*, August 24, 1998, p. 25.

242 The concept "well-worn . . . pedestrian." *Hollywood Reporter*, August 21, 1998, p. 8.

243 "I don't particularly . . . try to be satisfied." *Variety*, January 11, 1999, p. 57.

244 "It is a truism that . . . years of all time." Roth interview.

245 "There was failure . . . that's how it works." Roth interview.

246 "I want to take risks . . . Hire someone from Comedy Central.'" *Variety*, November 23, 1998, p. 21.

246 "I was a complete interloper . . . a short time to do it." Interview with Doug Herzog, September 12, 2003.

247 "I was literally thrown in . . . since Barry Diller was here." *Broadcasting & Cable*, September 20, 1999, p. 26.

247 "I'm sure a lot of people . . . the first six months." *Variety*, November 23, 1998, p. 21.

248 "I kind of scratch my head . . . Plain and simple." *New York Daily News*, July 2, 1999, p. 120.

248 "We tried to shrug it off . . . going out on a limb." Interview with Larry Wilmore, October 10, 2003.

250 "As far as the FOX Kids . . . the FOX Family Channel." Woods interview.

250 Tribune's Patrick Mullen . . . The leverage has shifted." Mullen interview.

251 "The FOX executives that are . . . demands placed upon us by FOX executives." O'Brien interview.

251 The blowup occurred . . . in a letter to the affiliates. *Variety*, April 12, 1999, p. 26.

252 "They don't call it affiliate relations . . . don't relate to their affiliates." Woods interview.

252 "What they were doing . . . national marketplace to sell an ad." Moran interview.
253 "There were certainly decisions to be made . . . time to conjure things up."
   Herzog interview.
254 Hill "was one of my few bigger, vocal supporters." Herzog interview.
254 "Our view was that . . . was not a smart thing to do." *Variety*, June 14, 1999,
   p. 18.

CHAPTER FIFTEEN: 1999–2000

255 "The idea of doing conventional sitcoms made me ill . . . a tough show to put
   over on a network." Herzog interview.
256 "It wasn't working . . . It kind of veered on camp." Herzog interview.
256 "Nothing is done till it's done . . . Whatever it is, we'll do it.'" Herzog interview.
257 "FOX sits at both sides of the bargaining table . . . serves its corporate interests." *Variety*, August 23, 1999, p. 27.
258 "I have a feeling we're part of a much bigger problem [at FOX]." *Variety*, November 1, 1999, p. 21.
258 "I literally almost had a heart attack and drove off the road." *Boston Herald*,
   May 25, 1999, p. 50.
258 "Everybody fell in love with David's idea . . . repurposing has become a staple
   of network television." Herzog interview.
259 "I was no longer the guy in charge . . . The dynamic had changed." Herzog
   interview.
259 "A guy who comes in in the middle of January . . . To blame Doug for this year
   is stupid." *Variety*, November 22, 1999, p. 29.
259 "Somebody on my comedy staff said . . . the funniest thing I had read since
   I got there." Herzog interview.
260 "Hey, get this out of UPN. We'll make this." Herzog interview.
260 "It was like 'Good luck, kid . . . Nobody cared about it." Herzog interview.
260 "He's not an A-list guy . . . He *is* the show." Herzog interview.
261 It was described as . . . wrote the magazine's editors. *TV Guide*, September 11,
   1999, p. 13.
261 "FOX was coming off a period . . . all they would be running." Herzog interview.
262 "Mike Darnell as so totally vexed . . . That sounds great.'" Herzog interview.
263 "It took something like this to make the Miss America pageant look good to
   me." *Boston Globe*, February 22, 2000, p. A1.
263 "I'm the guy who greenlit . . . And then the shit hit the fan." Herzog interview.
264 "You've got to balance a desire to win . . . you're certainly playing with fire."
   Variety, July 24, 2000, p. 23.
264 "The truth of the matter is, I never got a real at bat." Herzog interview.

CHAPTER SIXTEEN: 2000 AND BEYOND

267 "It's Fox's Dream Team—Stability in top exec ranks lead to ratings jump." *Variety*, August 11, 2003, p. 14.
268 "The revolving door stopped . . . been here a while." *Variety*, August 11, 2003,
   p. 14.

268 "Chernin in late 1999 . . . joined FOX in 1988." *Variety*, August 11, 2003, p. 45.

271 "We had our most competitive season . . . contender for prime-time leadership." *Variety*, May 28, 2001, p. 58.

271 "Initial episodes of *Idol* delivered . . . in those categories." *Variety*, June 24, 2002, p. 21.

272 Vocal coach Debra Byrd . . . had to have a doctor come to them." *TV Guide*, May 17, 2003, p. 17.

273 "We weren't playing with . . . unscripted guns in the fourth quarter. We didn't." *Variety*, January 27, 2003, p. 18.

273 "If you use reality properly, it infuses energy into the entire network." *Variety*, March 3, 2003, p. 35.

274 "Our goal is to have . . . shows to help scripted series." *Variety*, March 31, 2003, p. 23.

275 "We can't control the expectation . . . everyone threw their goods at us." *Variety*, November 12, 2001, p. 22.

276 "We'll have to reassess repurposing as a business." *Variety*, May 20, 2002, p. 71.

277 "I had a conceptual idea . . . but it's funny, too.'" Wilmore interview.

277 "They were hungry . . . the perfect fit at the right time." Wilmore interview.

277 "It's definitely a reminder that . . . color that counts in the end is green." *Variety*, January 7, 2002, p. 40.

278 "They always kept comparing it . . . didn't think the writing was good enough." Wilmore interview.

278 "We had great ratings . . . wrong about the show being good." Wilmore interview.

279 "Our brand is alive and well . . . should be on our air." *Variety*, April 29, 2002, p. 18.

280 "Mitch Stern is the cash cow . . . than anybody else. Period." Meidel interview.

280 "There's a sense of trust . . . this company moves very, very quickly." *Variety*, February 10, 2003, p. 27.

280 "The Chris-Craft acquisition . . . now it's unbelievably competitive." *Variety*, February 10, 2003, p. 27.

281 "The networks find it difficult . . . the game right now." O'Brien interview.

281 He recalled the early days . . . FOX is a hooker." Woods interview.

Bibliography

AUTHOR INTERVIEWS

Tom Allen (August 26, 1999)
Garth Ancier (September 10, 1999)
Ed Ansin (September 24, 1998)
Bob Bennett (August 16, 1999)
Jim Benson (July 15, 1999)
Tom Bergeron (October 1, 1999)
Stephen J. Cannell (June 23, 1999)
Michael H. Diamond (July 21, 1999)
Andrew Fessel (August 10, 1999)
Eric Gold (October 8, 1999)
Bob Greenblatt (July 23, 1999)
Lance Heflin (September 2, 1999)
Doug Herzog (September 12, 2003)
David Honig (April 6, 1999)
Ken Johnson (July 20, 1999)
Jamie Kellner (September 2, 1999)
Rob Kenneally (August 15, 1999)
Bob Leider (September 24, 1998)
Phil Lerman (September 1, 1999)
Margaret Loesch (July 22, 1999)
Brian Lowry (July 14, 1999)
Bob Mariano (July 23, 1999)
Paul McCarthy (April 16, 1999)
Greg Meidel (July 20, 1999)
Brad Moran (June 13, 1999)
Patrick Mullen (August 12, 1999)
Kevin O'Brien (July 22, 1999)
Preston Padden (March 9, 1999)

James Quello (March 11, 1999)
Peter Roth (July 19, 1999)
Mike Ruggiero (July 6, 1999)
Lucie Salhany (June 29, 1999)
Andrew Schwartzman (March 12, 1999)
Andie Sporkin (July 22, 1999)
Paul Stupin (July 21, 1999)
Anne Sweeney (September 10, 1999)
Gerry Walsh (February 11, 1999)
Kevin Wendle (August 5, 1999)
Larry Wilmore (October 10, 2003)
David Woods (June 9, 1999)
Joe Young (June 25, 1999)
Ken Ziffren (July 20, 1999)

BOOKS

Allvine, Glendon. *The Greatest Fox of Them All*. New York, Lyle Stuart, 1969.
Beck, A. C. *That Lawyer Girl: The Unauthorized Guide to Ally's World*. Los Angeles, Renaissance Books, 1999.
Block, Alex Ben. *Outfoxed*. New York, St. Martin's Press, 1990.
Boyle, Thomas F. *At Any Cost*. New York, Alfred A. Knopf, 1998.
Brown, Les. *Les Brown's Encyclopedia of Television*, 3rd ed. Detroit, Visible Ink Press, 1992.
Carter, Bill. *The Late Shift*. New York, Hyperion, 1994.
Farrand, Phil. *The Nitpicker's Guide for X-Philes*. New York, Dell, 1997.
Gross, Ed. *Alien Nation: The Unofficial Companion*. Los Angeles, Renaissance Books, 1998.
Hollywood Creative Directory. Santa Monica, Calif., Hollywood Creative Directory, Spring 1999.
Lowry, Brian. *The Truth Is Out There: The Official Guide to The X-Files*. New York, HarperPrism, 1995.
Mair, George. *The Barry Diller Story*. New York, John Wiley, 1997,
McNeil, Alex. *Total Television*, 4th ed. New York, Penguin Books, 1996.
Reeves-Stevens, Judith and Garfield. *Star Trek Phase II: The Lost Series*. New York, Pocket Books, 1997.
Rivers, Joan, with Richard Merryman. *Still Talking*. New York, Turtle Bay Books, 1991.
Royce, Brenda Scott. *Party of Five: The Unofficial Companion*. Los Angeles, Renaissance Books, 1997.
Shawcross, William. *Murdoch: The Making of a Media Empire*. New York, Touchstone, 1997.

Sheehy, Gail. *Understanding Men's Passages*. New York, Random House, 1998.

Solomon, Aubrey. *Twentieth Century–Fox: A Corporate and Financial History*. Metuchen, N.J., Scarecrow Press, 1988.

Spelling, Aaron, with Jefferson Graham. *Aaron Spelling: A Prime-Time Life*. New York, St. Martin's Press, 1996.

Television & Cable Factbook. Washington, D.C., Warren Publishing, 1997.

Wild, David. *The Official Melrose Place Companion*. New York, Harper-Perennial, 1995.

Zook, Kristal Brent. *Color by Fox: The Fox Network and the Revolution in Black Television*. New York, Oxford University Press, 1999.

ARTICLES

Adalian, Josef. "Foibles of Fox: When Hip Hits a Blip." *Variety*, October 25, 1999, p. 1.

——. "Frog Net Sez It Won't Grow Up." *Variety*, January 11, 1999, p. 57.

——. "It's Fox's Dream Team—Stability in top exec ranks lead to ratings jump." *Variety*, August 11, 2003, p. 14.

——. "Nets Turn Their Backs on Reality." *Variety*, March 31, 2003, p. 23.

——. "Webs, Affils Awash in War Over Revenue Stream." *Variety*, April 12, 1999, p. 25.

——. and Michael Schneider. "And the Winner Is . . ." *Variety*, May 28, 2001, p. 13.

——. and Michael Schneider. "Reality Changes the Rules." *Variety*, March 3, 2003, p. 35.

Advokat, Stephen. "Socialite Vigilante Bags *Married*, Sets Sights on Tabloids Now." *Variety*, March 8, 1989, p. 44.

Aucoin, Don. "Fox Divorces Itself from 'Reality' Show." *Boston Globe*, February 22, 2000, p. A1.

Bark, Ed. "Fox Sitcom Defends Pot Plot." *Boston Globe*, July 23, 1998, p. D8.

Bart, Peter. "Rupert on Rebound." *Variety*, January 21, 1991, p. 1.

Bauder, David. "Networks Find New Ways to Milk Popular Shows." *Boston Herald*, May 25, 1999, p. 50.

Benson, Jim. "Disney Socks Fox with 1-2 Punch." *Variety*, February 28, 1990, p. 37.

——. "Kidvid Rivals Talk About Teaming Up." *Variety*, January 17, 1990, p. 44.

——. "*Simpsons* Exemption Nuked." *Variety*, February 24, 1992, p. 86.

—— and Brian Lowry. "Fox Broadcasting to Affils: Play Along with the Team." *Variety*. February 1, 1993, p. 35.

Braxton, Greg. "*Ally* Returns to All That Attention." *Los Angeles Times*, September 9, 1998, p. F1.

——. "Fox Stirs Up the Pot with Sitcom." *Los Angeles Times*, June 20, 1998, p. F1.

Brodie, John. "Chevy: Built to Last?" *Variety*, September 20, 1993, p. 19.

——. "Conan, Chevy Chase Latenight Brass Ring." *Variety*, September 13, 1993, p. 19.

——. "Fox Puts 'Chevy' in for Repairs." *Variety*, October 18, 1993, p. 40.

Carter, Bill. "An F.C.C. Ruling on Fox's Ownership Leaves Rivals Wondering Which Way the Wind Is Blowing." *New York Times*, May 8, 1995, p. D8.

Daniels, Bill. "Fox Weblet Repeating Debuts to Boost Audience Sampling." *Variety*, December 24, 1986, p. 77.

"Demo Derby: The Great Divide." *Variety*, February 14, 1994, p. 68.

"Demo Derby: Fox Hits the Target." *Variety*, April 21, 1997, p. 28.

Dempsey, John. "Bart to Cos: Eat My Shorts." *Variety*. May 30, 1990, p. 1.

——. "Disney Intimidation Charges 'Ludicrous,' per Fox Affils." *Variety*, February 28, 1990, p. 37.

——. "Fox Affils Smiling Over Ratings But Frown Upon Raunchy Sitcoms." *Variety*, July 15, 1987, p. 41.

——. "Fox B'casting TV Competitors Attempt to Throw Cold Water on Fourth Net's Expectations." *Variety*, August 27, 1986, p. 65.

——. "Unhappy with Saturday Lineup, 3 Fox Affiliates Won't Renew." *Variety*, July 27, 1988.

"Fall Preview." *TV Guide*, September 11, 1999, p. 13.

Flint, Joe. "CNBC Boosts Bolster to Fill Slot Left by Ailes." *Variety*, January 22, 1996, p. 28.

——. "Fox Affil Powwow Strained." *Variety*, June 27, 1994, p. 104.

——. "Nets Court Gen 'X' and *Friends*." *Variety*, September 4, 1995, p. 33.

——. "Peacock Backs Off from Fox." *Variety*, February 20, 1995, p. 200.

—— and Dennis Wharton. "Rupert Regales Regulators." *Variety*, May 2, 1994, p. 1.

"Fox Affils, BVTV Warring Over Moving Disney Block to Rival." *Variety*, January 24, 1990, p. 166.

"Fox Gets Tough with Seattle Affil." *Variety*, February 14, 1990, p. 57.

"Fox Lowers Upfront Audience Estimates; Suggests CPM Hike." *Variety*, June 29, 1988.

"Fox's Use of *Color* Criticized." *Variety*, November 1, 1993.

Garron, Barry. "*Holding the Baby* (review)." *Hollywood Reporter*, August 21, 1998, p. 8.

Grego, Melissa. "News Corp.'s Power Play." *Variety*, February 10, 2003, p. 27.

Harris, Paul. "Fox's Recent Request for Exemptions from Government Regs Irks 3 Webs . . . For Now." *Variety*, July 27, 1988, p. 38.

Hontz, Jenny. "Fox Snips Tape on *Rewind*." *Variety*, September 1, 1997, p. 24.

———. "Fox to *Roar* into Summer." *Variety*, May 5, 1997, p. 225.

———. "Webmeisters Feel Power Outage." *Variety*, August 24, 1998, p. 1.

——— and Josef Adalian. "Moonves and Roth Keep Crix Content." *Variety*, July 27, 1998, p. 24.

——— and Richard Katz. "ABC, Fox Affils Tell Nets to Take a Hike." *Variety*, June 8, 1998, p. 19.

——— and Richard Katz. "Fresh Faces in High Places." *Variety*, November 23, 1998, p. 21.

Huff, Richard. "MTV & Fox Seek Talent, Develop Shows." *Variety*, May 11, 1992.

———. "Murphy Back in *PJs* Fold." *New York Daily News*, July 2, 1999, p. 120.

"*In Living Color* (review)." *Variety*, April 25, 1990, p. 108.

Jarvis, Jeff. "*Pacific Palisades* (review)." *TV Guide*, May 10, 1997, p. 16.

———. "*Profit* (review)." *TV Guide*, April 6, 1996, p. 12.

Johnson, Ross. "Bad Attitude." *Hollywood Reporter*, February 3, 1995, p. S-3.

Katz, Richard. "Affils Preempt *McBeal* Threat." *Variety*, March 30, 1998, p. 83.

———. "Networks May Have Gone Too Deep in Catching NFL." *Variety*, February 9, 1998, p. 35.

——— and Claude Brodesser. "Stations Punt NFL Fare Play." *Variety*, March 9, 1998, p. 30.

Kissell, Rick. "Fox Wants Reality to Rejuvenate Rest of Schedule." *Variety*, January 27, 2003, p. 18.

———. "Shaq Attack and Tiger Take Win for NBC." *Variety*, June 24, 2002, p. 21.

———. and Josef Adelian. "First Hour Doesn't Go Well for *24*." *Variety*, November 12, 2001.

Kissinger, David. "Affils Bristle as Fox Trots Out Trims." *Variety*, August 26, 1991, p. 1.

———. "Chernin Yearning to Get Fox Some Hollywood Respect." *Variety*, August 21, 1991, p. 21.

Levin, Gary. "Ad Buyers Study ABCs of Fall Skeds." *Variety*, March 31, 1997, p. 35.

———. "Four Series Take Home Peabodys." *Variety*, April 7, 1997, p. 53.

———. "Fox Bumps Bergeron from Table." *Variety*, July 14, 1997, p. 26.

———. "Fox Hopes Baseball Can Hit Promo Homer." *Variety*, October 21, 1996, p. 201.

———. "Rookie Clones Find Few Fans." *Variety*, September 25, 1995, p. 31.

———. "Webs Face Sked Aches." *Variety*, April 21, 1997, p. 1.

Lowry, Brian. "Disney, FBC Pass Peace Pipe." *Variety*, February 3, 1992, p. 26.

——. "Emmys Snub Bart for *Larry*." *Variety*, August 2, 1993, p. 23.

——. "Fox Affils Agree on Retrans Plan." *Variety*, June 14, 1993, p. 23.

——. "Matoian Preaches Patience." *Variety*, January 22, 1996, p. 34.

——. "Nets Flop Demo Desires." *Variety*, October 10, 1994, p. 33.

——. "Next Honchos Propose 52-week Season One Way to Survive." *Variety*, September 17, 1990, p. 30.

—— and J. Max Robins. "Webs Narrow Focus on '95 Season Shows." *Variety*, November 14, 1994, p. 23.

Loynd, Ray. "Gather 20th Under Fox, Inc. Umbrella." *Variety*, October 16, 1985, p. 5.

Marin, Richard. "*America's Most Wanted* Is a Runaway Hit for Fox." *Washington Times*, April 21, 1988, p. E-1.

Miller, Stuart. "Fox Affils Play Name Game in Latest Status Gambit." *Variety*, October 14, 1991, p. 63.

——. "Fox *Roc* 'n' Rolls in Male Demos." *Variety*, December 23, 1991, p. 26.

"Murdoch Entities Still in Limbo." *Variety*, April 6, 1988, p. 35.

"Murdoch Rescheduling Riles Bryant." *Variety*, November 13, 1985, p. 110.

"NAACP vs. Fox Station Ownership." *Variety*, December 6, 1993, p. 20.

Natale, Richard, and David Kissinger. ". . . As Rupert Rolls Up His Sleeves." *Variety*, March 2, 1992, p. 1.

"Orlando Fox Affiliate Dumps Saturday Lineup; Chris-Craft Backpedals a Similar Decision." *Variety*, December 30, 1987, p. 23.

Peers, Martin, and Joe Flint. "Probe May Stall Fox TV Affil Goal." *Variety*, March 20, 1995, p. 23.

Rice, Lynette. "Fox Network Loses Cassidy in *Hollyweird*." *Hollywood Reporter*, August 20, 1998, p. 3.

Richmond, Ray. "*Holding the Baby* (review)." *Variety*, August 24, 1998, p. 25.

"*Roar* Debuts Well." *Variety*, July 21, 1997, p. 17.

Robins, J. Max. "Fox Hunt for News Bags Few Affils." *Variety*, March 18, 1991, p. 27.

——. "Programming Guerrillas: Rebels with a *Cos?*" *Variety*, June 6, 1990, p. 39.

——. "Safe Bets Please Nets." *Variety*, April 25, 1994, p. 1.

—— and John Brodie. "Murdoch's Makeover." *Variety*, April 12, 1993, p. 1.

Schlosser, Joe. "Man of Action." *Broadcasting & Cable*. September 20, 1999, p. 24.

Schneider, Michael. "Fox Focuses on Fix for Fall." *Variety*, April 29, 2002, p. 18.

——. "TV Takes a Deja View." *Variety*, May 20, 2002, p. 1.

——. "Wider Pitch for Urban Niche." *Variety*, January 7, 2002, p. 40.

——. and Josef Adelian. "Reality or Bust for NBC, Fox." *Variety*, July 24, 2000, p. 17.

Seibel, Deborah Starr. "The Secret Idol." *TV Guide*, May 17–23, 2003, p. 16.

Shister, Gail. "Fox to Drop 'Reality Shows.'" *Boston Globe*, January 15, 2000, p. G12.

Stern, Christopher. "Fox Quits NAB Over Stations Tiff." *Variety*, June 14, 1999, p. 18.

"*The Simpsons Christmas Special* (review)." *Variety*, December 20, 1989, p. 48.

"Tracey Ullman Calls It Quits, Too." *Variety*, May 23, 1990, p. 74.

"Two Fox Affils Cancel Saturday Night Lineup." *Variety*, December 23, 1987, p. 48.

Wharton, Dennis. "Fox Might Dodge FCC's Big Bullet." *Variety*, April 24, 1995, p. 19.

——. "Fox Rebuts Ownership Beef." *Variety*, May 30, 1994, p. 24.

——. "Fox Takes Violence Hit." *Variety*, December 27, 1993, p. 38.

——. "Murdoch & Co. Do D.C. Shuffle." *Variety*, February 13, 1995, p. 29.

——. "Outlook for Fox Finsyn Requests: Yes & Maybe." *Variety*, February 7, 1990.

——. "Webs Won't Sour on Primetime Star Power." *Variety*, February 12, 1996, p. 1.

—— and Joe Flint. "NBC Slams Fox's Bids." *Variety*, November 28, 1994, p. 108.

WEBSITES

Amazon.com. (www.amazon.com)
Internet Movie Database. (www.imdb.com)
News Corporation. (www.newscorp.com)
Twentieth Century–Fox. (www.fox.com)

Index

A NOTE ON THE AUTHOR

Daniel M. Kimmel is the Boston correspondent for *Variety* and has written for numerous publications, including the *Boston Globe*, the *Christian Science Monitor*, *Film Comment*, and the *Worcester* (Massachusetts) *Telegram and Gazette*, where he reviews films. He also writes a column on classic science fiction films for *Artemis* magazine. In the 1990s he covered television first for his own syndicated column and then for the *Boston Herald*. Born in Long Island City, New York, he studied at the University of Rochester and received a law degree from Boston University. Mr. Kimmel has taught film and media-related courses at Emerson College, Boston University, and Suffolk University. He is co-author of the play *The Waldorf Conference*, about the birth of the Hollywood blacklist, and of *Love Stories*, a book of essays about Hollywood's most romantic movies. He lives in Brookline, Massachusetts, with his wife and daughter.